Ethics

for the Financial Services Professional

ISBN 1-57996-075-8

Ethics
for the Financial Services Professional

Ronald F. Duska
Richard A. Dulisse, Editor

Preface

In the last decade of the 20th century, the landscape in the financial services industry began to change rapidly. For more than 50 years, financial services were segmented. This was a direct result of legislation passed during the Great Depression of the 1930's. Banks could not sell insurance and insurance companies sold only insurance. The invention of new financial instruments, such as mutual funds and retirement funds; the increase in longevity, which made long-term care and retirement funds as important as, if not more important than life insurance; and the passage of the Financial Services Moderization Act (Gramm-Leach-Bliley) caused the development of new distribution systems. One-stop shopping became a possibility in financial markets. No longer did one need to go to an insurance agent for insurance, a bank for a loan, and a mutual fund salesperson for different investments. Financial planners began to look over clients' entire protfolios and recommend a variety of instruments and products, a balance of which best fit the now more complex needs of those clients.

Though extremely useful in the past, books such as *Piecing Together the Ethical Puzzle* and *Charting an Ethical Course*, which were created to instruct newly minted insurance salespeople in the ethics of insurance sales, needed to be modified and expanded to meet current-day realities.

Hence, this book addresses the basic ethical issues the financial services professional needs to be cognizant of today. While ethics that governs the scale of insurance is an important element in the picture, there are now other elements that are equally as important that govern the sales of other financial instruments.

Still, there is commonality to all of these products—they are used to help facilitate financial risk management and they have the benefit of removing the anxiety that might come from a client's lack of financial security. *Securities* are aptly named. They can create security for people and the freedom from worry, as does insurance. One cannot remove all anxiety and uncertainty from life, but by helping a client develop a well-balanced portfolio, a financial services professional can help produce benefits for clients that were undreamed of in the past, such as a degree of freedom from financial anxiety.

This is the noble goal of the financial services professional who, in his or her own way, is as important to the client as the client's doctor or lawyer. One of the conditions of happiness, according to the ancient Greek philosopher, Aristotle, is to have enough wealth so one's existence is not continually beset by financial worry. How a financial services professional can effect that laudable goal in an ethical manner is the subject of this book.

To acclimate to the changing realities, we will treat some subjects in a general way, such as the nature of ethics and the ethical responsibilities of being a professional, and the relationship between law and ethics. But we will also delve further into other more specific practices, such as what is ethically necessary in the sale of insurance as opposed to what is ethically necessary in the sale of securities.

The field of financial services is filled with a bewildering array of things to learn, ranging from sophisticated products to sales techniques. Perhaps, though, the most important thing to learn is how to do one's job in an ethical manner with integrity. How should I treat my employer, the companies I represent, my fellow financial services professionals and, most of all, my clients?

To paraphrase Shakespeare, we think being ethical makes you "twice blest." You are blessed because, as we will show, being ethical goes with having a *noble* purpose in life, which is essential for one to flourish as a human being and to fill life with immense satisfaction—a satisfaction money cannot buy. Secondly, being ethical also helps you stay out of trouble while gaining you a good reputation. Good ethics is good business.

Thus, our firm conviction is that for financial services professionals ethics is beneficial on both personal and financial levels.

Contents

The American College ix
    The Self-Study Learning Process ix
    Self-Study ix
    Chapter Review Quizzes ix
    Final Exam and Procedure x
    Study of Hints and Suggestions x
Acknowledgments xii
Special Notes xiv

CHAPTER 1
    Ethics in Financial Services 1-1

CHAPTER 2
    The Ethical Framework 2-1

CHAPTER 3
    The Legal Framework 3-1

CHAPTER 4
    Agency and Compliance 4-1

CHAPTER 5
    Professionalism 5-1

CHAPTER 6
    Fair Dealing and Suitability in Financial Products Marketing 6-1

CHAPTER 7
    Marketing Financial Products: Ethical Sales and Full Disclosure 7-1

CHAPTER 8
    Illustrations, Replacement, and Rebating 8-1

APPENDIX

LUTC Fellow Pledge A-1

NAIFA Code of Ethics... A-2

The American College Code of Ethics A-3

Society of Financial Service Professionals Code of Ethics A-8

Million Dollar Round Table Code of Ethics...................................... A-22

CFP Code of Ethics A-23

ACLI: What You Should Know About Buying Life Insurance............ A-43

Answer Key to Chapter Quizzes A-53

LUTC Forms

Index... Index-1

The American College

The American College is an independent, nonprofit, accredited educational institution founded in 1927 that offers professional certification and graduate-degree education, primarily on a distance-learning basis, to men and women seeking career growth in financial services.

The mission of The American College is to raise the level of professionalism of its students and, by extension, the financial services industry as a whole. By imparting expert knowledge—and by emphasizing that such knowledge must be regularly renewed and ethically applied—the College seeks to strengthen not only its students' professionalism but, ultimately and most importantly, the financial security of the individuals, families, businesses, and society they serve.

This course has been developed by the College and, although the effort has been made to assure the accuracy of the material presented here, the College does not warrant that accuracy and is not liable for any errors or omissions contained herein.

No reproduction of these materials is permitted without the express permission of The American College.

This course is designed to provide accurate and authoritative information in regard to the subject matter concerned. It is sold with the understanding that the publisher is not engaged in rendering legal, accounting or other professional service. If legal advice or other expert assistance is required, the services of a competent professional should be sought. —From a *Declaration of Principles* jointly adapted by a Committee of the American Bar Association and a Committee of Publishers and Associations.

The Self-Study Learning Process

Self-Study

This course is intended to be a self-contained, self-study course. That is, you should be able to complete the course and pass the test without any additional material. Although the chapters can stand alone, considerable thought has been given to their placement. The learning process will be most effective if you read and study each chapter in the order presented.

Chapter Review Quizzes

There is a short quiz at the end of each chapter. The multiple-choice questions cover material you will find on the final exam. The answers are located in the Appendix. The quiz is an excellent method to check your mastery of the material in the chapter. If you answer a quiz question incorrectly, it is best to go back and review the appropriate material immediately. You should be comfortable with the current material before moving on to the next chapter.

Final Exam and Procedure

The final exam is made up of 50 multiple-choice questions. The exam questions are similar to the multiple-choice questions in the chapter quiz sections. All the information you need concerning the exam is contained in the final exam packet to this course.

Final Exam Procedure—The final examination is administered online. To receive CE credit for this self-study course, you must pass the course examination.

The American College requires that a disinterested third party, over the age of 18, proctor the final course exam. The student is responsible to ensure that the proctor complies with the state's specific requirements for proctoring a final exam.

Information regarding proctor approval and access to the final examination will be provided as part of the course confirmation immediately after your course registration is received.

You have 6 months from the date of the course registration to take the final examination. Questions regarding the exam should be addressed to Customer Service at 877-655-5882.

Study Hints and Suggestions

Has it been a long time since you have taken a self-study course? Maybe this is your first experience with this method of learning. Several techniques have been developed to improve the results in a self-study environment. They have proven to be extremely effective and are worth your consideration.

Set a Goal for Completion—Set a target date for completing your studies. Do not try to do too much at once. Many people set a goal of one or two chapters per week. Put your goal in writing and post it in a prominent place.

Schedule the Time You Need—Block out the necessary time in your planner or appointment book. Consider this time as important as a sales call and resist changing it.

Study When You Are Fresh—Pick study times that occur when you are well rested and at your peak. This will maximize your retention of the material.

No Distractions—Find a quiet place to work where you are able to minimize interruptions. Try not to allow telephone, coworkers, or children to disturb you.

Highlight—Use a highlighter to emphasize important points in the text. This can improve your retention and facilitate your review for the final exam.

Review: Take the Chapter Quizzes—Take each chapter quiz and, if you have incorrect answers, review the appropriate material immediately. Record your answers on a blank piece of paper. This will allow you to take the quiz again.

Implement Ideas—The text is full of ideas that can enhance your practice while limiting malpractice liability. However, you have to use the ideas to reap the benefits.

Exercises—The text contains short exercises within each chapter. Complete these exercises during your reading. If you attend a seminar, be prepared to discuss your answers during classroom training. (Note: You will not be responsible for the information contained in the exercises for the final examination.)

Acknowledgments

This book and its accompanying course is the result of taking the best of two LUTC ethics books, *Piecing Together the Ethical Puzzle* and *Charting an Ethical Course*, along with part of The American College book, *The Regulation of the Life Insurance Business* by Jon S. Hanson, melding their content together, thoroughly revising that content, and adding a substantial amount of new material. We greatfully acknowledge the generosity of innumerable organizations and individuals who assisted in developing those courses with their advice, suggestions, and/or contributions of material.

Such a book is not possible without the joint effort of numerous people. I would like to thank them for what is worthwhile about the book, while holding none of them responsible for any of its shortcomings.

Specifically, I owe a great debt of gratitude to the following people at The American College. Samuel H. Weese, President and CEO, who encouraged the production of a new book and a new course for the use of LUTC candidates, as well as by financial services professionals in general. Gary K. Stone, Executive Vice President; Shirley P. Steinman, Vice President, Student Services Administrative Division; and especially C. Bruce Worsham, Associate Vice President and Director of Educational Development. These persons, in their administrative capacities, helped shepherd the book through the peaks and valleys of the various departments involved in such a production. Walt J. Woerheide, Vice President and Dean of Academic Affairs, as my immediate supervisor, contributed his support to the project. Edward E. Graves, Associate Professor of Insurance, helped by checking the manuscript for fidelity to existing regulations and procedures in the financial services marketplace. Renée Heron, a senior editor, lent her considerable talents to editing the text, along with senior editors Todd Denton and Maria Marlowe, and editors Keith dePinho, Wendy dePinho, and Elizabeth Fahrig, and editorial assistant/permissions editor Patricia Cheers. Teresa Kobylarz, assistant editor, did thorough and detailed work in helping to identify areas of commonality in the two LUTC books to assure that no important topics were omitted. Evelyn M. Rice contributed her fine production skills to the project. Jake Remaley did a yeoman's job on early designs and instructor's manuals as well as writing exam questions, and Joe Brennan designed the striking cover.

But there are several people without whose efforts none of this would have been done. Thanks are due to the production efforts of Charlene McNulty, production group leader, who unfailingly typed and rearranged piles of manuscript and text that quite often bordered on the illegible. Richard A. Dulisse, an LUTC program author/editor also deserves enormous thanks. He served almost as a co-author, writing the final drafts of the objectives and the exam questions. He also served as a valued organizer of text, indicating the placement of certain topics and suggesting the topics that were most relevant for discussion in the contemporary world of financial services. My gratitude also goes to Lynn Hayes who, as Director of Editorial Services, oversaw the project from its earliest days. Above and beyond her overall helpful comments and editorial expertise, she formatted the layout to create this dynamic and aesthetically pleasing text.

My final thanks go to all the students of the past several years who, in the classes I teach at The American College, have furnished me with untold numbers of ethical situations in the financial services industry along with wise solutions to any number of those situations. I have learned much from them.

Ronald F. Duska
Professor of Ethics
The American College

Special Notes

Text Materials Disclaimer

This publication is designed to provide accurate and authoritative information about the subject covered. While every precaution has been taken in the preparation of this material to insure that it is both accurate and up-to-date, it is still possible that some errors have eluded detection. Moreover, some material may become inaccurate and/or outdated either because it is time sensitive or because new legislation will make it so. Still other material may be viewed as inaccurate because your company's products and procedures are different from those described in the book. Therefore, the authors and The American College assume no liability for damages resulting from the use of the information contained in this book. The American College is not engaged in rendering legal, accounting, or other professional advice. If legal or other expert advice is required, the services of an appropriate professional should be sought.

Caution Regarding Use of Illustrations

The illustrations, sales ideas and approaches in this book are not to be used with the public unless you have obtained approval from your company. Your company's general support of The American College's programs for training and educational purposes does not constitute blanket approval of the sales ideas and approaches presented in this book, unless so communicated in writing by your company.

Use of the Term Financial Services Professional or Financial Advisor

Use of the term "Financial Services Professional" as it appears in this book is intended as the generic reference to professional members of our reading audience. It is used interchangeably with the term "Financial Advisor" so as to avoid unnecessary redundancy. Financial Services Professional takes the place of the following terms:

Account Executive	Life Insurance Agent
Agent	Life Underwriter
Advisor	Planner
Associate	Practitioner
Brokers (stock or insurance)	Producer
Financial Consultant	Property & Casualty Agent
Financial Planner	Registered Investment Advisor
Financial Planning Professional	Registered Representative
Health Underwriter	Senior Advisor
Insurance Professional	

Answers to the Questions in the Book

The answers to all essay and multiple choice questions in this book are based on the text materials as written.

1

Ethics in Financial Services

Learning Objectives

1-1. Describe the main reason that this ethics course was developed.

1-2. List five key reasons why the financial services marketplace has changed in recent years.

1-3. Explain why there are now increased industry career risks.

1-4. Explain the impact of the Gramm-Leach-Bliley Act on the financial services industry.

1-5. Identify seven unethical practices that have lowered the insurance industry's integrity in the eyes of the general public.

1-6. Identify three major ethical requirements facing today's financial services professionals.

Chapter Outline

Ethics in Financial Services

Introduction 1-3
    Reason for This Course 1-3
The Changing Face of the Financial Services Industry 1-4
The Making of Today's Financial Services Environment 1-5
Changing Marketplace 1-7
    Educated Consumers 1-7
    Technological Advancements 1-8
    Changing Demographics 1-9
    Changing Legal Environment 1-9
    Integration of Financial Services 1-11
Unethical Practices in the Financial Services Industry 1-12
    1—Misuse of Illustrations 1-13
    2—Unnecessary Replacement and Twisting 1-14
    3—Product Misrepresentation 1-14
    4—Improper Licensing 1-15
    5—Lack of Competency 1-16
    6—Fraud 1-17
    7—Forgery 1-17
    8—Insolvency 1-18
Major Ethical Requirements Facing the Financial Services
        Industry 1-18
    Identifying and Meeting Customer Needs 1-19
    Proper Identification of Skills 1-19
    Honest Marketing 1-20
Conclusion: The Need for Ethical Training 1-21
Chapter 1 Review Questions 1-23

Ethics in Financial Services

Introduction

A well-known financial planner wrote the following: "It strikes me, or I should say, it struck me, a few months back when the scale of these corporate-world problems (Enron, WorldCom, etc.) began to become apparent, that the planner's desk really is a major buck-stopping point.

"There will always be some public company execs who go too far. There will always be some accountants/consultants/lawyers who either advise it or facilitate it. There will always be some extent to which those we pay to preclude/catch it (the regulators and the analysts) just fall flat; for whatever reason or reasons, they miss it until it's too late. These are fully predictable 'isnesses' that the 'shadow side' of our human existence manifests. The only real variable over time is the extent to which these things happen.

"In our profession, we need to be exceedingly clear about what being ever and 'duly' diligent means. Recognizing and avoiding those very real-to-the-point-of-inevitable unethical acts is fundamental to our role; it is a primary responsibility of a trusted financial services advisor. The opportunity to buffer clients from some of the difficulties inherent in the real world is a substantive underpinning of our developing profession's existence."[1]

Put more simply, taking care of clients is why financial services professionals exist. What that involves is being ethical.

Reason for This Course

Over the last few decades, the public has been demanding the highest ethical standards from their professional advisors. In the free-market world, there is an emphasis on the necessity for corporations, those

---

1. Reprinted with permission by the Financial Planning Association from a message posted by Guy Cumbie online at the JFP Voice Web site on Friday, August 30, 2002, in response to the talking point: "A Set of Rules or a Moral Code to Follow? Our Role and Responsibility."

employed by corporations, and those selling products of corporations to act in an ethical manner. Companies have created compliance departments and/or chief ethics officers. Organizations and professional groups have developed ethical codes. Financial services professionals must know both their legal obligations and their ethical obligations. They need to understand how their personal value system can mesh with their day-to-day business activities, thereby ensuring that they uphold their integrity. They must be aware of how the richness of life can be enhanced by functioning ethically in the financial system.

This course has been developed to help financial services professionals respond to the expectations and responsibilities the public has placed upon them.

The course provides a framework for recognizing and analyzing the ethical issues that financial services professionals encounter. It discusses general ethical principles and rules as well as government regulations, emphasizing the practical application of those ethical principles and legal regulations to day-to-day business conduct. Although the term *ethics* encompasses a wide range of issues and a variety of perspectives, this course concentrates on the question, "What are the financial services professional's ethical responsibilities?"

The Changing Face of the Financial Services Industry

Financial services is looked upon as a profession. One of the primary reasons why financial services providers claim professional status is the increased complexity of the financial planning activity and the important role financial services professionals play in helping individuals and companies identify and meet their complex financial needs.

Over the years financial transactions, instruments, and needs have become more complicated. Until recently, financial planning, for most people, consisted of having adequate life insurance to protect their families and loved ones from premature loss of income. Pensions and Social Security took care of retirement needs. Estate planning was necessary only for wealthy individuals. For most people, a simple will was sufficient. With greater life expectancies, the rise of mutual funds, and the demise of company-controlled pension plans, more and more individuals depend on their own retirement plans, long-term care policies, annuities, and investments in financial instruments to guarantee their financial security after retirement. Planning for living longer became more urgent than planning for premature death.

Insurance, which protects against risk, remains one of the most important tools to meet financial needs. Millions of individuals rely on property and casualty insurance to safeguard their homes and other property from unfortunate events. They depend on life insurance to ensure the general welfare of their families should premature death occur. But, they depend on various other investments along with insurance to provide for their retirement, to help fund the payment of their mortgages, to provide for their children's education and the dispositions of their estates.

The person who helps to identify financial needs, provides necessary insurance coverage, recommends other financial products, advises on the disposition of estates, and helps to set up trusts to provide for a secure comfortable retirement, becomes a trusted advisor. The financial services professional acting as such a trusted advisor is responsible for ascertaining the financial needs of a client and then matching those needs through a multitude of complex products.

The fact that the public recognizes the need for financial advisors allows the financial services industry to prosper. That recognition brings with it increased demands for professionalism by those in the industry, because the primary aim of any professional is to ensure that the client's needs are met. Thus, today in the world of financial transactions, millions of clients rely on financial services professionals for help in fulfilling their needs with competence and integrity. It is a sacred trust, bearing much ethical responsibility.

The Making of Today's Financial Services Environment

Examining where we have been often enables us to better understand not only where we are but also where we are going. This rule applies not only to society in general but to business in particular. Financial services is a specific industry with a substantial history and strong presence in the American business landscape.

There have been broad changes in the landscape of the industry over the last 20 years. Financial planning and estate planning have grown out of the insurance field. The experienced professional (as well as the novice) often expresses surprise at the notion that the insurance industry was once considered highly stable and was the only game in town. The new professionals cannot believe there was a time when agents were not faced with the same marketplace practice issues they currently face.

What were these changes and what caused them? The history of the American economy provides an answer. For many years following the Second World War, the American economy experienced productivity-driven growth. Inflation and interest rates were both low and stable, thus encouraging individuals to save.

Traditional whole life insurance products with set premiums and guaranteed cash values fit well into such a system and answered the needs of many consumers. The stable economy enabled insurers to surpass anticipated published dividend scales. As a result, public confidence in the insurance industry was high. Term insurance represented the one basic alternative to the traditional whole life product. A stable product line marked the era with stable product performance against the backdrop of a stable economy.

During the 1970s and early 1980s, the American economy began to change. Productivity growth stagnated. Demographically, the economy was faced with a huge influx of inexperienced baby-boom workers. Foreign cartels were formed to control the price of oil and other natural resources. Shockwaves reverberated throughout the world monetary system while inflation and interest rates soared. Tempted by the high rates of the newly popular money market funds and other financial instruments, consumers borrowed against their insurance policies. The insurance industry began to experience a massive disintermediation of funds. In response, the industry developed universal life products that reflected the high interest rate yields offered by short-to-intermediate-term investments. Premiums were no longer standardized at set levels. Life insurance policy guarantees were reduced.

Sales techniques also changed. Advances in technology facilitated the use of customized proposals. Policies were frequently sold on the basis of illustrations rather than needs. Clients often made judgments based not on guaranteed values, but on illustrated projections reflecting the then high interest rate environment. Customers liked the new products but often were not familiar with their operation. Nor were they always cognizant of the impact of the economy on the products. When interest rates dropped, so did product performance. Many universal life policyholders were caught unaware when premium notices arrived indicating the need for additional cash infusions to keep policies in force. At the same time, to take advantage of the investment markets, mutual fund agents were recommending that their clients "buy term insurance and invest the rest."

Public approval ratings of the insurance industry began to plummet and dropped farther as the decade of the 1990s opened with a recession and a solvency crisis within the industry. As the economy moved into the 90s, mutual funds became popular as depositories of IRAs and investment companies flourished, in some cases, dwarfing the size of the insurance companies. Other factors outside the industry also impacted the public's perception. Insurance became closely allied in consumer's minds with the difficulties and scandals faced by other branches of the financial services sector. The savings and loans crisis sparked public skepticism about financial institutions as one bank after another fell victim to ineptitude and poor business planning by its high-level executives. The greed of Wall Street brokers and their manipulation of the marketplace, including federal securities, added to this cynicism. To add fuel to the fire, highly publicized charges of improper marketplace practices against several insurance agents and home office executives followed on the heels of these developments.

As the 20th century came to a close, the old-line insurance companies became financial services institutions. With the collapse of Enron, Adelphia, WorldCom and many other companies and the bursting of the stock market bubble, the role of the financial services professional becomes even more important.

Changing Marketplace

Because of the changes mentioned above, the current marketplace is clearly different from the marketplace of 30, 20, or even 10 years ago. Not only have financial products changed in response to a changing economy but consumer awareness, attitudes, and expectations have also changed. Let's look at the elements that make up this changing marketplace.

Educated Consumers

The consumer of financial instruments is generally better educated and less docile than the consumer of the past. He or she approaches purchases in a sophisticated manner. Rather than simply doing what they are told to do, today's consumer responds best to a consultative selling environment. Today's consumer seeks to fully understand a product before reaching a decision to buy. The best transactions in this type of environment are participative in nature. Educating consumers about financial products is an integral part of the sales process. Today's consumer has higher expectations regarding the type of service to be provided, which places added responsibilities on the shoulders of today's financial services professional.

Technological Advancements

Advances in technology have also raised the expectations of the consumer regarding the type of information to be provided as part of the sales process. The consumer of financial instruments is accustomed to bank ATM statements as well as quick market quotes from stockbrokers. In the insurance and money market fields, the demand for greater technology has expanded to the wide use of computerized illustrations, of expected return on investment financial planning software, and client service on a faster-than-ever turnaround basis. An illustration no longer takes a week or two to make its way from a centralized department in the home office. Instead, it can be faxed within a day. In some cases, illustrations are generated within hours at an agency. In other cases, the illustration is generated on a PC within minutes by an agent and then e-mailed from his or her mobile office.

Today, financial services products are bought and sold on the Internet, leading companies to develop entirely new marketing and delivery systems. The functions of the agent—advising, selling, and servicing—are being bundled and given to different people. Advice and products are being blended together and one-stop-shopping for financial plans' products and services is provided by multidisciplinary firms that offer financial, tax, legal, and accounting advice. The financial services professional, driven by the increasingly complex marketplace, can no longer be all things to all clients and adequately fulfill his or her responsibility to provide competent service.

Technological advances have both pros and cons. On one hand, the rapid pace can fulfill client expectations and offer the opportunity to speed the ultimate closing of a sale. On the other hand, the rapid pace leaves far less time for reflection and increases the ethical burdens of financial services professionals to provide better information for client choice.

Changing Demographics

Another important cause of change in the financial services marketplace is the dramatic demographic change that occurred in the last half of the 20th century. As mentioned, the American population is living longer. This creates new concerns about how to manage risk. The problem today is not so much premature death, a factor that makes life insurance necessary, but outliving the source of income, which makes wise investment for retirement years a major concern. Studies have shown that even relatively prosperous members of the baby-boom generation have expressed fears about living too long, thereby outliving their source of income.

This fact creates a temptation to recast life insurance as a retirement vehicle. Life insurance can certainly supplement income needs in later life; however, the primary function of that product is protection from premature death. Clients should clearly understand that in some cases life insurance is not the product the client needs.

Financial advisors should not ignore the opportunities presented by the changing demographics. The shift toward an older population means that financial services professionals should look at their clients' financial and estate plans. Life insurance can play a significant role in supplementing retirement needs whether this entails the use of cash values during life or of benefits by a survivor following death. But other products also need to be utilized. Annuities may be needed to provide income in old age. Disability and long-term care protection also represent an increasing part of the package clients are likely to need. All these different products offer financial services professionals the opportunity to cross sell and increasingly turn one-purchase consumers into lifelong clients. Beyond mere insurance-based products, there is an increasing need for other products, such as mutual funds and stock investments used to fund 401K plans or other retirement vehicles. Old-line life insurance agents need to diversify along with their companies.

Changing Legal Environment

Financial services professionals today are increasingly perceived by the public as professionals. Inherent in such recognition is added responsibility and increased risk of legal liability. Simply put, higher legal standards are being applied to financial services professionals and their companies. Consumer protection, not *caveat emptor* (buyer beware), guides today's court decisions. There is also an increased trend to hold a company liable for the actions of its agents.

Consider the following—a June 3, 2002, Supreme Court ruling, which found in favor of a Securities and Exchange Commission action against a broker, stated that the securities market's regulations introduced in the 30s "sought to substitute a philosophy of full disclosure for the philosophy of caveat emptor, and this to achieve a high standard of business ethics to the securities industry." Thus, *caveat emptor* is not sufficient. Analysts may have a legal duty of care for their retail customers, which means they need to offer them only such advice as they would give to themselves.

In short, the switch from *caveat emptor* to *caveat vendor* (seller beware) means the financial services professional must be careful. Because we live in a litigious society, malpractice can affect any professional. Most of us are familiar with malpractice in relation to the practice of medicine. But malpractice lawsuits are not limited to the medical field; they are increasingly instituted against members of all professions, including those engaged in financial services. Financial services professionals and the companies they represent can become targets of such lawsuits when something goes wrong, either because they have caused the harm or simply because they are perceived as having deep pockets.

The combination of a marketplace in transition, an aging population, and evolving judicial standards translates into increased legal liability and career risks for the financial services professional. Today's consumer is not afraid of challenging a big company in a lawsuit. There are firms that specialize in representing the little guy against an entire industry. Failure to understand these increased risks can result in the loss of license, reputation, and even career.

Financial services professionals are not immune from the growing mistrust of the public. A litigious environment has arisen, partly because society has decided that businesses should be held responsible for the harm they can do to consumers. Society has concluded that ethics counts in business activities, and those companies that are not concerned with ethical behavior should be held responsible. In the early 1990s, the U.S. sentencing guidelines took ethics so seriously that they developed a scale that made fines levied against companies with an ethics program smaller than fines levied against companies without an ethics program. Conducting business in an ethically conscious, litigious environment requires vigilance and attention to the details of both law and ethics.

This attention requires not only increased client service but also increased record keeping. Financial services professionals are well-advised to be aware of their moral responsibilities as well as the legal risks, and to take proactive steps to service their clients as well as possible and to take defensive steps to protect themselves from lawsuits, whether founded or unfounded.

In this course, we look at the ethical principles of the proactive approach as well as the precautionary defensive approach, which involve compliance with state laws and regulations and with agents' contracts. Ethics and compliance are issues that are treated in great detail throughout this text. These topics can enhance the quality of your client relationships and add to your professional protection. Read them carefully and put the ideas into use.

Use of an ethical framework that includes the study of legal requirements as the first step, followed by an investigation of industry codes, will provide you with an essential part of the guidance needed to reach objective business decisions. Compliance issues can then be added to the equation in order to provide you with defensible positions for your actions. One purpose of this course is to help you construct such an operational framework.

Integration of Financial Services

There is another factor that has served to change the legal environment in which we do business. That is the blurring of lines between the sectors of the financial services industry. Traditionally, one set of rules has applied to the securities industry and another to the insurance industry. With the entry of variable products into the insurance portfolio, this distinction is becoming blurred.

The Gramm-Leach-Bliley Act made the path toward financial integration of banking, underwriting, and agency activities in securities and insurance possible. This means that financial services companies can use banks as distribution centers, which will have implications for the entire financial services distribution system.

Gramm-Leach-Bliley Act

The Gramm-Leach-Bliley Act (GLBA) implemented the most sweeping overhaul of financial services regulation in the United States in over 60 years by eliminating the barriers between banking, investment banking, and insurance. It allows for affiliations between banks and other financial companies who may now establish so-called financial holding companies that can include commercial banking, securities underwriting, insurance underwriting, and merchant banking. This act lays the groundwork for significant further consolidation in the U.S. banking and financial industry.

The act also addresses consumer confidentiality. Section 502 generally requires that a financial institution may not, directly or indirectly, or through any affiliate, disclose to a nonaffiliated third party any nonpublic personal information, unless the institution has provided the consumer with notice of its intent to do so.

Unethical Practices in the Financial Services Industry

Enron, WorldCom, Tyco, Waste Management, Arthur Andersen—these are names of formerly admired companies that now represent pervasive unethical behavior. Accountants who cook books, investment banks that cover up financial slight-of-hand, executives who line their own pockets while violating their fiduciary responsibility to look out for the best interests of the shareholders are just a few of the unethical practices that have damaged public confidence in the financial market system's ability to carry out its mission to society.

One part of the financial services industry that was especially hard hit by suspicion was the insurance business, particularly in the early to mid-90s. In the late 80s and early 90s, unnecessary replacements of life insurance policies that benefited only the agent and the company, as well as the misuse of illustrations and the misrepresentation of insurance as an investment vehicle, led to billion-dollar law suits against several

---

Review Item

Appropriate Recommendation?

Agent Abraham Adams (young agent):

"I have good news. Your medical report came back and you're in good health. In addition, our company has just released a new variable universal policy."

Client Zoe Zingler (older client):

"That's wonderful. I'd like to establish an educational fund for my granddaughter. I live on a fixed income. I have just one question. Is that new product appropriate for me?"

How would you respond? What sort of product would be most appropriate given the client's needs and desires?

Log your answer in the space below.

---

insurance companies. Because of those scandals, according to a U.S. News and World Report in the mid 90s, the general public ranked the integrity of insurance agents only slightly higher than that of used car salespeople. Annual surveys conducted by the American Council of Life Insurance offer insight into the current status of the insurance industry with the public. ACLI survey results confirm the fact that consumers remain skeptical of the industry and its agents. An analysis over a period of years indicates a steady erosion of the public's trust.

Obviously, such negative views make it difficult for financial services professionals to gain and maintain the trust advisors' need to effectively practice their profession. It also increases the risk of legal action by individual clients and evokes calls for more government regulation. So that we can avoid repeating the same mistakes, let's look at some of the specific situations and practices that have tarnished the reputations of the insurance/financial services professional. Many of the scandals could have been avoided through adherence to the professional codes of the industry.

Let's look at eight areas in which abuse of professionalism has occurred.

1—Misuse of Illustrations

The misuse of product illustrations created problems for the insurance industry and mutual fund sales forces. With the introduction of universal life policies in the early 1980s, some agents began to use high-return illustrations whose projections turned out to be unrealistic. Predicted interest rates of 15 percent, for example, did not remain at that rate for long. Clients who bought policies during the high interest rate era were later required to increase premium payments. Those added premiums were not just for increasing the cash values of the policy. They were increases necessary to keep the policies in force. Many of those clients realized that the illustrations they had received were just that— illustrations, not contractual obligations of the company. However, those clients felt their agents had deceived them by portraying projections as guarantees. The clients became disgruntled; many believed they had received improper advice or that improper promises had been made. Such stories added to the layer of suspicion that tarnished the reputation of the insurance industry and its agents.

Some of this dissatisfaction could have been avoided with proper client education. Clients who are clearly taught that illustrations are mere "for instances" and not contractual promises by the company and who understand the basic assumptions underlying illustrations are better able to understand why those notices of increased premiums arrive. They can also understand that the life insurance they bought is still a very good product. However, some agents, who want to paint their product in the best possible light can leave the impression that these high-return illustrations are guaranteed. In short, they push for the sale rather than to educate the client.

What's the price of the subsequent client dissatisfaction? A tangible measure of that price is the increased regulation of insurance illustrations by state insurance departments. The era when agents could simply pick a set of illustration assumptions is over.

2—Unnecessary Replacement and Twisting

One way to make a quick buck is to replace a client's insurance policy. In some cases, an insurance policy replacement can serve a valid purpose. However, there are often times when policy replacement is not in the best interests of insurance clients and is only in the best interest of the agent, if he or she gets a fresh commission on the sale. Such a practice is not confined solely to the insurance industry. There is the general practice by some financial services professionals of activities called twisting, churning, and piggybacking—actions by which a financial services agent turns over a client's product, not for the sake of the client, but to generate new business for him/herself and/or the company, thus generating new commissions. This refers to improper replacements.

Stories have been presented to the public of unscrupulous agents seeking out policyholders who have built up cash values within policies. The cash values are tapped to finance new, unnecessary policies, solely to provide new business commissions for the agents.

The result, once again, has been the loss of trust by the buying public, which negatively impacts honest professionals and encourages more government intervention. On the insurance side, state regulators have addressed the replacement issue with new and more strict legislation, which has resulted in increased paperwork and record keeping.

3—Product Misrepresentation

There is a tendency among salespersons to present their products in the best light possible. Advertisers sometimes make claims about products that are untrue in order to sell a product. When the life insurance market slowed down as a result of the change in demographics and when insurance agents, because of the negative publicity, got a bad name, some financial services professionals (primarily insurance agents) became reluctant to identify the product they sold by its proper name: life insurance. They described their products as *savings vehicles* or *retirement plans*. They called premium payments *deposits* or *capital transfers*. They referred to themselves as *retirement representatives* instead of *insurance agents*.

Review Item

Paying Attention to Client Education

Client Albert Young:

"Those papers with all the numbers are confusing."

Agent Brenda Boxer:

"Don't worry about understanding them. My company stands by its word. Just sign here."

What do you think of the way Agent Boxer handled this situation? Would you have taken a different approach?

Log your answer in the space below.

Practices such as these confused consumers and brought an onslaught of complaints to insurance departments. This led to legislation where failing to describe an insurance product as insurance is prohibited by state consumer protection laws. What's more, failure to abide by these laws has effectively ended the once promising careers of several top insurance industry representatives.

4—Improper Licensing

Another problem that afflicts financial services professionals in general, and insurance agents in particular, is improper licensing. Agents are required to have the proper licenses to sell their products. However, licenses to sell insurance differ from licenses to sell securities products. If one ventures from insurance to securities products, a different set of licenses is necessary. Some insurance representatives do not have those proper licenses when they change from insurance to securities products. More often, license infractions involve the improper crossing of state jurisdictional boundaries to obtain a nonresident license. The improper licensing situation tarnished the image of the industry and brought about regulatory reaction. If you are not licensed to sell a product, don't sell it.

Review Item

Market Tip

Agent Charles Coughlin:

"This fund is guaranteed to make you money. It's a growth fund. . .no, it's a value fund. That's it! A growth value fund."

Client Bradley Walters:

"I've never heard of a fund offering guaranteed returns. This certainly sounds interesting to me."

Does it sound like Agent Coughlin understands the type of mutual fund he is selling? If not, does this present an ethical problem? Would you have any concerns if Agent Coughlin was just halfway through an NASD licensing review course?

Log your answer in the space below.

5—Lack of Competency

Even more serious than improper licensing was the problem of the financial services professional misunderstanding the nature of their own products. The growing complexity of financial instruments with varying commission structures and diverse tax implications makes it difficult, at times, to ascertain what products are most suitable for clients. Some clients with a low risk tolerance are sold high-risk products. Others are sold products that have adverse tax consequences and that penalize clients with unexpected surrender fees. This can result in clients being sold products that are not appropriate for them. Such clients can become, rightfully, disgruntled. It's important to sell with competence. If you don't understand a product, get help.

6—Fraud

Another difficulty, and perhaps the most serious, is fraud. Fraud is defined as "intentional misrepresentation, concealment, or omission of the truth for the purpose of deception or manipulation to the detriment of a person or an organization. Fraud is a legal concept and the application of the term in a specific instance should be determined by a legal expert."[2] Much misrepresentation, if it is done deliberately, constitutes fraud. Some particularly disturbing practices of fraud turned up in the financial services area.

Misrepresentation or omission that is carried out to manipulate the client intentionally is a form of fraud and is unethical. There are too many instances of agents and brokers, who for the sake of sales and commissions, disregarded the good of clients and either lied to them or failed to disclose relevant information. Such activities hurt the clients and, when discovered, besmirched the reputation of the entire financial services profession.

7—Forgery

A recent case came to light concerning an insurance representative who forged a client's signature on an automatic checking withdrawal authorization form. The funds went to pay for a high-commission product that the client had previously rejected.

Some agents have signed a client's name to a document in the belief that they were expediting the underwriting process. Their rationale was that they were helping the client obtain the desired product. While signing a client's name is sometimes done with good intentions, to save an extra visit to the client or to save the client more aggravation, sometimes it is done to take advantage of the client. That is unethical. The bottom line is that signing a client's name to a document, no matter what the reason, without a power of attorney is technically forgery, and it is illegal.

Signing clients' signatures on insurance forms was once a common practice and was called *windowing*. But the practice was abused enough

---

2. Money's Complete Guide to Personal Finance and Investment Terms, p. 148.

to receive wide attention and has been thoroughly rejected as an acceptable practice.

8—Insolvency

The decade of the 1990s opened with an economy in recession, which impacted the insurance industry. An industry with a reputation for financial soundness and conservatism became linked with risky bonds and devalued real estate.

Retirees dependent on uncertain annuity income streams became regulars on the evening news as they questioned the advice they had received from their insurance representatives. Some wondered whether their agents had ever studied the financial picture of the companies in which they had invested their clients' hard-earned dollars. Some wondered if the agents had simply placed business on the basis of which company paid the highest commissions. Elected officials called for government intervention. The solvency crisis caused many policyholders to reevaluate the stability of the insurance industry and question agents' abilities to serve their needs. The market decline of the first years of the 21st century also brought a new concern for solvency because of the extensive sale of variable annuities in the late 90s. A declining market made it difficult for companies to meet their guaranteed annuity payouts.

Major Unethical Practices

- misuse of illustrations

- unnecessary replacement and twisting

- product misrepresentation

- improper licensing

- lack of competency

- fraud

- forgery

- insolvency

Major Ethical Requirements Facing the Financial Services Industry

The types of misconduct just described demonstrate the harm that can be done to both clients and the financial services industry by the failure to think and act ethically. An analysis of these few instances that have shaped public perception indicates that the financial services industry faces major ethical challenges. Key issues with which the industry continues to deal include the failure to uncover client needs, misrepresentation of products and services, and poor product performance compared to client expectations. The following are responsibilities with which the financial services professional should be concerned.

Identifying and Meeting Customer Needs

Agents sometimes fail to identify customer needs. Merely writing down a "guesstimated" figure on a yellow pad does not suffice as a needs analysis. When these needs go unidentified, clients are often sold inappropriate products. Every financial services provider should question the appropriateness of the product in each client situation prior to making a recommendation.

Suitability is the new watchword. Is the product *suitable* for the client? When the suitability requirement is not met, it can usually be attributed to a lack of knowledge. Some financial services professionals are reluctant to admit that they are not experts in all financial planning fields. This represents an educational need. To properly uncover needs and make appropriate recommendations, agents need knowledge of the products available and what the products do. Without this knowledge, the situation is ripe for client dissatisfaction.

Agents, sometimes pressured to sell the latest product either by their company or by the promise of a great commission, do so without ever investigating their clients' needs. Some young professionals, new to the business and without much knowledge of the various products, are pushed to sell. They are often taught only a few products and licensed to sell only those few. To make their quotas, they then sell one product to everybody, convinced that one size fits all. This practice reveals a lack of competence and understanding of the complex products in the field.

Proper Identification of Skills

The competition that currently exists within the financial services industry leads some individuals to promote themselves as being more capable than they actually are. This leads to confusion on the part of the public and can also lead to charges of misrepresentation against both individuals and the financial services industry as a whole.

We need to market ourselves and identify our skills. An illustrative example of an identity crisis is with insurance agents. It is significant that the American Society of Chartered Life Underwriters has changed its name to The Society of Financial Service Professionals. At the very time when many life insurance agents were promoting themselves as professionals, they began to call themselves financial services professionals. As we have seen, some agents fail to identify themselves as insurance agents or their product as insurance because they fear not getting an interview or not making the sale. They feel that the word *insurance* turns people off. However, if you are primarily an insurance agent, then that is what you are. To hide behind another description is self-defeating and it's simply not a good business practice. It creates suspicion. If life insurance is your field and some other product is more suitable for your client than life insurance, then it is proper that you disclose this fact to the client.

There is no reason to be ashamed of the products you represent. The public is becoming increasingly sophisticated in understanding the products you offer. The labeling of the product by another name hides its basic essence and prime benefit. You must identify the product in sales presentations. The only thing to be ashamed of is selling the product to someone who does not need it and for whom it is not suitable.

Honest Marketing

At times, some agents fail to act with integrity or honesty when dealing with clients. The worst cases often involve fraud. When personal gain is pursued at the expense of a client, this indicates a complete ethical failure. When the actions of an agent might not clearly be fraudulent, they are nonetheless open to criticism. It is wrong to misrepresent the characteristics of a product, sell an inferior product to get a larger commission, or sell products that the client does not need. Such sales arise from a lack of honesty, integrity, or objectivity where the agent fails to put himself in the place of the client. Not only does such behavior open financial services professionals up to criticism, but it is poor business practice. For the professional, the client's welfare should be the main focus. Additionally, the professional's reputation is one of his or her most valuable assets, an asset that sleazy marketing practices will undermine.

Thus, we should ask the following questions. Do your clients understand what they are buying? If it is insurance, do they understand it is insurance? Do they understand the type of insurance they are buying? Can your past clients say the same? Do you refer to insurance as an investment? A retirement fund? A tax shelter? Consumers have cited these euphemisms for insurance in lawsuits brought against agents and their companies. It is tempting to call the insurance product something else. It may seem like a much easier way to approach a prospect and close a sale. Avoid that temptation.

The same can be said of the way in which we choose to identify ourselves. How do we identify ourselves when we first introduce ourselves to prospects? It is easy to mislead a client about your role and the type of product you sell.

Another related area is how you identify the type of financial instruments being offered. Does your client understand the difference between insurance and investment? Between a traditional whole life policy and a blended policy? What about a universal life policy and a variable universal policy? Between insurance and an annuity? Between annuities and mutual funds? You may inadvertently forget that your sophistication and understanding of the products are far greater than that of your client.

Take the time to carefully explain who you are and what you are selling. A client who does not understand the product he or she has purchased is like a launched torpedo that has the potential to blow up your career. If you are reluctant to disclose something, either about your product or yourself, ask yourself why. If the answer is that you think you will not make the sale if the client knows the truth, a red flag should go up. To treat clients with respect means you must allow them to make their own decisions about what is best for them—based on the best possible information you can give. That is the essence of honest marketing.

Conclusion:
The Need for Ethical Training

Good business practices can be learned.

An examination of the recent scandals that have beset the financial services industry indicates that agents often fail to realize that their actions could be considered unethical. For example, agents selling their first retirement cases may be unfamiliar with all of the technical terms and requirements of installing qualified retirement plans. Bad advice may be given to clients through ignorance. As a further example, clients may be told that individual retirement accounts (IRAs) can be funded on the basis of unearned income. The retired client, who receives no wages, relying on this advice, sets aside $3,000 of dividends received during the year and takes a tax deduction only to be called by the Internal Revenue Service for an audit. Did the agent intentionally twist the tax facts to get the sale? Probably not. The greater likelihood is that the agent simply failed to investigate the rules. The client was sold an inappropriate plan. The agent now faces threats of legal action and a tarnished reputation due to ignorance of good business practices. Don't be caught in the same trap. Recognize the limitations of your own expertise. Get expert advice when you need it. It's often readily available through your agency or your home office.

Review Item

Misinterpretation of the Tax Code

Agent David MacDonald:

"Mrs. Vogel, why don't you use the interest from this bond fund to make an IRA contribution? I'm sure it doesn't matter that you're retired. We set up an IRA for you while you were still working."

Client, Mrs. Vogel:

"That sounds like a good idea. I'm always interested in ways to lower taxes."

Do you see any problems if the advice Agent MacDonald is giving proves inaccurate? Can you think of any steps Agent MacDonald could take to provide clients with accurate information?

Log your answer in the space below.

Don't be tagged as unethical simply because you are ignorant. Education adds to your expertise. It also increases your awareness of the ethical questions that can arise in a variety of sales situations.

What is all of this talk about ethics? Is it simply a matter of doing right or wrong? In one sense, yes. There are some things that are clearly wrong, like fraud and manipulation. But there are some areas in which things get a little less black and white. We should probably become aware of these sensitive gray areas and develop some tools with which to handle them. That is the focus of the next chapter in this course.

Chapter 1 Review Questions

Answers to Review Questions start on appendix page A-53.

1. An important cause of change in the financial services marketplace is the demographic change that occurred in the last half of the 20th century due largely to
   - (a) individuals outliving their income source
   - (b) computers
   - (c) the emergence of the two-earner family
   - (d) approval rating resurgence

2. Higher legal standards that are being applied to financial services professionals and their companies have created a business ethic environment where
   - (a) caveat emptor is still sufficient
   - (b) caveat emptor is not sufficient
   - (c) caveat vendor is not sufficient
   - (d) caveat vendor is not applicable

3. This ethics course has been developed to help financial services professionals
   - (a) respond to the increased legal pressure that the public has placed upon them
   - (b) respond to the expectations and responsibilities the public has placed upon them
   - (c) deal with the allegations the public has charged them with
   - (d) help insurance companies, banks, and securities firms deflect their increased exposure to legal liability

4. The Gramm-Leach-Bliley Act caused
   - (a) the deregulation of the insurance industry
   - (b) the construction of barriers between the banking, investment banking, and insurance industries
   - (c) the elimination of barriers between the banking, investment banking, and insurance industries
   - (d) the reversal of the McCarran-Ferguson Act

5. The term windowing refers to
   (a) agents using illustrations that may be deceptive in nature
   (b) agents signing clients' signatures on their insurance forms
   (c) agents' omission of facts to the client's detriment
   (d) agents selling products without a clear understanding of them

6. In today's marketplace, the financial services professional is exposed to
   (a) increased legal liability and career risks
   (b) a stagnant level of legal liability and career risks
   (c) decreased legal liability and career risks
   (d) a low-level legal liability and career risks

7. Compared to the consumer of the past, today's consumer of financial products is generally
   (a) better educated and more docile
   (b) better educated and less docile
   (c) less educated and more docile
   (d) less educated and less docile

8. All of the following are major unethical practices in which the abuse of professionalism has occurred EXCEPT
   (a) misuse of illustrations
   (b) necessary policy replacement
   (c) product misrepresentation
   (d) forgery

9. All of the following are major ethical requirements facing the financial services professional EXCEPT
   (a) proper identification of skills
   (b) identifying and meeting customer needs
   (c) the need for compliance training
   (d) honest marketing

10. All of the following are key factors that have contributed to the changes in the financial services marketplace over the past 10 years EXCEPT
    (a) technological advancements
    (b) a changing legal environment
    (c) an increase in the financial services workforce
    (d) the integration of financial services

2

The Ethical Framework

Learning Objectives

2-1. Demonstrate an ethical awareness in analyzing business situations.

2-2. Define what ethics means.

2-3. Identify the possible consequences and penalties of unethical conduct for the financial services professional.

2-4. List the four major ethical principles.

2-5. Identify the six steps of the ethical decision procedure used to evaluate the ethical appropriateness of an action.

2-6. List the six major constituencies to whom the financial services professional has ethical obligations.

2-7. Describe what *role morality* is.

Chapter Outline

What Is Ethics?

An Ethical Sensitivity Exercise   2-3
Your Responses to These Scenarios   2-6
   Areas of Agreement   2-6
   Areas of Disagreement   2-8
   How to Score the Exercise   2-11
Ethics Defined   2-11
Why Ethics Is Important   2-14
Penalties for Unethical Behavior   2-15
Ethics As a Set of Beliefs of What is Right or Wrong   2-16
The Purpose of Ethical Rules   2-17
Evaluating Our Ethical Beliefs   2-18
Four Basic Ethical Principles   2-20
Six Questions to Ascertain the Ethics of an Action   2-21
   Is the Action Good or Harmful for Me?   2-21
   Is the Action Good for Others?   2-22
   Is the Action Fair or Just?   2-22
   Is There a Commitment?   2-23
   Does It Preserve My Integrity?   2-24
   Is the Action Legal?   2-24
A Decision Procedure   2-24
Role Morality   2-26
Ethical Obligations to Six Constituencies   2-27
   Obligations to the Client   2-27
   Obligations to the Company   2-27
   Obligations to the Profession   2-27
   Obligations to Allied Professionals   2-28
   Obligations to Oneself and Others Related to Us   2-28
   Obligations to Society and Its Laws   2-28
Summary   2-29
Conclusion   2-29
Chapter 2 Review Questions   2-30

What Is Ethics?

An Ethical Sensitivity Exercise

During our lives, we often need to decide whether acting in a certain way is or is not ethical. That is when we exercise our ethical judgment. Let's start with a set of scenarios that describe an action and see what you think of them. In the exercise that follows, you will consider some actions and be asked if you have any ethical reservations about them.

- If you have no ethical reservations about the action described, put a check in the box labeled "None."
- If you have serious reservations about performing the action, put a check in the box labeled "Major."
- If you have only have minor reservations about the action, check the box labeled "Minor."
- If you have more moderate reservations about performing the action, check the box labeled "Moderate."

Whichever way you feel, put a check in the appropriate box to indicate the degree of your reservations about performing the action described in the exercise.

Some of these scenarios might be a bit ambiguous. That is okay for now. We will worry about the ambiguity later. Just use your imagination to fill in the blanks in each scenario so you will be able to indicate your level of ethical concern.

Now look at each of the scenarios in the Ethical Sensitivity Awareness Exercise, which is on pages 2-4 and 2-5, and check the box that best represents your level of ethical concern.

We'll explain the scoring on page 2-11.

Test Your Ethical Sensitivity/Awareness

Ethical Dilemma	Level of Ethical Concern				Score
	None	**Minor**	**Moderate**	**Major**	
1. You don't inform a wife who has limited ability to manage funds when her husband asks you to draft a codicil to his will increasing the amount put in trust for the minor children.					
2. You take full credit for an ingenious use of a product that one of your agents developed.					
3. You inform the children of an elderly man about the erratic changes he has made in his will. A recent widower, he asked you to change his will to leave most of his money to the SPCA, with whose director he claims to have fallen deeply in love. The director's son, a financial planner, will make the changes if you do not.					
4. You give NFL box seat tickets to the human resource director of a company to expedite negotiations on an employee benefits package you want to sell to that company. (Such gifts are an expected perk in the director's company.)					
5. You join a service club in the city where your agency operates in order to network.					
6. You advise your client's husband how to reduce her share of his estate because he thinks she is suffering from dementia.					
7. You give your wife a gift to make up for not going with her to the theater as you promised, because you had to meet with a client who had asked for an impromptu meeting.					
8. You don't mention a replacement product's downside to a client.					
9. You lower fees for services for new clients without a corresponding rate decrease for older clients.					
10. You put off completing the annual financial report for your child's scouting organization so that you can finish a presentation to an important client.					
11. You indicate on a life insurance application that a client is a nonsmoker, even though you know he smokes.					

Test Your Ethical Sensitivity/Awareness (Continued)					
Ethical Dilemma	**Level of Ethical Concern**				**Score**
	None	**Minor**	**Moderate**	**Major**	
12. You provide a friend with confidential knowledge that your company plans to merge so he can buy stock in the company, thus making a quick profit on the merger.					
13. You bring a competent colleague in to help you with a planning case that is a bit beyond your reach because you feel the client doesn't trust you to do it alone.					
14. You decide to use a financial planner of dubious competency from your multidisciplinary firm to help you with a difficult case, even though you know that there is a more capable planner available who is not part of your firm.					
15. You encourage your client to sign multiple fund transfer forms in blank and give you verbal approval to use them at your discretion.					
16. You turn over your lower-income clients, to whom you promised originally to serve as their lifelong agent, to a junior colleague because their accounts are not lucrative enough to be worth your while financially.					
17. You do not reveal information to your manager about the possible market conduct violations of one of the producers affiliated with your office.					
18. You place a young agent under the supervision of a mentor to improve his production prior to his possible dismissal.					
19. You set up a charitable remainder trust for the benefit of your client and offer it to a charity for a commission of 5 percent of the funding amount.					
20. You expedite the transactions for a middle-aged client with minimal investment experience who insists on investing a significant portion of her total assets in high-risk funds.					
Your Score	x0	+x1	+x2	+x3	= Total

Your Responses to These Scenarios

Areas of Agreement

No Reservations—Let's look first at areas where most people would probably agree. To begin, I'll bet there were some scenarios where you had no reservations. Did you have any difficulties with number 5, joining the local service club? Probably not. Most people don't. Services organizations help people. Why would you have a problem with someone joining one? Doing good is laudatory. But wait. Every once in a while someone has a problem with your joining a service club, because doing so helps your business networking. They are objecting to your doing a good thing for the wrong reasons. They are considering an aspect of an ethical issue that is very subtle. You not only should do the right thing, but you should also do it for the right reasons, or your motives should be pure. Well, I'm inclined to think there is nothing wrong with doing something that helps you. But if that's your only reason for doing something, then you are in trouble morally.

Did you have any difficulty with number 13, bringing in a competent colleague to help you with a planning case that is a bit beyond your reach because you feel the client doesn't trust you to do it alone? Isn't that exactly what the competency requirement of most codes of ethics would demand? If you aren't competent, you should get help.

Let's look at another scenario. How about number 18? You are placing a young agent under a mentor's supervision to improve his production prior to possible dismissal. What could be wrong with that? It seems like you are trying to help someone with potential who desperately needs assistance to fulfill that potential. Some might think that such an action is going too far for a manager, being too nice, but by and large, most people would have no reservations about such activity.

Those are three scenarios about which most people would agree they have no reservations. And that should tell us some things about ethics. The first thing is that there are areas in ethics where all, or most, people agree. The second thing is that all of ethics is not about the hard cases. Ethics permeates all of our lives. It deals with the good actions and the bad actions of people. There are things we do that we are supposed to do, and we should have no reservations about doing them. At best, we should have reservations about not doing them.

Serious Reservations—Now let's take a look at some scenarios with which most people have serious reservations.

How about number 2, taking full credit for a product that one of your agents developed? Most people think that is wrong. It is not fair and it does harm to your peer by taking credit away from him to you.

How about number 11, filling out a life insurance application for a client you know smokes? You indicate she is a nonsmoker, because she claims your job is simply to write down the answers she gives. She'll find another agent if you don't. Most people have serious reservations about this. Why? Because it involves lying, and most of us think it's wrong to lie, even if you do it to help a client and yourself.

How about number 12, mentioning to a friend confidential knowledge that your company plans to merge so your friend can buy stock in the company? Most people also have serious reservations about this, because it involves insider trading, a practice that is generally frowned upon in financial circles, not to mention that it is illegal.

How about number 15, encouraging a client to sign blank multiple fund transfer forms and to give you verbal approval to use them at your discretion? Most people from the insurance industry have serious reservations about this behavior although there may be nothing intrinsically wrong with it. For example, if I give a signed blank check to my wife whom I trust with my life and tell her to fill out the amount when she needs the money, there is absolutely no ethical problem with that. If two people trust each other, one may get the other to sign a blank check or a fund transfer form to be utilized at the other's discretion. It may be imprudent and unwise, but it is not unethical. The reason so many agents have reservations about it is because of the abuse of this business practice back in the late 1980s and early 1990s.

There may be other scenarios with which you have serious reservations, and we will get to those. Right now we are concentrating on the situations with which almost all people have serious reservations. If you have serious reservations about scenarios 2, 11, 12, and 15, you are in agreement with a large number of fellow financial services professionals. What this agreement shows is that there is unanimity, a like-mindedness, about ethical issues. And where there is like-mindedness, there is an ethical community or culture. After all, the word *ethics* comes from *ethos*, which means culture; the word *morals* comes from *mores*, which means the way of doing things.

One of the things we will do in this course is to look at issues where there is a great deal of agreement about proper ethical behavior, what we call "no brainers." For example, you should not falsify an application because that is a lie. This is a "no brainer" because it is clear what should and should not be done.

However, it's important to note that because we shouldn't do something doesn't mean we won't go ahead and do it. We are all familiar with the phenomenon of doing something we know is wrong. None of us is perfect, but the fact that we do something wrong, or that a lot of people do something wrong, doesn't make it right. We will return to this issue.

Areas of Disagreement

In addition to those areas in which we have agreement, there are those with which there is legitimate and real disagreement. I've assumed agreement about scenarios 2, 5, 11, 12, 13, 15, and 18. That comprises more than a third of the scenarios. But it also leaves about two-thirds for which there is usually some disagreement.

Sometimes there is disagreement because we just don't have enough facts. Sometimes there is disagreement because we operate by different sets of rules. And sometimes there is disagreement because there is some deep conflict about values and/or principles. Let's briefly look at each of these scenarios and at the possible reasons for the disagreement.

Scenario 1—not informing a wife about her husband's request that he asked you to draft a codicil to his will increasing the amount put in trust for the minor children. The wife appears to have limited ability to manage funds. This scenario usually generates a great deal of discussion and disagreement, because it involves a complexity of relationships. Are both the wife and the husband clients? If so, do you need to inform the wife about the husband's request? Can you continue to be an advisor to both of them? How far does confidentiality bind you when it requires you to keep a confidence of one client, which may violate the other client's right to know?

Scenario 3—informing the children of an elderly male client about his strange, erratic behavior. (A recent widower, he asked you to change his will to leave most of his money to the SPCA, with whose director he claims to have fallen deeply in love. This raises questions similar to those in scenario 1 about confidentiality.) What is your responsibility to your client, who is apparently suffering from some sort of dementia? Do you follow his wishes if you suspect he is not capable of making decisions for his own benefit? How seriously are you bound by the rule to look out for a client's best interest, particularly when those best interests will not be served if you do not accede to the client's wishes? Who are you to determine what is in the client's best interest? Shouldn't you just do what the client asks even if, in your best professional judgment, it is not suitable?

Scenario 4—giving box seat tickets to an NFL game to the human resource director of a company to expedite the adoption of an employee benefits package you are pushing. (This would be an expected perk in his company.) There is usually disagreement when evaluating that action and it can generate much discussion. Is giving tickets to a client to encourage him to give you business appropriate? Is it similar to a bribe or is it just the way we do business? Is it okay if you are an RIA (Registered Investment Advisor)? After all, there is a monetary limit to the size of gift you can accept. Would this be okay if it were tickets to a minor league baseball game instead of an NFL game? Tickets to minor league baseball games are much less expensive than those to NFL games. What are the rules governing giving and receiving gifts for insurance agents, financial planners, and investment advisors? Are they the same or not? Here we need more facts. We also need specific knowledge of the particular rules of the associations to which you belong.

Scenario 6—advising your client's husband how to minimize his wife's share of his estate because he thinks his wife, your client, suffers from dementia. It's his second marriage, there are no children, and your client has her own assets. The scenario involves violating your client's rights to your services, but it is probably for the long-run benefit of both her and her husband. More facts are needed about your relationship to the husband and the client. There are best-interest issues as well as confidentiality and fiduciary issues involved.

Scenario 7—substituting a gift for a theater date with your spouse because you have to meet with a client for an impromptu meeting. This scenario raises an issue about what to do when faced with a conflict of loyalties, if not conflicting commitments. There is an ever-growing concern over the struggle between the demands of a personal life and the demands of a business life. How are we to resolve these competing demands?

Scenario 8—not mentioning or adequately discussing the replacement of your client's old traditional life policy prior to her signing an application for a new policy because of her busy schedule. There is a general consensus that this is, at least, moderately problematic. Most suggest it is the agent's responsibility to insist that the client make the time to meet with the agent. If the client refuses, the agent should not finalize the transaction. But there are those who maintain that it is the client's decision about how informed the client should be.

Scenario 9—lowering fees for services for new clients without a corresponding rate decrease for older clients. This generates a great deal of disagreement because lower fees mean less income. The question revolves around what is fair.

Scenario 10—delaying completion of an annual financial report needed by your child's scouting organization so you can complete an important client presentation. Here, you are faced with a common ethical problem: a conflict of obligations. You have an obligation both to the scout club and to the client. Who gets precedence? The disagreements about what to do are often solved with more information. If the annual report is not due immediately, you can postpone it because no one will be harmed. If it can't be postponed, you may have to delay the client presentation. We face conflicts like this quite often. They are not always easy to resolve. One of the goals of this course is to give you some tools that will enable you to evaluate a situation and perhaps come up with a practical solution that is also an ethical one.

Scenario 14—deciding to use a financial planner whose judgment you question from your multidisciplinary firm to help you with a difficult case, even though you know there is a more capable planner available who is not part of your firm. This raises a serious question faced by those who work, or are contemplating working, in a multidisciplinary financial planning firm. Is one's obligation more to the firm than to the client?

Scenario 16—turning over your lower-income clients to a junior colleague because they are not lucrative enough to be worth your while financially. You originally promised those clients you would be their lifelong agent. This is a situation with which more and more high-end agents wrestle. It appears to involve breaking one's word to the client. Some argue that it is in the client's best interest to step aside and let the clients be serviced by someone who can give them more time. At any rate, it raises the issue of what would be a good reason for setting aside or not abiding by a promise. Are there times when it is all right not to do what one promised?

Scenario 17—not revealing information to your manager about possible market conduct violations of one of the producers affiliated with your office. This circumstance raises issues about how responsible we are to blow the whistle to keep our profession ethical and honorable. Obviously, because deciding when and if blowing the whistle is required is such a hard issue, one can expect much disagreement about this course of action.

Scenario 19—setting up a charitable remainder trust for your client and offering it to a charity for a commission of 5 percent of the funding amount. There is often disagreement in the area of finder's fees, but it is a violation of the code of ethics of the Association of Fundraising Professionals, which prohibits finder's fees or compensation based on percentages of contributions. Such compensation creates conflicts of interest.

Scenario 20—going along with a middle-aged client with minimal investment experience who insists on investing a significant portion of her total assets in high-risk funds. This action raises the issue of what it means to look out for the client's best interest, particularly when what the client wants is clearly not in her own best interest. If a product is not suitable, can I sell it to a client anyway, simply because the client wants it? Or does my professional status require that I refuse to do what is clearly not in my client's best interest?

As we indicated, two-thirds of the scenarios are likely to generate disagreement and discussion about the proper course of action. Discussing these scenarios, deciding what you believe, and discovering what specific rules govern your behavior are the central activities of ethical analysis.

How to Score the Exercise

This activity should help you to discover how sensitive you are to the ethical dimension of some situations you face in your day-to-day existence. Some people are too sensitive; some are probably not sensitive enough. If you want to compare yourself to others, add up your score—you get 0 points for None, 1 point for Minor, 2 points for Moderate, and 3 points for Major. The majority of planners who have done this exercise fall in the range of 29 to 36. We make no claims for its scientific validity; simply use this range as a guide for how you compare with a large number of other financial services professionals. Look at figure 2-1. Wherever you fall in the sensitivity range, it is important to be aware that every action has an ethical dimension.

Ethics Defined

What is ethics? Ethics deals with the question, "What should one do?" It doesn't apply in *all* situations, of course, for you can ask, "*Should* one put the fork on the left or the right of the plate?" or "How often *should* one change the oil in a car?" or "*Should* one add more color to the corner

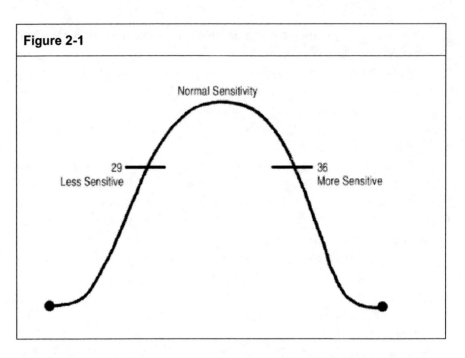

Figure 2-1

of the painting to give it balance?" Those are simply cases of etiquette, car maintenance, and aesthetics. Ethics deals with what people should do in situations where actions can seriously affect their own well-being or the well-being of others. If you put the fork on the right, no person's well-being is seriously affected for better or worse. If you fire a loyal employee, however, that employee's well-being is seriously affected.

As mentioned, the word *ethics* is derived from the ancient Greek word *ethos*, which means customs or habits. Ethics, therefore, refers to the rules people live by or the customary way of doing something. People internalize the rules and customs of their society while they are growing up, sometimes to such an extent that they are not even aware that they are following those rules and customs. Consider how many people, without even thinking about it, bring a notebook to class and automatically take notes. They learned that behavior long ago, and they internalized it so much that they don't even think about what they are doing. Certainly taking notes is not an ethical rule, but the example is indicative of how we follow rules we have internalized without thinking. Most of us learn ethical principles at home, in our schools, through the religious institutions with which we are affiliated, or through the stories we are told, we read, or we absorb through the media such as television.

The purpose of the rules is, of course, to make society an orderly place. As we also mentioned, the word *morals*, which for all practical purposes is synonymous with ethics, is derived from the Latin word *mores* and also refers to societal customs and rules. Any society requires rules to exist in an orderly fashion and will have its own ethics or mores. To the extent that it successfully socializes or civilizes its members, that set of rules will be incorporated into the thinking processes and attitudes of the group's members. Hence, any adult of any group comes equipped with a set of moral or ethical rules that he or she has "inherited" from his or her culture.

There is historical evidence that moral codes have existed at all times in all places. They are a necessary part of the human order. Without them there would be chaos. These codes have been applied in various forms in diverse situations and circumstances, and have developed in different ways. Some moral codes developed in conjunction with religious beliefs. Others developed as a result of customs to promote human harmony. For example, in ancient Egypt, strong secular leaders established precepts which, in combination with a strict religion, affected the behavior of all members of Egyptian society. In Israel, the Judaic religion guided moral behavior. Its tenets were spelled out in the commandments of the Mosaic law and members of Hebrew society were expected to follow these standards without question. Early Christian thought focused on the role of God to achieve good—God's help was necessary; will and intelligence alone were insufficient. However moral codes developed, it is instructional to remember how similar the various moral codes are. (Christianity shares a common theme with all the major religions of the world as expressed in the Golden Rule: Whatsoever you wish that men do to you, do so unto them.)

Ancient Greek thinkers—including Socrates, Plato, and Aristotle—were the first to theoretically speculate about what constitutes right or wrong behavior. They helped identify some of the major principles underlying most moral codes.

The Golden Rule

The Golden Rule is a universal ethical norm, utilized by most, if not all, the major religions. Consider the following six versions:

1. Good people proceed while considering that what is best for others is best for themselves. (Hitopadesa, Hinduism)

2. Thou shalt regard thy neighbor as thyself. (Leviticus 19:18, Judaism)

3. All things whatsoever ye would that men should do to you, do ye even so to them. (Matthew 7:12, Christianity)

4. Hurt not others with that which pains yourself. (Udanavarga 5:18, Buddhism)

5. What you do not want done to yourself, do not do to others. (Analects 15:23, Confucianism)

6. No one of you is a believer until he loves for his brother what he loves for himself. (Traditions, Islam)

Modern secular thinkers held that ethics provides a sort of social contract that gives us guidance on how to flourish in society. Adam Smith in *The Wealth of Nations* provided us with an ethical framework for modern business. It is often called the *enlightened self-interest model*. Smith claims that the free enterprise system, which espouses liberty and autonomy, works and has prospered because it benefits the common good when constrained by justice. We will examine the different theories and see what they have in common.

Why Ethics Is Important

There are those who feel that ethics is an esoteric subject, one reserved for scholars and not for business people. Some say, "There's no such thing as business ethics." But what are those people indicating? That they can cheat? That they can steal? That they are not to be trusted? Ethics is absolutely essential to business running well. Without ethics in business, there would be no trust. Without ethics, no one would keep promises. There would be no reliability. It would be a dog-eat-dog world of the survival of the fittest. There would be no real giving of advice, which requires looking out for the best interest of the advisee, not the advisor. Ethics is necessary for, and allows, human beings to get along together so they can flourish. This especially applies in the financial services industry.

When a member of the public buys a financial product, the very nature of the transaction is usually lopsided. It involves what is called *knowledge asymmetry*. The agent generally knows far more about the product than the client. The contract is drafted by the company, not by competing teams of attorneys representing both sides. Trust is the key ingredient. Without a sense of trust that (1) the agent is looking out for the client's interest, (2) the agent is fairly representing the product, and (3) the company will honor its obligations, few consumers would be willing to purchase financial products like insurance. Trust is an elusive concept. It takes years to build but can be torn down quickly. When the scandals of Enron, Adelphia, and World Com came to light, people lost trust in the integrity of the financial markets.

The financial services industry is now at a crossroads. Over the years, the industry has honored its obligations, and consumers have had faith in what they were told in sales presentations. Unfortunately, recent events have now undermined this trust. The need to restore public trust is urgent. Each of our livelihoods is at stake. Each of us has a role in this process. Our actions and the way we conduct our business affairs must become an important part of the equation. Restoring the public trust involves going beyond the mere letter of the law to a full-fledged effort on the part of agents to act in an ethical manner—to take that extra step to do what is right. Good ethics is good business.

Review Item

Proper Product Representation

Agent Holland:

"This policy is just like a mutual fund, even better. It will take care of your retirement needs."

Do you detect an ethical problem?

Log your answer in the space below.

Penalties for Unethical Behavior

There is another reason to behave ethically.

As we have learned from the Enron and World Com scandals, the penalties for ethical lapses are severe. Not every breach of ethics is detected, but where unethical behavior is discovered, its costs can more than outweigh any potential gains. Ethical breaches end careers more quickly and more definitely than any other lapse in business judgment. The proof is in the headlines of articles on the financial services scandals. Will any of those professionals ever work in the industry again?

Not every ethical breach is subject to the broad light of public scrutiny. In many cases, the individual involved in unethical behavior keeps his or her job. But a reputation is developed. It's not a bright and shining one. It's tarnished. The individual becomes known as someone more concerned about personal gain than the interests of others.

Finally, and perhaps most important, being unethical can erode your very soul. Most successful financial services professionals realize that business is just a part of life, that their work life cannot be completely separate and apart from their private life.

These lives are interwoven; the ethical tenets these professionals practice carry over and are a part of both areas of life. A well-grounded value system provides these successful individuals with a full ethical professional life and a full ethical life with friends and family.

There is no guarantee that through the study of ethics you will become a better person. But it can help you realize the ethical implications of some behaviors you might not have considered and give you a systematic tool for dealing with tough ethical situations. A study of ethics increases your awareness of the reasons for your judgments as well as the direct consequences and indirect implications of your actions.

Sometimes people simply don't realize that what they are doing is ethically problematic. We all know what happens when a financial services trainee comes under the direction of an unscrupulous trainer, whose only thought is to make money. The trainee starts to think that coercive salesmanship is the norm in the industry. "Everyone acts that way" becomes a rationalization used to justify unacceptable behavior. Sometimes people need to be taught the right way to do things. Sometimes people without experience have just never thought about certain activities as being unethical. People often need tools to help resolve a difficult situation. Ideally, the study of ethics can help in these areas.

Ethics As a Set of Beliefs of What is Right or Wrong

Let's elaborate on the importance of a point we made earlier about the source of our ethical beliefs. As we mentioned, no person grows up isolated from some group or society. The person would not survive. We all inherit our attitudes or beliefs about right or wrong from the group that nurtured us. We learn ethical rules when we are young, and the rules become so internalized that we rarely think about them; they become almost second nature to us. If we think of our mind as a kind of file cabinet in which these rules and ethical beliefs are stored, with a little effort we can take inventory of our beliefs. For example, a person might believe euthanasia is wrong, capital punishment is wrong, lying is wrong, and so on. The list of beliefs and attitudes concerning actions and social practices can go on indefinitely.

Our attitudes and beliefs come from many areas of society—family, religion, school, TV, peers, the workplace, and so on. While some learn their attitudes and beliefs from the Ten Commandments, their parents, or their church or synagogue, it is possible in this day and age that just as many people learned their rules from television. Think of all the rules of sharing and of being kind and considerate that a child learns from *Sesame Street* or from the TV characters Barney and Scooby Doo, where it is always clear who is good and who is bad. No matter where the rules are learned or how they are learned, these attitudes and beliefs form a set of ethical or moral rules for behavior.

The Purpose of Ethical Rules

It is important to note that the primary purpose of ethical rules is to help society function smoothly, so people can get along and flourish together, not fight and destroy each other. Society is a web of relationships, and a well-functioning society is based on healthy relationships. Hence, the purpose of morality and ethics is to help relationships that are healthy not only to survive but also to flourish.

According to Stanley Cavel, morality is a "social institution (and/or God-given set of laws), composed of a set of standards about practices, defining right or wrong, for the purpose of rationally adjudicating disputes while allowing relationships to continue."[1] This definition is crucial, for it points out that the purpose of morality is to help settle disputes while preserving relationships that are necessary for the society's well-being. There are, of course, nonethical ways of settling disputes. For example, we can settle disputes by using brute power or force, but if we do that, we fall into the law of the jungle, where might makes right.

Human beings do not have to revert to the use of pure force. People have the ability to use reason, to figure out the ways to resolve their disputes and maintain relationships. Reason helps in the development of ethical or moral codes. For example, our reason tells us if we don't share some things, life will be nasty, brutal, and short, to paraphrase the 17th century English philosopher Thomas Hobbes. So we teach our children to share and to be fair at a very early age. We recommend that they don't

---

1. Stanley Cavel, *The Claims of Reason.*

fight over a toy, and we show them that it will be much better if they take turns and cooperate. When we get older and more sophisticated, we recommend to our colleagues that they seek win-win situations.

Our attitudes about who has a right to what, and who deserves what, reflect our ethical beliefs and give us ways to resolve disputes while allowing relationships to flourish. Humans talk about and attempt to reach agreement about what's just or fair. Those agreed-upon beliefs comprise their ethics or morality, which are the means for resolving disputes. If we never had disputes, we would not need ethics because we could all just do what we want.

It follows that it would be a mistake to think ethics is a purely subjective or personal matter. As we have seen, the main purpose of ethics is the resolution of interpersonal disputes in which the individual is only one player among many. We are not the source of our ethical beliefs, and the purpose of ethics is not to help us achieve what we want. Such a view is frightfully egocentric. Most of our beliefs came from outside us and were impressed on us by members of the culture into which we were born.

We can, of course, reflect on our beliefs to see if we should submit to being governed by them. It is when we become reflective about these beliefs that we enter the domain of ethics referred to as the philosophical subject, but the beliefs are there long before we begin such reflection. In that sense, we *have* ethics (our set of beliefs and attitudes) before we *do* ethics (reflect on and evaluate our beliefs and attitudes). The answer to the question of whether or not we should submit to the rule of our beliefs is not determined by whether or not we want to submit to them, but by our examination of their purpose and whether that purpose is justifiable.

Evaluating Our Ethical Beliefs

At some time in our lives, our moral beliefs will either conflict with each other or be challenged. The challenge will arise from harsh reality or from someone who holds an opposing opinion. At that point, a cognitive/affective disequilibrium will occur, and we will have to reflect on the adequacy of one or more of our beliefs. It is then that we begin to *do* ethics—the philosophical discipline—through the analysis and evaluation of our ethical beliefs.

For example, Huck Finn grew up believing slavery was okay, that slaves were the property of their masters, and that runaway slaves needed to be returned to their masters. Huck's beliefs were challenged when he traveled down the Mississippi with Jim, the runaway slave. Jim looked as human to Huck as any other man. So Huck began to question the ethical rules with which he grew up. How was it right to treat two people who are the same differently? Huck confronted the issue of justice. We all go through such epiphanies when our values or moral beliefs are challenged. We either ignore the challenge or do ethics. That is, we begin to analyze what we believe and then evaluate whether those beliefs are adequate.

Young financial services professionals may fall under the spell of an unscrupulous mentor who teaches them exploitative sales techniques and then justifies them by saying, "That's the way we do it in this business. Just make the numbers." The ethical professional will smell something wrong in such a situation and try to get out of it.

We can't avoid doing ethics even if we want to. One of the most popular phenomena of today is talk radio, more particularly sports talk radio. But after talking about who is the better baseball or basketball player, the talk often moves on to ethical issues. Should the Dallas Cowboys renegotiate Emmett Smith's contract? Should Pete Rose be allowed back into baseball? Should a basketball player be suspended for violating a league drug policy? Should players honor their contracts? Do players have a duty to be role models? The answer to any of these questions requires that a person has a set of beliefs about what's fair or just, a set of beliefs he or she uses to adjudicate disputes. In short, the answer to any of these questions requires having an ethic and doing ethics.

Doing ethics is engaging in philosophical speculation about how we ought to live. In its most academic form, ethics is that branch of philosophy concerned with analyzing, explaining, and/or justifying the rules of right and wrong. The part of ethics that analyzes and evaluates is reflective. It reflects on our learned customs and mores to judge what they demand of us or others and whether those demands are sufficient or appropriate.

Let's take a simple example of rules being subject to various interpretations. Does the commandment "Thou shalt not kill" simply prohibit killing human beings, or does it extend to animals and plants? Albert Schweitzer thought it referred to all living creatures. Does it even extend to all humans? Are there exceptions? Defenders of capital punishment argue that it does not apply to all humans. Do other animals have rights? To answer these questions, we must engage in ethical analysis.

What about situations in which standards or rules conflict with one another? Suppose the obligations of family life conflict with those of work. Suppose your obligation to your company conflicts with your obligation to your client. How do you resolve those conflicts?

Finally, consider situations in which our rules and standards conflict with those of other people. Think of the conflicts over abortion, euthanasia, or capital punishment in our society. Consider the conflict over the acceptability of rebates or disclosure of commissions in the field of life insurance. Are there ways to resolve these disputes?

Four Basic Ethical Principles

To solve ethical disputes, we need to make judgments about alternative courses of action. We make such judgments by investigating the *reasons* why some actions are deemed ethically appropriate and others are not. For example, we have seen that we should not falsify an application because that is a lie. We could ask, "Why is lying wrong?" And we would get a host of answers: "Lies hurt people." "Lies use other people." "To lie is not to play fair."

There are a number of reasons why we approve or disapprove of our actions. One basic reason why we approve of an action is that the action is beneficial. We disapprove of actions that are harmful. These reasons provide us with a basic ethical principle: "Do good and avoid harm." A second reason why we approve of an action is that it is just or fair. Fairness concerns lead us to the principle of respect for others: "Do unto others as you would have them do unto you," the Golden Rule. A third reason why an action should be carried out is that a person has promised to do it. This leads to the principle: "Keep your word." Finally, actions that allow a person to keep his or her integrity are acceptable. This leads to the principle: "Be true to yourself."

On a practical level, ethics attempts to apply these four ethical principles to specific situations. Sometimes situations are complicated and the principles conflict—for example, when an action benefits me but damages others or when keeping a commitment will bring harm. Another example: when I sell a product the client does not need to gain the commission, I violate the Golden Rule. There are actions in which we are detached from the consequences, but where principles still conflict. Should I do something unlawful, such as verify a false statement, to help a client get a better rate?

These principles give us a clear set of reasons that ethically justify actions. Let's review the reasons. If the action benefits me or society, that is a good reason to do it. If the action harms me or society, that is a good reason *not* to do it. If I promised to perform the action, that is a good reason to do it unless it is somehow harmful to me or society. If it is unfair or unjust, that is a good reason *not* to do it. If the action violates someone's rights, that is a good reason *not* to do it. Remember: Ethical issues or problems arise only when there are good reasons to perform and good reasons not to perform actions. To ascertain whether there are good reasons for an action, such as those mentioned above, there is a set of questions, which depend upon those reasons.

Six Questions to Ascertain the Ethics of an Action

Is the Action Good or Harmful for Me?

In judging an action, one should always ask, "Will it hurt or help me?" Obviously, if an action is beneficial to the person performing the action, that is a good reason for that person to do it. For example, a very important reason to work is that work is beneficial. It provides the wherewithal to live and, ideally, it allows a person to engage in fulfilling activity. Meaningful work is work that is beneficial to the person. We have a need to be creative and productive, and meaningful work can help us fulfill that need. Hence, it is good for us.

However, as we saw in the earlier example of the service club, some people are suspicious of self-interested motivation and are, therefore, hesitant to defend actions that are beneficial to themselves. That is a mistake. Healthy self-interest is a good thing.

If you don't concern yourself with your own benefit, who will? However, a caveat is necessary. What benefits you is not necessarily what you want or desire. Our wants and our desires are a mixed bag. I want the piece of pie, but it is not good for me because I am on a diet.

We must further clarify what is meant by *good*. For our purposes, let us say that which fulfills basic human needs is good, although there may be other things that are also good. Human beings have different levels of need. There are physical needs for food, shelter, and clothing. There is the need for health, for some minimum wealth, and early solid training in how to get along in society. Because human beings are social, there are needs for relating to other people, as in friendship. These are the needs of the social dimension of human beings. Finally, because human beings are potential producers, there is a need for meaningful activity for projects and goals and actions with a point to them. These are the needs that fulfill the creative level. To provide these needs for oneself is an important reason for performing an action. In short, we can often justify our belief that an action is good simply by showing that it is good for us.

Is the Action Good for Others?

The second question to ask of any action is whether it is going to be good for others. When we think ethically, we do not usually stop to consider the benefit of the action for ourselves; we go further and think of its benefits for everyone affected. Not every action performed in the world affects us. In the fall of 1982, since neither I nor anyone else I knew used Tylenol, whether Johnson and Johnson pulled it from the shelves because cyanide-laced capsules had killed five people really didn't affect me. It was neither good nor bad for me. Nonetheless, I can say removing Tylenol from the shelves was a good thing to do, because removing it probably benefited all those who might have used it. Simply, if a good reason for doing an action is that it benefits me and if everyone counts as much as I do, then the reason is true for everyone. The more people benefited, the better. Of course, when the action benefits society but does harm to me, there is a problem. We will discuss this. (Note that the questions about benefit or harm deal with the consequences of the action. The next set of questions deals more with the action itself.)

Is the Action Fair or Just?

It is only logical to believe that if two things are the same, they should be treated in the same way. How can you justify treating one differently from another if there are no relevant differences? Of course, someone might have two identical people in need and only enough goods for one of them. In that situation, we would not know to whom to give the goods.

In such a case, flipping a coin is as fair a solution as any. Hence, if there is no relevant difference between two children, they are both being given a piece of cake, and there is enough cake to go around, they should each get a piece of roughly the same size. One cannot justify giving one child or the other a larger piece. However, if it were one of the children's birthdays, then the children are not the same in all relevant respects, and it would be fair for the birthday child to get a larger piece. The birthday creates a good relevant reason for one child to get a bigger piece of cake.

The principle of justice, which is in many ways the basis of ethical thinking and puts limits on the pursuit of self-interest, holds that "the same should be treated the same." We all recognize and use this principle. To see that, you need only to reflect on how annoyed you get when someone, who you think is no better than you are, gets special treatment. You think that person does not deserve it any more than you do.

Thus, if an action treats people unfairly—for example, differently, without a good reason—it is ethically suspect.

Is There a Commitment?

The fourth important question to ask is, "Is there a commitment?" Were any promises made to do something? If there were, they ought to be kept. Keeping promises is a good reason for doing something.

We need to note that there are commitments that go beyond those that result from explicit promises and contracts. Any lasting relationship rests on implied promises and expectations of guaranteed behavior in spite of the contingencies of the future. Customers expect to get the benefits promised in insurance advertisements and do not expect to be cheated because of disclaimers in the small print. A professor commits himself or herself to show up for a class a certain number of times at a certain time for a certain length of time. Our commitments penetrate the future and bind us to a course of action, no matter whether we feel like keeping our promises or not. Human beings are unique promise-making animals. Although other species act largely by instinct, human beings set up their relationships with each other on the basis of expectations and promises. Hence, we can say that the basis of any ethics is to keep one's commitments. It is what distinguishes us from the rest of the animal kingdom. Our social structure depends on promises and cannot function if these promises are not kept. Thus, another very good reason for doing something is that you have made a promise or commitment.

Does It Preserve My Integrity?

This question is related to the previous one. If people keep their commitments, they are true to their word. In one sense, someone's word defines a person. Our promises and commitments define what we are, and failure to keep them makes us irresponsible and unfaithful to our word. Keeping one's word is as much a part of integrity as being honest. But there is another aspect of integrity. The word *integrity* comes from the field of integers in mathematics. Integers are whole numbers. Integrity, therefore, means wholeness. A person who acts one way in business and another in his or her personal life lacks integrity. A business decision that is not in conformity with personal values fractures a person and can destroy his or her integrity.

Is the Action Legal?

This is the final question to ask when evaluating an action: "Is it legal?" The law is society's instrument for enforcing morality and imposing sanctions. Assuming, then, that laws are in conformity with what is ethical and beneficial to society, it is good to obey them. Breaking the law can lead to punishment. All financial services professionals are familiar with the many regulations and laws that govern their practice and the burden imposed on them by compliance. Ethics and the law are not identical, and there can be unjust laws. The relation of the law to ethics is so complicated, we will defer an examination of it until the next chapter.

> ### Ethical Decision Procedure
>
> Six questions to ask when evaluating an action or practice from an *ethical point of view.*
>
> - An answer of "yes" to all means we have an unqualifiedly good action or practice.
>
> - An answer of "no" to all means we have an unqualifiedly bad action or practice.
>
> - "Yes" and "no" answers mean we have a complicated ethical issue that needs sophisticated analysis.
>
>   1. Does it benefit me?
>   2. Does it benefit all the others affected by the action?
>   3. Is it fair?
>   4. Does it meet my commitments?
>   5. Does it preserve my integrity?
>   6. Is it legal?

A Decision Procedure

By using the questions above, we can set up a decision procedure to discover what we should do. If I answer "yes" to all of the questions, I have an action that clearly should be done, an action we could call unqualifiedly good or right. If I answer "no" to all of them, it is an action that should not be done, one unqualifiedly bad or wrong. If I am thinking of selling a financial product that brings a profit to the company, a commission to me, benefits others, and doesn't in the process treat anyone unfairly or violate some promise or commitment, because there are nothing but good because there are nothing but good reasons for doing it, it should be done. However, if I am tempted to fraudulently sell off defective products, and I see that it is not beneficial to me, the company (because we will be sued), its executives, or the general society, then that action would be deceptive and, hence, unfair. It would also violate the relationship of trust that we have with the community. In this case, all the answers are "no," and there is every reason for not performing the action.

Review Item

There's Always Another Client, Right?

Agent George Wright:

"Frank, aren't you concerned that Mrs. Smith won't be able to pay the premiums you're suggesting? Perhaps another type of policy would be more appropriate."

Agent Frank Marley:

"Who cares if the client won't be able to keep up the policy. I'm a realist. My commission is what counts. I can always prospect for more clients."

What do you think of Agent Marley's approach to selling? What would you do in this situation?

Log your answer in the space below.

Thus, we have a decision procedure for deciding what to do and what not to do. If an action benefits me and others, does not violate fairness or a commitment, and preserves my integrity, it should be done. If, on the other hand, an action does not benefit me or others, is unfair, requires breaking a commitment, or violates my integrity, it should not be done. If I get mixed answers of "yes" and "no" (if, for example, the action benefits society but is unfair or vice versa), then I am faced with an ethical dilemma. Ethical dilemmas are difficult, sometimes impossible, to resolve because, in a sense, you are "damned if you do and damned if you don't."

Role Morality

Keeping promises is at the basis of what is called *role morality*. It might be that the best way to do well and to avoid harm while being fair is to honor one's commitments. We have seen that ethics, largely the product of society, allows a society to flourish. One of the ways in which society flourishes is by cooperation, which requires the building of relationships and the division of labor. We get along because we have rules and relationships, which gives each person in society a set of responsibilities. The growth of market economics has made the delivery of financial services an essential factor in developing a flourishing society. Hence, society as it has developed needs the services of the financial planner and advisor.

Review Item
Need a Recommendation?
Prospect Alicia Dougherty:
"Mary, I need to find an insurance agent. Whom do you use?"
Mary Frankel, Purchaser of Insurance (thinking):
I wouldn't recommend Agent Ralph Clover to Alicia. She's my friend. He never returns my calls unless it involves more money. I also heard there were some questions about the way he handles money.
Would you want this type of recommendation? Has Agent Clover's reputation impacted his sales?
Log your answer in the space below.

The fact that you decided to enter the field of financial services means you have made a commitment. Financial services professionals have different constituencies with whom they have relationships and, consequently, toward whom they have responsibilities. Those various constituencies include clients, companies, the profession, yourself, other professionals, and the law. Assuming an important ethical obligation is to do our job—one taken voluntarily—it is necessary to examine what that job entails to determine our responsibilities. Doing our job involves servicing clients in a professional way by using products of companies and services of other related professionals under the existing laws. We enter into a relationship with each of these constituencies, which means that we have ethical responsibilities toward each of them. To get a full picture of the financial services professional's ethical responsibilities, we need to look at all the constituencies and what is owed to them.

There are six major constituencies to whom the financial services professional has ethical obligations as a result of relationships that are based on explicit or implicit promises.

Ethical Obligations to Six Constituencies

Obligations to the Client
Generally, the obligation to look out for the client's best interest is seen as the primary responsibility of the financial services professional. We will examine issues of how this is best done and look at specific practices that either fulfill or undermine those obligations.

Obligations to the Company
Each individual agent or service provider operates to some extent as an agent or broker for a company that creates the product that is being recommended or sold. It is important to look at the various types of relationships that exist between an agent or broker and the company, because they can be quite dissimilar and carry different responsibilities. In chapter 4, we will look at the agency/principal relationship to investigate to what extent truth and loyalty are owed to companies. For example, some agents deceive the company to get it to insure a client who, if the truth were known, would be uninsurable. That is unethical.

Obligations to the Profession
We, as financial services professionals, are by our very name designated as professionals. That means we possess specialized knowledge and

operate in a position of trust. We should conduct our practices according to a professional code. In chapter 5 we will look at what is involved in being a professional as well as what the various codes typically require. Professional status can be a two-edged sword: With increased recognition comes increased responsibility, and with increased responsibility comes increased liability.

Obligations to Allied Professionals

More and more each day, given the increased complexity of financial products, it is necessary for planners and advisors to depend on people from allied professions, such as law and accounting, to give proper advice to clients. As a result of this dependence, and a multidisciplinary approach to financial services, some ethical difficulties arise.

Obligations to Oneself and Others Related to Us

A sometimes overlooked obligation is the obligation to oneself. We sometimes think it is okay to do what we want with our lives at the same time we condemn others for wasting their talents. We each have an obligation to ourselves to create a worthwhile life of integrity. As John Donne said, "No man is an island." We live with others and, consequently, have responsibilities toward them. We are extremely close to some of those people, such as our family, who are often extensions of our own ego. We often hear a person justify making a problematic sale as doing it not for himself or herself, but for his or her family.

Those to Whom We Have Obligations

- the client
- the company
- the profession
- other allied professionals
- oneself and others related to us
- the law

Obligations to Society and Its Laws

Financial services professionals are an essential part of society. Society needs them and, to make sure its needs are well met, has established laws and regulations to help achieve those needs. Financial services professionals, in general, and insurance agents, in particular, are regulated by both the federal and state governments. Although this course cannot examine all the regulations in every state, we will cover key elements of regulations that have a commonality from state to state and are demanded by the federal government. The law is the public's way of legislating morality and gives us a glimpse into what society expects ethically. If something violates a law, it usually also violates morality.

Knowledge of the various laws is important. It helps financial services professionals to stay out of trouble and avoid the heavy penalties that can be applied for violations. These penalties can include license suspension or revocation—the type of penalties that can end a career. (We will look at the requirements of the law in the next chapter.)

Summary

From a societal point of view, we can probably reduce most of ethics to keeping one's commitments. Ethics is a reflection of the rules of behavior we have learned from our society to help us determine what we ought to do and how we ought to live. These rules constitute our everyday knowledge of what's right or wrong. If we are to take control of our own lives, we must reflect on those rules, accept or reject them, then either make them our own or replace them with other rules. Socrates claimed that the unexamined life was not worth living. Examination requires reflection on the rules of behavior. This reflection, which involves analysis and evaluation of these rules, constitutes doing ethics and is part of this course.

Conclusion

Practicing a career as an ethical financial services professional can provide you both financial gain and personal growth and fulfillment. Clients will recognize that you are acting as a trusted professional in their best interests. Your actions will gain the respect of the companies you represent or serve. Your role as an ethical financial services professional will benefit society as a whole as you undertake service after service on behalf of your clients. Your reputation will grow. People in your community will want to do business with you. And what is probably most important, you will be able to look in the mirror and like what you see. Good ethics *is* good business.

Chapter 2 Review Questions

Answers to Review Questions start on appendix page A-53.

1. Which of the following best describes the term *ethics?*
   - (a) Ethics asks what should be done in a given situation.
   - (b) Ethics deals with what is done in a given situation.
   - (c) Ethics is the process of planning philanthropy.
   - (d) Ethics means living in a self-interested manner.

2. What is the purpose of rules?
   - (a) to control the lives of citizens
   - (b) to make society an orderly place
   - (c) to reveal who are the followers and who are the leaders
   - (d) to create conformity to a standard of behavior

3. According to Stanley Cavel, a "social institution (and/or God-given set of laws) composed of a set of standards about practices, defining right or wrong, for the purpose of rationally adjudicating disputes while allowing relationships to continue" is called
   - (a) rules
   - (b) ethics
   - (c) love
   - (d) morality

4. What is the essential message in the Golden Rule?
   - (a) You shall not commit adultery.
   - (b) One is motivated by an inner drive to improve the quality of life.
   - (c) The pursuit of one's interest is at the expense of another.
   - (d) Do unto others as you would have them do unto you.

5. Adam Smith in *The Wealth of Nations* provided us with an ethical framework for modern business that is often called the
   - (a) Golden Rule model
   - (b) enlightened self-interest model
   - (c) planned philanthropy model
   - (d) utilitarian model

6. All of the following statements concerning morals are correct EXCEPT
   (a) All cultures have the same basic moral principles.
   (b) Any adult of any group comes equipped with a set of moral or ethical rules in his or her head that he or she "inherited" from his or her culture.
   (c) In some cases, moral codes are developed in conjunction with religious beliefs.
   (d) In some cases, moral codes are developed as a result of customs founded to promote human harmony.

7. The text states that ethics is essential to business for all of the following reasons EXCEPT
   (a) If there were no ethics in business, there would be no trust.
   (b) If there were no ethics in business, no one would keep promises.
   (c) If there were no ethics in business, there would be no lawsuits.
   (d) If there were no ethics in business, there would be no reliability.

8. All of the following are situations which cause ethical reflection EXCEPT
   (a) when the standards or rules we were taught are not clear and subject to interpretation
   (b) when the rules and standards have been accepted by all those around us
   (c) when the rules or standards conflict with one another
   (d) when those standards or rules conflict with those of other groups of people

9. All of the following are general ethical principals EXCEPT
   (a) Be fair.
   (b) Keep your word.
   (c) Be true to yourself.
   (d) Always have goals.

10. All of the following are major constituencies to whom the financial services professional has an ethical obligation EXCEPT
    (a) the client
    (b) the company
    (c) the law
    (d) the state

3

The Legal Framework

Learning Objectives
3-1. Describe the relationship between law and ethics.
3-2. Identify the legislation that is responsible for the federal regulation of the insurance industry.
3-3. Describe the NAIC and its function.
3-4. Explain the effect of the Securities Act of 1933 on the sale of stocks.
3-5. Identify the duties of the Securities and Exchange Commission.
3-6. Describe the responsibilities that an RIA assumes.

Chapter Outline

The Legal Framework

The Law and Ethics   3-3
   Business Law and Business Ethics   3-5
   The Law and Compliance   3-6
Sources of Positive Law   3-8
The Laws and Regulations That Govern the Insurance Industry   3-8
   State Role in Insurance Regulation   3-8
   Federal Role in Insurance Regulation   3-10
Laws and Regulations That Govern Other Financial Services   3-11
   Similarities between Life Insurance and Securities Sales   3-11
   Federal Regulation of Registered Products   3-12
   National Association of Securities Dealers   3-14
   NASD Rules of Conduct   3-15
   Rules of Conduct—An Application to Insurance Agents   3-15
   Mandated Securities Continuing Education   3-16
Legal Obligations and the Roles of Consultants and Financial
        Planners   3-17
   Emergence of Financial Planning Services   3-17
Registration As an Investment Advisor   3-19
   Who Is Subject to the Investment Advisers Act?   3-19
   Security Advice Test   3-21
   Security Business Test   3-21
   Compensation Test   3-22
   Regulation under the Act   3-23
   Future Regulatory Trends and Developments   3-25
   Avoiding Registration As an RIA For Insurance Agents   3-26
   RIA—Weighing the Responsibilities, Advantages, and
        Disadvantages   3-27
State Regulation in the Securities and Insurance Marketplace   3-28
Insider Information   3-30
Case Study: Investment Advice—NASD Rules   3-32
Key Points to Ponder   3-33
Chapter 3 Review Questions   3-35

The Legal Framework

What does the law have to do with ethics? What laws and regulations apply to financial services professionals? This chapter discusses several topics.

- First, it compares and contrasts legal and ethical behavior.
- Second, it looks at the laws and regulations that govern financial services professionals, both those who sell insurance and those who are investment advisors and/or security dealers.
- It looks briefly at the history and content of both federal and state laws that cover the financial services of selling insurance and financial planning.
- It also discusses the concepts of agency that bind financial services professionals to their carriers, and the special relationship of brokers to both carriers and individual clients.
- It concludes with a discussion of why compliance with the law does not sufficiently cover all ethical matters.

The Law and Ethics

There is a false dichotomy between ethics and the law that is expressed by the cliché, "You can't legislate morality." Clearly this is not universally true. We legislate morality all the time, and if we reflect for only a few moments, we can see how law and ethics are intertwined.

Any community develops its customs—forms of life that citizens can follow when making decisions. It is what leads to ethical rules against lying, cheating, killing, stealing, and other unethical practices. Initially, these customs and rules are uncodified. However, these uncodified customs of a culture often are not enough to ensure acceptable behavior. At that point, governmental units, such as cities or countries, develop laws that prescribe a framework for what the governing unit considers to be minimal standards of conduct that will allow the community to survive and help its citizens flourish. Sanctions are established to discourage people from violating those laws. Ethical theorists make a distinction between the moral law (which refers to ethical rules) and positive laws (which refers to laws of governments). All laws are rules and have a shared goal and a shared origin—the common good.

The positive law seems relatively clear to the extent that it is written down. Hence, lawyers, police officers, and court officials who are all employed in the justice system have a body of legislation by which to determine if a law is broken. Of course, there are disagreements about the interpretation of these written laws. However, even as those interpretations evolve, there is a concrete and accessible legal system in place.

Unlike positive law, the moral law (ethical rules) is not written except in places like the Bible. It is in the hearts of human beings. There are commonly accepted rules and standards of behavior regarding the basic rules that govern the moral life. These include such rules as

- Do not kill.
- Do not deceive.
- Do not cause pain.
- Do not disable.
- Do not cheat.
- Keep your promises.

These are all commonly held expectations about how to live in our society. They reflect our values of individual rights and obligations to others. Some of these rules have corresponding civil laws, while others do not.

Viewed in this way, the positive law is "the public's agency" for translating moral laws into explicit social guidelines and practices and for stipulating punishments for violations of those guidelines. In other words, if some members of society break the ethical rules, the government must step in and insist on proper behavior by threatening punishment for transgressions. This is how to legislate morality.

But it is not only the government that passes laws to regulate behavior. Frequently, industries and/or specific business organizations develop their own codes of ethical conduct, statements of values, rules of conduct, and so on, because there are areas of behavior that the law does not address. Because people aspire to standards more demanding than the law, these standards become a higher benchmark against which the organization's ethical conduct is measured. That higher benchmark is often referred to as the spirit of the law as contrasted with the letter of the law.

Ethics, via the law and codes, gives us rules and standards of conduct that govern us as citizens of a nation, members of an organization, or simply in our individual/societal lives. To the extent that one is part of a group, culture, or organization, one more or less voluntarily accepts the standards of that group, culture, or organization.

However, we need to examine the relationship between law and ethics more closely. As shown here, law and ethics overlap but each also has its own domain. The dotted line at the intersection of law and ethics represents a mutable boundary. As we have seen, laws are largely ethical standards that society has codified in order to enforce certain behaviors. Ethical issues that are deemed sufficiently important may become laws; conversely, laws considered to be excessive or unjust may be either ignored or struck down in court proceedings. Indeed, for a number of philosophers, positive laws are not laws at all if they violate objective moral law.

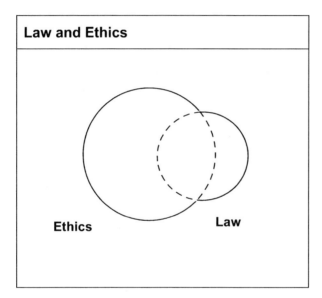

Law and Ethics

Ethics

Law

Business Law and Business Ethics

To further illustrate the complex relationship of law to ethics, it is helpful to contrast business ethics with business law.

Business ethics and business law overlap regarding such issues as the fulfillment of contractual agreements, laws against fraud, agency law, contract law, liability law, labor law, and employee rights law—including nondiscriminatory treatment of different racial groups in hiring and promotion decisions and meeting minimal quality-control and safety standards in manufacturing processes.

Within the realm of business ethics (but outside the realm of business law) are areas either not covered or insufficiently covered by existing laws, (such as layoffs, downsizing, and manipulative marketing

overlap

practices, which are not fraudulent), as well as concerns (such as the acceptable level of toxic waste emitted or dumped into the environment) regarding companies' knowledge of inadequate or nonexistent legal standards. Other examples include verbal abuse in the workplace, manipulative sales practices, and intimidation of subordinates.

Business law includes trade regulations, product specifications, and contractual relationships with suppliers, customers, the community, shareholders, and investors. However, many "purely legal" rules quickly become ethical issues if they are violated, intentionally misinterpreted, or ignored. If a law or regulation is passed to serve the common good, then it would usually be unethical to violate that law. In fact, as we have seen, laws represent codified ethical standards. The positive laws are the minimum moral requirements that we have agreed to demand for society as a whole.

The Law and Compliance

The distinction between law and ethics highlights a common misunderstanding. The term compliance is often used as if it were synonymous with ethics. *Compliance* means obedience to the law. Some argue that a compliance emphasis may undermine ethics because it is targeted at meeting legal requirements rather than addressing the causes of ethical misconduct. For instance, Lynn Sharp Paine states that "legal compliance is unlikely to unleash moral imagination or commitment. The law does not generally seek to inspire human excellence or distinction. Those managers who define ethics as legal compliance are implicitly endorsing a code of moral mediocrity for their organizations."[1]

Law and ethics, working in harmony, are essential for any civilization to continue. Neither is sufficient unto itself. Both are social institutions developed to help civilization survive (and what is true for society at large is true for business in general and the financial services industry in particular). However, it is important to note that what validates a law is the spirit of the law, its basic purpose, and finding the spirit is an ethical matter.

Let's examine this relationship in the area of financial services. We begin by asking the purpose of a financial institution. Such institutions are developed to help people liberate themselves from the fear and risk of a fortuitous and unmanageable financial loss "and in noninsurance cases,

---

1. Lynn Sharp Paine, "Managing for Organizational Integrity," *Harvard Business Review*, March–April, 1994, pp 3–4.

produce a financial gain." Because compliance and ethical rules must be functionally organized to bring about such benefits for clients, the spirit of the law is defined as serving these clients. Financial institutions were created to serve the public. Neither the compensation and rewards system for agents and shareholders nor avoiding litigation and fines is the main purpose of financial institutions.

So we see that, in many cases, the law simply sets minimum requirements for behavior. It does not set optimum standards for professional behavior. However, because what is legal is usually an expression, no matter how minimal, of the ethical, one usually needs to follow the law to be ethical. Therefore, if you follow the requirements of the law as a financial services professional, you have started on the path to ethical behavior. If you act without regard for the law or against the law, you could be acting unethically and could invite professional ruin. Acting within the parameters of the law immediately adds credibility to actions undertaken by the financial services professional. We will say more about the relationship between ethics and compliance later.

It is possible that the cliché "You can't legislate morality" developed because people in older democratic societies with market-based economic systems began to think of ethics as a private matter. Modern thought ushered in the age of the individual and created a distinction between the private and public spheres. When considering the rights to privacy, thinking followed that what a person does in private is no business of the government, so do not legislate morality. However, as we saw in the previous chapter when we reflected on the original meaning of the words *ethics* and *morality*, ethical codes are fundamentally public enterprises. They originated as public affairs. From the meaning of the terms, we saw that ethics or morals originally referred to the public rules societies set up to allow them to survive and, hopefully, flourish. Hence, ethics is not a purely private matter and we can legislate morality.

However, society cannot legislate all morality; laws cannot be made to cover every situation that arises. (If an attempt were made to define and regulate all moral behavior, it would be impossible to enforce.) Laws cannot mandate decent treatment and concern for other human beings. That is clearly an ethical issue. Also, not every possible behavior can be spelled out. There must be a reliance on an understanding of the law and an interpretation of the law, which is in accord with the laws' spirit. For example, the commandment "Thou shalt not kill" does not specify what the scope of the law is, whether it applies to all living creatures including plants and animals, or whether it applies to all or just to some human beings. Civil laws may be more precise than moral laws in distinguishing between the degrees of murder and manslaughter, for example, but even in these instances the civil laws cannot specify all possible behavior. It is imperative to look for the spirit of the law and to determine where and to what extent it applies. The spirit of all law—civil, common, positive, or moral—is always guided by the purpose of law, which is to promote the common good or the public interest.

Citizens in democratic countries generally prefer fewer laws and greater personal freedom. With a significant increase in laws governing individual behavior, courts and prisons would be even more crowded. People want a certain amount of personal independence to resolve their ethical dilemmas, but they also must adhere to some common moral standards because their decisions about such dilemmas inevitably affect others.

Sources of Positive Law

Let's turn our attention to the positive or civil laws, which consist of the laws promulgated by elected officials. In the United States, both federal and state laws regulate the two major areas of the financial services industry:

- insurance
- financial planning and investment

We will begin by examining the laws that govern the insurance industry.

The Laws and Regulations That Govern the Insurance Industry

State Role in Insurance Regulation

The major responsibility for regulation of the insurance industry rests with state governments and is carried out by state insurance departments. These departments regulate insurance in three primary areas: company authorization, agent licensing, and insurance sales practices. These responsibilities include monitoring the ethical conduct of licensed agents. State judicial departments act as a primary source of common law rules governing the insurance industry.

Company Authorization—State insurance departments determine the companies that are eligible to do business within their borders. Factors taken into consideration in granting this authorization include financial stability and adherence to state laws. Once a company has been authorized to do business within a state, it must also seek approval of each product it wishes to sell within that state. This approval must be obtained before consumers can be approached regarding the product's purchase.

> ## State Versus Federal Jurisdiction
>
> The insurance industry is technically subject to both federal and state law. Historically, however, the federal government has stepped aside and permitted the insurance industry to be regulated primarily through the states. This pattern was established as a result of the Supreme Court decision in *Paul vs. Virginia,* decided over a century ago in 1868. Congress reaffirmed this pattern when it passed the McCarran-Ferguson Act in 1945. The McCarran-Ferguson Act spells out the role of the federal government in regulating the insurance industry.

Agent Licensing—All states require agents to be licensed or authorized before they can sell insurance within their borders. Sales of policies by either an unauthorized insurer or agent are illegal. For some agents, this may mean maintaining just one license in the state in which they live and do business. However, today's transient population means that many agents serve clients in more than one state. As a result, more agents must maintain nonresident licenses and, therefore, have to comply with the rules and regulations of more than one state. Varying continuing education requirements are one example of how differing state rules can affect an agent.

Insurance brokers are also subject to state licensing rules. An agent or broker who does business in more than one state may be required to hold a nonresident license(s). When in doubt, it is a good idea to obtain a license.

Sales Practices—All states have rules regarding how insurance can be sold. Typically, those rules cover the issues of product misrepresentation, replacement, and rebating. For example, presenting insurance as a retirement annuity or a mutual fund is a form of impermissible misrepresentation. In a replacement situation, failure to compare a policy that has already been issued to a newly proposed policy is also an area typically of concern to state regulators. Also, paying a client "commission kickback" is a violation of the sales practice rules in almost every state.

State insurance laws are not uniform, but they do contain common themes. All states, through laws and regulations, establish rules of practice. These rules provide ethical guidelines by spelling out what an agent may or may not do.

Typically, state laws and regulations cover the following matters:

- **Approved Policies**—Agents may sell only policies that have been filed with and approved by state authorities.
- **Misrepresentation**—Agents are forbidden to misrepresent policy terms or coverage.
- **Replacement**—Agents in most states must follow strict guidelines when replacing coverage.
- **Rebating**—Rebating is forbidden in most states.
- **Timeliness**—Agents are required to perform their duties toward clients in a timely manner. This includes, for example, prompt submission of a completed insur-ance application.

Federal Role in Insurance Regulation

Even though the insurance industry is predominately regulated by the states, the insurance professional will encounter federal regulation in several areas. In particular, it is important to know how federal regulations affect clients.

- Federal rules apply to the area of antitrust regulation. You become aware of this when you attend industry meetings and receive warnings regarding the exchange of company information, such as product pricing.
- Federal rules apply in the area of taxation of insurance companies. This may be an area far removed from a field agent, but federal taxation affects the cost of products. The Internal Revenue Code contains specific provisions that spell out how both mutual and stock carriers are to be taxed, as well as provisions that affect the tax status of products sold by insurance carriers. For example, the Internal Revenue Code provides for the tax-deferred build-up within a life insurance product as well as income tax-free death proceeds. Knowledge of product-related

---

NAIC

Common statutory themes exist from state to state despite the many jurisdictions involved in the regulation of insurance. This is due in great part to the influence of the National Association of Insurance Commissioners (NAIC).

The NAIC is an organization of state insurance supervisory officials formed in 1871. Its role is to act as a forum for the exchange of ideas and provide a medium for standardization of state regulatory practices. This is accomplished through meetings and issuance of uniform statutes and regulations. The NAIC has issued model legislation affecting every facet of the insurance business.

tax provisions is particularly important to the insurance professional. Providing clients with inaccurate information about the tax consequences of various insurance-related transactions can be an invitation to a lawsuit.

- Federal rules apply in the area of labor and pension regulation. Many financial services companies have large pension departments. Many professionals sell qualified retirement plans, which are subject to both Internal Revenue Service and Labor Department rules and regulations. The landmark piece of legislation in this regard is the Employee Retirement Income Security Act of 1974 (ERISA). Pension and retirement planning legislation is an evolving area. Agents who practice in this area must stay abreast of up-to-date developments. Running afoul of these rules can subject the insurance agent to broad-based liability.

- Federal securities rules apply to the insurance industry, particularly in regard to the promotion and sale of variable life and annuity products. These products have at their core investment-type subaccounts similar to mutual funds. This means there is an oversight by the Securities and Exchange Commission (SEC) that is carried out through the licensing procedures established by the National Association of Securities Dealers (NASD). We will discuss more about this later, when we look at laws governing investment advisors.

- In recent years, the federal government has shown increased interest in the regulation of the health insurance industry. At the present time, this has resulted in the standardization of Medicare supplemental policies. The design of long-term care insurance has been influenced by indirect health care legislation in the form of federal tax regulations. In the future, federal oversight may affect basic health care policies and access to care provided by health maintenance organizations (HMOs).

Laws and Regulations That Govern Other Financial Services

Similarities between Life Insurance and Securities Sales

We are witnessing a slow crossover of activity between life insurance and securities sales. More agents are selling variable products and mutual funds, in great part because of client expectations and demands.

Consequently, as we have already seen, many agents now find themselves dealing with dual licensing requirements at the state and federal levels. As a result, the legal rationales and considerations that once applied only to the securities industry have found their way into life insurance and annuity sales.

Federal Regulation of Registered Products

Historical Background—It has been many years since the 1929 stock market crash, but the regulatory responses to this crisis remain with us. Federal investigations at the time of the 1929 crash recognized that market manipulation, overextension of credit for stock purchases, and unfair dealings with clients were abuses in need of correction.

In response, Congress enacted several major laws that changed the structure of the securities markets in the United States. These acts provided a definition of securities, guidelines for the issuance and registration of security products, and rules regarding the conduct of security marketplace operations. These acts also provided for the establishment of self-regulatory organizations such as the National Association of Securities Dealers (NASD).

A general familiarity with three of these federal acts is helpful to understand what is appropriate conduct for businesses in today's financial services marketplace. These acts are the Securities Act of 1933, the Securities Exchange Act of 1934, and the Investment Advisers Act of 1940. All share a common statutory theme—providing the proper disclosure, which is necessary to a free and open marketplace. From an ethical standpoint, the acts share a common focus of fair and honest dealings in the securities marketplace.

Securities Act of 1933—The Securities Act of 1933 provides statutory guidelines that must be followed before a company can sell new issues of its stock to the public. These guidelines emphasize disclosure of information. This disclosure is accomplished through the completion of a registration statement, which must be reviewed by the Securities and Exchange Commission (SEC). Following the filing of the registration statement, a prospectus is prepared. The prospectus summarizes the information contained in the registration statement and must be made available to all interested buyers.

Securities Exchange Act of 1934—While the Securities Act of 1933 concerns newly issued securities, the Securities Exchange Act of 1934 extends federal regulation to the ongoing trading of securities that have already been issued. The 1934 Act charged the SEC with the enforcement of these directives.

Provisions of the 1934 Act require disclosure of information by publicly traded companies, prohibit market manipulation, and restrict the amount of credit that may be extended for the purchase of securities. The 1934 Act also requires security brokers and dealers to register with the SEC. In addition, the 1934 Act provides for SEC supervision of national security exchanges, industry associations, and securities information processors.

The primary function of the SEC is to review information provided in the registration statement and other forms submitted to its offices. The SEC does not provide the public with investment advice. It is up to individual investors and/or their advisors to evaluate the securities registered with the SEC.

Investment Advisers Act of 1940—The Investment Advisers Act of 1940 seeks to protect the public from harmful and fraudulent conduct of persons who are paid to advise others on buying and/or selling securities. It was aimed at two categories of advisors: those who publish market reports or newsletters for paying subscribers that contain recommendations concerning securities and those who advise to individual clients about securities. A major purpose of the law was, and still is, to reveal conflicts of interests that may cause the advisor to make recommendations more in his or her own interest than in the client's interest.

This Act sets out a scheme of federal regulation for investment advisors. The key question for financial services professionals posed by the Act is whether or not they are considered investment advisors. If they are, they are required to register with the SEC. For example, if an insurance agent is in the business of providing investment advice for compensation, in addition to selling insurance, the registration provisions of the Act apply.

There are some instances, however, in which it is unclear whether or not an agent is an investment advisor. For example, if an agent advertises a financial planning designation, is he or she providing financial advice in the ordinary course of business? In a few cases, state law points to a "yes" answer. In other cases, the answer is unclear; in still others, the answer is "no." Failure to comply with the law's provisions carries heavy penalties, so many legal commentators suggest that agents should register, if in doubt.

One other thought to keep in mind: registration under the Investment Advisers Act is just registration. It is not an endorsement of competence or expertise by the SEC. This means financial services professionals should avoid the temptation to imply SEC endorsement when speaking to clients—such action would point to unethical and possibly illegal behavior. (We will return to a more thorough study of the Investment Advisers Act later in this chapter.)

National Association of Securities Dealers

The SEC is not the sole source of rules and regulations under the federal securities laws. Congress, in drafting the Depression Era legislation, recognized that the nation's stock exchanges had long been regulating the trading activities of their own members. With this in mind, self-regulatory organizations (SROs) were incorporated into the regulatory structure of the securities industry.

The National Association of Securities Dealers (NASD) is part of this self-regulatory structure. It was established under authority granted by 1938 amendments to the Securities Exchange Act of 1934. The principle behind the enabling legislation is voluntary self-regulation of broker/dealers under SEC oversight.

The NASD has the power to require and monitor compliance with standardized rules of fair practice for the industry. NASD regulatory responsibilities include registration and testing of securities professionals, review of members' advertising and sales literature, and services such as arbitration of investor disputes. Registered representatives must provide the NASD with personal information including prior employment and any history of securities-related disciplinary action.

Life insurance agents who sell variable products are considered registered representatives of the insurer's broker/dealer and are required to be both cognizant of and compliant with NASD rules. Agents must sit for qualification tests to demonstrate professional competence before selling variable products.

The reach of the NASD does not just stop with testing; it goes much further into the everyday sales practices used by agents. Sales literature, advertising, and most public-oriented written communications are subject to NASD regulatory review. Therefore, when selling securities products it is important not to step inadvertently into a compliance quagmire by sending out specially prepared sales materials without first consulting the manager. Sometimes this can mean obtaining the approval of the company's compliance officer. At other times, it can also mean that materials will have to be filed with the NASD prior to their use. Home office employees involved in the sale and distribution of variable products are also subject to NASD rules and registration.

NASD Rules of Conduct

The NASD sets forth its expectations for the ethical treatment of customers in its Rules of Conduct. These rules spell out two fundamental steps, which must be followed in order to fairly deal with clients. The agent must

- understand the client's current financial status
- understand the client's financial goals

Only with these two pieces of information is it possible to offer appropriate advice to a client.

For example, an older client who has accumulated a relatively modest retirement nest egg and who seeks some income along with preservation of capital would be an unlikely candidate for a financial product that stresses high-risk emerging growth funds. Changing client circumstances are also part of the fair dealings equation. For example, in midlife, successful clients have accumulated more assets and may be able to tolerate greater risk in order to seek higher return. On the other hand, clients near the end of their working careers may find that the high-risk strategies, which enabled them to achieve earlier financial success, no longer fit their needs.

Rules of Conduct—An Application to Insurance Agents

The essence of the NASD Rules of Conduct is not really all that different from needs selling. Those who sell insurance, whether variable or traditional whole life, by uncovering client needs and goals are already substantially following the NASD guidelines. Financial advisors who conduct periodic reviews of their clients' insurance policies are taking into account changing client circumstances, needs, and goals.

The various insurance products available today can be characterized by different levels of risk and potential return, elements that have long been considered in the promotion and sale of securities. Ethics, backed increasingly by corresponding regulatory principles, requires financial advisors to consider these factors when recommending the purchase of an insurance product.

The result is that the spirit of the NASD Rules of Conduct will continue to influence the sale of insurance. Financial advisors can expect a continued emphasis on disclosure, both about the products they sell and the methods used in the sale of those products. In addition, financial advisors should expect that both regulators and the courts will focus on whether or not a particular product was appropriate in light of the client's financial condition, risk tolerance, and goals.

Mandated Securities Continuing Education

Securities industry regulators recently recognized the need for relevant training to keep pace with changing regulations and the innovative products that are surging into the marketplace. Therefore, all registered persons in the financial, insurance, and banking industries are now required to participate in a two-part program of continuing education that consists of a regulatory element and firm element.

The SEC mandates that each person shall complete the Regulatory Element on the occurrence of their second registration anniversary date and every three years thereafter, or as otherwise prescribed by the NASD. The Regulatory Element is designed to focus on compliance, ethics, business conduct, sales-practice standards, and other regulatory concerns.

Persons Exempted from the Rule—Persons who have been continuously registered for more than 10 years on July 1, 1998, shall be exempt from participation in the Regulatory Element programs for registered representatives, provided such persons have not been subject within the last 10 years to any disciplinary action as enumerated in paragraph (a)(3).

Persons who have been currently registered for 10 years or less as of July 1, 1998, shall participate in the Regulatory Element within 120 days after the occurrence of the second registration anniversary date and every third year thereafter.

The Firm Element requires an organization to annually develop its own training plan for covered registered persons. The goal of the Firm Element is to ensure that these persons are trained regularly in the investments or services in which they deal and to keep them current on matters relating to their particular areas of responsibility.

Let's look more carefully at the nature and responsibilities of the financial planner and registered investment advisor.

Legal Obligations and the Roles of Consultants and Financial Planners

Emergence of Financial Planning Services

Until the early 1980s, personal financial planning services were primarily available only to the wealthy. Such services were provided by the so-called "old line" investment advisors at a significant cost. However, with the advent of relative prosperity, middle-income Americans became more financially astute. But while gross personal incomes rose, mounting inflation and taxes absorbed greater portions of that income. To meet their retirement and other future financial needs, many individuals increasingly relied upon their own personal financial plans, either as a supplement to employer and/or government programs or, in some situations, as the primary foundation for their financial future. In doing so, however, many found that prudent selection from among a variety of investment and insurance alternatives had become an increasingly complex task. Thus, a substantial demand for relatively low-cost financial planning services emerged.

Who is considered a financial planner? In the context of life insurance, an agent who sells only insurance products and provides little or no other financial services would not be deemed a financial planner. However, when an agent moves beyond simply advising upon and selling life insurance and offers financial advice in general, he or she has moved into the realm of financial planning.

Sensing an opportunity, like other financial institutions, many life insurers began to position themselves within the newly emerging financial services marketplace not only to offer an array of diverse financial products (especially investment-oriented products), but also to expand the scope of their activities to provide financial planning services.

Furthermore, by the 1980s, the competitive trend toward products with lower premiums, including less expensive term insurance, portended lower commissions for insurance agents per unit of sale. Life insurance agents felt threatened not only by this trend, but also by inflationary and other cost pressures of doing business. Consequently, life agents (as well as their companies) sought additional strategies for increasing income. Within this environment, many agents responded affirmatively to the opportunity to offer more comprehensive financial services, including not only more diverse insurance and/or other products, such as mutual funds, but also a broader scope of financial planning services.

Financial planning has been described as follows:

> Financial planning typically involves providing a variety of services, principally advisory in nature, to individuals or families regarding the management of their financial resources based upon an analysis of individual clients' needs. Generally, financial planning services involve preparing a financial program for a client based on the client's financial circumstances and objectives. This information normally would cover present and anticipated assets and liabilities, including insurance, savings, investments, and anticipated retirement or other employee benefits. The program developed for the client usually includes general recommendations for a course of activity or specific actions to be taken by the client. For example, recommendations may be made that the client obtain insurance or revise existing coverage, establish an individual retirement account, increase or decrease funds held in savings accounts, or invest funds in securities. A financial planner may develop tax or estate plans for clients or refer clients to an accountant or attorney for these services.

> The provider of such financial planning services in most cases assists the client in implementing the recommended program by, among other things, making specific recommendations to carry out the general recommendation of the program, or by selling the client insurance products, securities or other investments. The financial planner may also review the client's program periodically and recommend revisions. Persons providing such financial planning services use various compensation arrangements. Some financial planners charge clients an overall fee for developing an individual client program while others charge clients an hourly fee. In some instances, financial planners are compensated, in whole or in part, by commissions on the sale to the client of insurance products, interests in real estate, securities (such as common stocks, bonds, limited partnership interests, and mutual funds), or other investments.[2]

Or more succinctly, a financial planner is a person who offers individualized advice on investments, life insurance, and the overall

---

2. SEC Rell. No. IA-1092, October 8, 1987.

general management of financial affairs with a view toward planning, implementing, and maintaining a program designed to meet the client's future financial needs.

There are three types of personal individual financial planners. First, there is the "fee-only" type who charges his or her clients a fee for the development of a financial plan but does not recommend specific investments, insurance contracts, and/or other type of products. Second, there is the "commission-only" type of planner who charges no fees for the development of a financial plan, but collects a commission on the securities, insurance, or other products or services that he or she sells to the client. And third, there is the "fee-commission" type who charges the client a fee for the planning services rendered and receives commissions for the sale of products. Regardless of the approach adopted, the offering of financial planning services was, and still is, seen as a means to increase one's wealth and/or income.

Furthermore, the emergence of financial planning services on a broader basis to the less affluent population has not been confined to life insurers and their agents. As the demand for financial planning increased, accountants, lawyers, banks, and securities firms became increasingly involved. Boundaries of traditional disciplines were breached as these persons and institutions advertised themselves as full financial planners.

Within this environment, both actual and potential abuses occurred. Many of the so-called financial planners lacked even the most basic qualifications to competently perform the financial planning task. Often they used their financial planning status to sell securities of issuers or insurance of insurers with which they were affiliated. Because of the rapid growth in the number of persons and firms offering financial planning services and the accompanying abuses associated with such growth, there has been increased focus upon the applicability of both federal and state regulatory law to the financial planning phenomenon. The activities of financial planners, both individuals and organizations, cut across various regulatory disciplines at both the federal and state level, giving rise to a complex system of dual federal and multistate regulation.

Registration As an Investment Advisor

Who Is Subject to the Investment Advisers Act?
The SEC takes the position that the Investment Advisers Act of 1940 governs the regulation of financial planners. In the 1980s, the SEC issued

three tests that could be used to determine whether or not an individual must register as an investment advisor. If all three tests are answered in the affirmative, registration is required. If any of the tests is answered in the negative, there is no need for the individual to become a Registered Investment Advisor (RIA).

It is important to remember that the purpose of the SEC in devising the three tests is to protect clients from fraud and other abusive situations. The SEC does not guarantee the competence or investment abilities of any individuals who register under the act; it merely seeks to provide a mechanism for discouraging unethical behavior, principally via full disclosure to clients.

The Act defines an investment advisor as any person who, for compensation, engages in the business of advising others as to the value of securities or the advisability of acquiring or disposing of securities. Any person who falls within the Advisers Act's definition of an investment advisor (unless expressly excluded from the definition or exempted from the registration requirements) and who makes use of the mails or any instrumentality of interstate commerce is required to register with the SEC pursuant to the Act.

The Supreme Court defined what constitutes a security in the 1946 landmark case *SEC v. T.W. Howey Co.* In that case, the Court ruled that

> "The test is whether the scheme involves an investment of money in a common enterprise with profits to come solely from the efforts of others."

Under this test, virtually every investment which a financial planner might recommend for his or her client would appear to qualify as a security. The term *security* has been interpreted to include not only marketable securities traded on an organized exchange (such as the New York Stock Exchange) but also such instruments as limited partnerships, mutual funds, certificates of deposit, commercial paper, variable annuities, and variable life insurance, as well as other types of interest-sensitive life insurance products.

However, merely dealing with a security does not, by itself, make someone an investment advisor. In 1987, the SEC issued the Investment Advisers Act Release No. 1092, which defined three elements that must be met if persons or entities want to qualify as investment advisors under the Act:

- They must give advice or analysis concerning securities.
- They must be engaged in the business of advising others regarding securities.
- They must be in receipt of compensation.

Security Advice Test

In determining of whether or not an individual must become a RIA, the SEC looks first at the type of services being provided. If an individual renders advice about the purchase or sale of securities, this indicates that registration is necessary.

In this regard, a very broad definition is applied to the term security. A security is not just a stock or bond. It may also be a variable annuity or a variable life insurance policy. This broad definition of security means that many life insurance agents can pass the first test required for registration.

If an individual provides advice or issues reports or analyses regarding specific securities, clearly this test is met. However, the advice need not relate to specific securities, but may focus on the advisability of investing in securities in general. The SEC has determined that a person who deals with securities in general or who advises as to the advantages and disadvantages of investing in securities vis-à-vis other financial vehicles (for example, life insurance) meets this test. Also, most analyses or reports that incorporate judgments concerning securities are considered to be investment advice. Given the breadth of the definition of a security, virtually any person who presents himself or herself as a financial planning professional almost assuredly will render advice concerning securities.

Security Business Test

Is the individual engaged in the business of providing such services about securities? Providing advice with some regularity, even when it is not the person's primary business activity, is an important factor in subjecting the person to the Act. Whether a person is "in the business" is determined by a facts and circumstances analysis, including consideration of the frequency of the activity. Furthermore, a person is deemed to be "in the business" if he or she does any of the following:

- holds himself or herself out as an investment advisor
- receives separate or additional compensation that is a clearly definable charge for providing advice about securities

- provides specific investment advice in other than isolated instances

Another way of looking at this is to examine how the individual presents his or her business to the public. For example, what name and type of business description appears in the telephone book or on the front door? Does the individual's business card or letterhead suggest he or she is an investment advisor or stockbroker? If the way an individual presents his or her business to the public suggests that investment advice is provided, the second test provides another factor indicating the need for the individual to be a Registered Investment Advisor (RIA).

Investment Advisor Tests

If any of the tests are answered in the negative, there is no need for the individual to become a Registered Investment Advisor (RIA).

- securities advice test

- securities business test

- compensation test

Compensation Test

Does the person provide such services for compensation? The compensation can be in any form and from any source. Even though a person who provides advice concerning a security does not charge a separate fee for such advice, if he or she receives some form of economic benefit (whether as an advisory fee, a fee relating to total services rendered, a commission, or some combination thereof) in connection with such advice, the compensation test is met. In meeting this test, it is not necessary, that the advisor's compensation be paid directly by the person receiving the services, but only that he or she receive compensation from some source (for example, an insurance company) for such services. The criterion is whether the individual derives earnings from the sale of securities. The exact manner in which these earnings are obtained does not matter. The test is answered affirmatively if either a *fee* or *commission* is paid for securities-related investment advice. For example, if Mr. Smith earns his living by charging fees for investment advice, this indicates the need for registration. Similarly, if Ms. Jones earns commissions from the sales of securities products, this also indicates the need for registration.

Under this three-pronged definitional test (that is, providing advice or analysis concerning a security, engaging in the business, and receiving compensation), all of the elements must be present to classify the person as an investment advisor under the Act. However, given the broad scope of each of the definitional elements, those engaged in financial planning activities are highly likely to be included in the Act's definition of an investment advisor unless they come within some exclusion under the terms of the Act.

Review Item

Testing for RIA Status

Colin Murphy, Financial Advisor:

"Hi! I'd suggest that you invest 20 percent of your savings in MBI Corporation, 20 percent in ABD Mutual Fund, and buy a single premium life insurance policy with a face amount of $100,000."

"How do I get paid?" you ask. "Through a combination of fees and commissions," you're told.

Does this agent appear to be acting as an investment advisor? If so, what should he do to comply with securities laws?

Log your answer in the space below.

Regulation under the Act

The basic regulatory mechanism of the Advisers Act is the requirement that any person falling within the definition of an investment advisor, unless excluded or exempted by another section of the statute, must register with the SEC. A financial planner, as an investment advisor (which is usually the case, unless for some reason, the person is exempted or excluded), is subject to a number of legal obligations in addition to the registration requirement.

First, under its broad rule-making authority, the SEC has imposed extensive record-keeping and reporting requirements. The SEC generally requires that an investment advisor maintain typical accounting books and records (such as checkbooks, banking statements, and written agreements), as well as certain additional records (including personal securities transactions entered into by the advisor and his or her employee) to ensure compliance with fiduciary standards.

Second, an investment advisor is subject to inspection and examination by the SEC. Inspections are of two types—routine and "for cause." Inspectors especially look for evidence of churning, scalping, practices contrary to the client's interest, unsuitability, deceptive advertising, and improper record-keeping.

Third, while almost any basis of compensation may be used (as long as it is not fraudulent), an investment advisor is prohibited from entering into an investment advisory contract if the contract provides for compensation based upon a share of the capital gains or capital appreciation of the client's funds. Underlying this prohibition is the concern that the investment advisor might undertake undue investment risks with the client's funds in efforts to enhance the advisor's compensation.

Fourth, every investment advisor, when entering into an advisory contract, must deliver a written disclosure statement (often referred as the "brochure") to the prospective client at least 2 days before the advisory contract is entered into or at the time of entering into the contract if the client can terminate the contract within 5 days. This statement must include information concerning the advisor's background, education, experience, types of services offered, and the investment techniques to be employed.

Fifth, the Act prohibits an investment advisor from representing that he or she is an "investment counsel" unless his or her principal business consists of action as an investment advisor and a substantial portion of the business consists of providing investment advisory services.

Sixth, an investment advisor is permitted to pay finder's fees, but only if certain conditions are met. There must be a written agreement between the advisor and the finder of the business. The finder must provide the prospective client with not only a copy of the advisor's brochure but also a separate disclosure statement that outlines the arrangement between the advisor and the finder, including the compensation to be paid by the advisor to the finder and whether the client will be charged for this service in addition to the advisory fee. The SEC does not look favorably on this method of obtaining new business, so if this method is used, great care should be taken to comply with all requirements.

Seventh, during the legislative process leading up to the enactment of the Adviser Act, much emphasis was placed on the importance of trust and confidence between an investment advisor and his or her clients. As a consequence, the Act contains an antifraud section detailing various types of conduct considered to be violative of the fiduciary nature of the investment advisory relationship. Among other things, the Act specifically prohibits the use of the mails or any means of interstate commerce to "employ any device, scheme, or artifice to defraud a client or prospective client" or "to engage in, any transaction, practice or course of business which operates as a fraud or deceit upon any client or prospective client." The United States Supreme Court elaborated in defining an investment advisor as a fiduciary owing his or her clients an affirmative duty of utmost good faith and full and fair disclosure of all material facts, as well as an affirmative obligation to employ reasonable care to avoid misleading his or her clients.

The SEC has stated that the duty of an investment advisor to refrain from fraudulent activity includes the affirmative obligations to

- disclose all material facts as to any potential conflicts of interest so the client can make an informed judgment whether to enter into or to continue the relationship with the investment advisor
- disclose fully the nature and extent of any interest the advisor has in any given recommendation
- inform clients of their right to execute recommended investment purchases or sales through other broker-dealers
- disclose whether the advisor's personal securities transactions are inconsistent with advice rendered to a client
- avoid engaging in any conduct that might result in the advisor preferring his or her own interests to those of clients.

The antifraud provisions of the Advisors Act apply to any person who is an investment advisor as defined by the Act, whether or not such a person is required to be registered with the SEC as an investment advisor. Although persons who are excluded from the definition of an investment advisor are not subject to the antifraud provisions, those who fall within the definition of an investment advisor, even though not required to be registered, are subject to the antifraud provisions of the Advisors Act and the rules promulgated thereunder.

Future Regulatory Trends and Developments

The merger of financial services is likely to have a regulatory as well as a marketing impact on insurance professionals and their companies. For example, the sale of insurance through banks has invited the scrutiny of the Office of the Comptroller of the Currency and the Federal

Reserve. In the future, federal regulation may provide a clear answer about jurisdiction over these types of sales. In the meantime, be prepared to comply with increased and sometimes conflicting rules and regulations.

Avoiding Registration as an RIA for Insurance Agents

Many insurance agents involved in the sale of variable products will find it difficult not to answer the compensation test in an affirmative manner. Therefore, the second test (security business) becomes the key issue. In other words, if you do not wish to be an RIA, do not present yourself as a full-fledged financial planner to the public. Exercise caution when developing a name for your business.

Example—Consider the case of an independent insurance agent named Maria M. Conte. Maria may wish to lend a greater professional tone to her business by printing cards and stationery with MMC Investment Advisors, Ltd. after her name. This may sound very professional, but it may also mislead the public into thinking Maria is providing services beyond the sale of insurance.

Also, take a look at your state's law. Some states, such as Maryland and Washington, have very strict criteria as to what constitutes being a financial planner. For instance, using designations such as Chartered Financial Consultant (ChFC) can be enough to trigger registration. Insurance agents who wish to avoid registration should also keep four other factors in mind:

- Make it clear to your clients that you are a financial advisor who is selling insurance. Do not try to hide the identity of the product. Trying to recast an insurance policy as a mutual fund would be one example of not only violation of ethics, but a legal matter that would indicate the need for compliance with SEC registration requirements.
- Up-front fees may be a tempting source of income, but if you want to avoid registration, do not charge clients for your professional advice.
- Base your income on regular commissions. Again, to avoid registration, do not charge advisory fees.
- Follow your company guidelines. If your company is affiliated with a broker-dealer, in all likelihood it has specified methods of

operating the business in a manner that can avoid the necessity of registering as an investment advisor. Ignoring these guidelines is an invitation to becoming an RIA.

RIA—Weighing the Responsibilities, Advantages, and Disadvantages

An individual who becomes an RIA assumes a series of responsibilities. For some individuals, the advantages offered by RIA status outweigh any potential disadvantages. For others, these responsibilities outweigh the advantages of being an RIA.

Whether or not you choose to register as an investment advisor depends in part on the type of practice you wish to develop and the guidelines developed by your company. Some insurance companies discourage their agents from being RIAs mainly because of the potential for added legal liability shared by both the company and the agent. Other companies leave registration up to the discretion of their individual agents. (See table 3–1 for a list of the responsibilities of an RIA.)

Summarized below are some of the advantages and disadvantages you may wish to take into consideration before deciding whether or not to conduct your practice as an RIA.

Advantages—If you are a registered investment advisor, you have the ability to charge fees for your professional advice and planning services. For those who wish to move away from a dependence on commissions, this can be a very substantial reason to become an RIA.

Registering as an investment advisor also affords an agent far greater latitude in how he or she advertises and promotes his or her practice. Your cards and letterhead can indicate you are engaged in providing investment advice. As an RIA, you can indicate that you develop financial planning programs and investment achievement strategies for clients. You can expand your practice in investment planning and asset management, and you can move into other markets that are collateral to the sale of insurance, such as limited partnerships.

Disadvantages—To register as an investment advisor, you must pay application fees. While these are not onerous, they are a factor to be considered.

Being an RIA also involves substantial paperwork. As an RIA, you must maintain meticulous records regarding the advice given to clients and must also comply with regulatory reporting requirements.

Perhaps the greatest disincentive to being an RIA is the potential for substantial legal liability. You are clearly inviting clients to rely upon your expertise and investment advice. If your expertise is limited or your investment advice imprudent, you are likely to find yourself named in a lawsuit. In addition, an RIA is legally held to a higher professional standard than that normally applied to an individual who is engaged solely in the sale of insurance.

State Regulation in the Securities and Insurance Marketplace

Federal securities laws do not necessarily preempt state authority. In fact, various federal securities laws specifically preserve the regulatory power of the states, and all states have so-called blue sky laws[3] regulating securities activities in their respective states. This means that both home office and field personnel must comply with both state and federal regulations in the areas of company investment decisions and client planning.

For example, most states follow the broad definition of advertising set forth in NAIC model legislation. At the same time, the NASD has also developed rules regarding advertising and the literature that may be used in the sale of registered products such as variable annuities. The NASD rules do not override the state rules; they supplement them.

Another example would be the fact that both state laws and NASD rules apply to sales practices of variable products. In other words, both state and federal regulators have guidelines as to what we say and what we do as part of a sales call. Simply using approved materials is not enough. We must use them in a proper fashion that will not mislead our clients.

---

3. The name "blue-sky" comes from a statement made by a U.S. Supreme Court justice, who referred to "speculative schemes that have no more basis than so many feet of blue sky." The Uniform Securities Act (USA) serves as model legislation that each state may follow or adapt to its own needs.

TABLE 3–1
Responsibilities of a Registered Investment Advisor (RIA)

The major responsibilities of an RIA include:

1. **Registration**—The first step in becoming an RIA is to register with the SEC. Registration involves the completion of a detailed questionnaire (Form ADV) and the submission of a one-time filing fee.

2. **Records**—RIAs are required to keep extensive records regarding the many aspects of their practices. This record keeping involves retention of sales brochures, client communications, and recommendations. It also involves maintenance of financial records in accordance with generally accepted accounting principles.

3. **Fee Restrictions**—RIAs are subject to the fee restrictions developed under SEC rules. As a general rule of thumb, the fee restrictions tend to be stricter for clients with assets of less than $1 million dollars.

4. **Designation Prohibition**—The term "RIA" cannot be used as a designation as one would use LUTCF, CLU, or ChFC. This is because it merely represents a registration, not an educational achievement. However, the rules do permit those registered, to fully spell out and refer to their status as registered investment advisor(s) when dealing with clients.

5. **Informational Brochure**—RIAs must develop and distribute a brochure to clients, which includes substantial information about their education, business background, and clientele. The brochure must also indicate the type of informational sources used and the investment strategies pursued.

6. **Client Reassignment**—RIAs cannot arbitrarily reassign their clients to other RIAs. Clients must clearly consent to any reassignment. This rule stresses the personal nature of the relationship and the uniqueness of services provided by RIAs.
   (This is also a factor that RIAs must keep in mind when planning for their retirement. Simply put, RIAs cannot decide to sell their practices without notifying clients. Preretirement succession planning thus becomes an important element for any RIA. In this way, clients can get to know the "newcomer" during a transition period and can then make informed decisions as to how they wish their accounts handled.)

7. **Fiduciary Role**—The Investment Advisers Act of 1940 contains strict anti-fraud provisions. These provisions have the effect of recognizing RIAs as fiduciaries who owe their clients affirmative duties. These duties include the obligation to deal in good faith and to provide full and fair disclosure of all material facts that surround an investment recommendation.
   As fiduciaries, RIAs must also be careful not to place themselves in ethically questionable situations that involve a conflict of interest.

The overlap of state and NASD guidelines means agents need to be aware that two sets of rules must be considered as they develop strategies involving the sale of today's sophisticated financial products. How can agents retain all this information when securities laws vary greatly from state to state? The answer lies in studying the three common themes that can be found in most state statutes:

- The laws prohibit fraud in the sale of securities.
- There are state registration requirements for those involved in the sale of securities.
- There are registration and disclosure requirements for securities sold within the state.

Although securities laws may seem to be targeted toward home office investment officers, they apply to field staff as well. Field underwriters need to be aware, for example, that many states have strict requirements regarding the practice of financial planning. In these jurisdictions, an agent may not solicit business as a financial planner or investment advisor unless state registration guidelines are followed. Failure to follow these rules can lead not only to charges of unethical behavior but also to the loss of a license.

Insider Information

We move from the consideration of the responsibilities of RIAs to other legal considerations—insider information and the legal concept of agency. Both of these areas place ethical and legal obligations on the financial services professional because many financial services professionals have access to important financial information before it becomes available to the public.

For example, you may have clients with substantial sums of money in highly responsible positions. As part of total needs selling, they may be privy to confidential information regarding the companies for which they work or in which they hold substantial ownership positions. Hence they may obtain important financial information before it becomes generally available to the public.

This important (material) information might indicate, for example, an upcoming loss or profit decline. On the other hand, it might indicate the expansion of a new product line with the likelihood of increased and substantial profitability. In each instance, the information may involve a firm whose shares are publicly traded and from which substantial personal profits could arise.

This type of financial data is considered "insider" information. Personal stock purchases or sales based upon this data constitute insider trading and are considered illegal under federal securities laws.

Both the NASD and the national stock exchanges monitor trading activity in their respective markets. One purpose of this surveillance is to detect unusual activity that could indicate insider trading based on material, nonpublic information.

The courts have broadly applied the insider-trading laws. Their application is not just limited to company officers. In one instance, insider-trading issues arose when a printer read reports that he was preparing for publication. In other instances, parties who have received information from corporate executives have been held in violation of the law.

For example, insider-trading allegations have arisen where a corporate executive casually mentioned information to his wife and son. The executive did not trade on his own account. However, his wife and adult son purchased stock for their own accounts. Charges were pressed even though the parties later became concerned about potential securities laws violations and voluntarily brought their trading activities to the attention of regulatory authorities.

Picture yourself updating your client's estate plan. It is conceivable that you could find yourself in a similar situation. Be aware of the insider-trading rules and their implications. You can spare yourself much grief and aggravation by simply not acting on an innocently given stock tip.

The insider-trading rules do not stop here. For example, the regulatory authorities have also strictly interpreted when information becomes public. Just because information has been released to the financial press does not mean it has become public. Insiders must wait until the news can reasonably be expected to appear and circulate within the media before engaging in trading activities.

What lessons can be learned from these cases? For starters, allegations of insider trading by regulatory authorities are likely to continue. In fact, the financial excesses of the 1980s resulted in two pieces of legislation designed to stiffen insider trading sanctions—the Insider Trading Sanctions Act of 1984 and the Insider Trading and Securities Act of 1988.

This means financial services professionals must exercise extra caution in handling and discussing financial data. Err on the side of propriety in handling your personal finances. Failure to do so could result in a ruined reputation, heavy legal expenses, and stiff financial penalties.

Treat financial information you receive as confidential information. This is another example of mixing good ethics with good business. Clients need to know they can trust you with private matters. You will receive more information through fact-finding, which in turn will enable you to satisfy a greater number of needs as a financial services professional.

Case Study

Investment Advice—NASD Rules

Marvin Atwood has been an insurance agent for the past 7 years. From the start, he has been licensed to sell traditional life, health, and annuity products. Last month, Marvin obtained a Series 6 license. This permits him to sell his company's recently introduced variable life insurance product portfolio.

During the past year, he has also completed financial planning courses that permit him to use a designation. He is currently debating whether to change his business card to read, Marvin Atwood, Atwood Certified Financial and Investment Planning."

For the past year, he has been following the movement of the stock market. Day after day, he has read about the growing shift of household wealth into financial assets. Marvin now feels he can put this knowledge to work. He believes that the new variable product line will open many new sales opportunities. In fact, he has scheduled an appointment with a new client, Loretta Charles, and intends to make his first variable life sale.

During his meeting with Loretta, Marvin used a company-provided fact finder. At the initial interview, Marvin learned that Loretta recently inherited a half interest in a condominium from her father. The property is under contract and Loretta expects to net $30,000 from its sale. Loretta has followed the stock market headlines but has traditionally placed her savings in certificates of deposit and money market funds.

Marvin also learned that Loretta is a middle-aged single mother. She bears the full financial responsibility for raising her 16-year-old son, Jeffrey. During their meeting, Loretta expressed two concerns in regard to her parental financial responsibilities. Number one, she is concerned about having funds available to meet Jeffrey's needs should she die prematurely. Number two, she is concerned about meeting college tuition bills.

That evening Marvin went through the investment books and magazines he had gathered during the last year. He clipped a few articles on the growth opportunities offered by the stock market. He even found an article that mentioned a mutual fund (ABCO Growth) sold through his company. Marvin put these together with a personal note directing Loretta to read the materials. He felt these are superior to the dry materials drafted by his home office.

The following week Marvin met with Loretta again. He started the meeting by providing her with an embossed folder—Financial and Investment Plan for Loretta Charles. Marvin then proceeded to review his recommendations. He first recommended that Loretta provide for her life insurance needs through the purchase of a variable universal life policy. He then recommended that Loretta place at least half of her expected inheritance in the ABCO Growth Fund. Marvin bases his recommendations on the long-term upward trend of the stock market as cited in the previously sent articles.

Loretta thanked Marvin for his work and indicated that she will need at least a week to think over his recommendations. Marvin ended this meeting by reminding Loretta that a delay could mean a major market movement and a missed opportunity to time the market.

Key Points to Ponder

Write down your thoughts.

1. Is Marvin selling on the basis of needs analysis or preconceived needs? If he is selling on the basis of preconceived needs, does this technique raise ethical issues? Explain.

2. Is it advisable to use company-approved materials in selling to clients? Why?

3. Are there any compliance rules that must be followed when selling equity-type products? Explain.

4. Has Marvin taken into consideration the dictates of the NASD Rules of Conduct in his dealings with Loretta? Explain.

5. Is Marvin properly representing his professional role in this sales situation? Explain.

Chapter 3 Review Questions

Answers to Review Questions start on appendix page A-53.

1. Federal regulation of the insurance industry is accomplished through the
   (a) NAIC Model Code
   (b) Uniform Commercial Code
   (c) McCarran-Ferguson Act
   (d) Smith-Cooley Act

2. Legal jurisdiction over the insurance industry has historically been primarily a function of
   (a) the federal government
   (b) the NAIC
   (c) the state insurance departments
   (d) the U.S. Trade Commission

3. State insurance departments have primary legal responsibility over
   (a) pension plan regulations
   (b) antitrust regulations
   (c) taxation of life insurance products
   (d) insurance product approvals

4. Regarding the relationship of laws to ethics, laws usually establish
   (a) minimum requirements for behavior
   (b) optimum standards for professional behavior
   (c) standards that only the most ethical individuals could follow
   (d) rewards for those who act ethically

5. Registration under the Investment Advisers Act
   (a) is an endorsement of competence by the SEC
   (b) is not an endorsement of competence by the SEC
   (c) may inform clients of their SEC endorsement
   (d) allows for the sale of all financial products

6. On the second anniversary of his or her registration and every 3 years thereafter, every registered representative (unless exempted) must complete a uniform computer-based continuing education training program called the
   (a) firm element
   (b) regulatory element
   (c) securities element
   (d) registration element

7. The NAIC is
   (a) an organization of state insurance supervisory officials formed in 1871
   (b) an organization of federal insurance formed in 1905 that supervises officials
   (c) an agency of the federal government formed as a result of the Armstrong Commission findings of 1905
   (d) a state insurance organization formed in 1991 in response to federal solvency investigations of the industry that supervises officials

8. The NASD is
   (a) a self-regulatory organization of Congress
   (b) a self-regulatory organization of the securities industry
   (c) a federal authority administered by a consortium of major insurance carriers
   (d) a federal authority created by Congress

9. The Securities Act of 1933
   (a) provides for the registration of previously issued securities
   (b) provides for the registration of newly issued securities
   (c) requires the publication of confidential financial data in the financial media
   (d) requires corporate officers to own corporate stock in order to maintain the integrity of the marketplace

10. All of the following are federal acts aimed at providing proper disclosure regarding the solicitation and sale of securities products EXCEPT
    (a) the Securities Act of 1933
    (b) the Securities Exchange Act of 1934
    (c) the Investment Advisers Act of 1940
    (d) the Securities Act of 1942

4

Agency and Compliance

Learning Objectives
4-1. Identify the core concepts of agency.
4-2. Specify the differences among the four types of agent authority.
4-3. List the obligations that an agent has to the carrier.
4-4. Identify the four primary legal implications of an agency contract between an agent and an insurer.
4-5. Describe the distinction between compliance and ethics.

Chapter Outline

The Concept Of Agency
What is an Agent? 4-3
Agency Principles 4-3
Types of Agent Authority 4-4
   Express Authority 4-4
   Implied Authority 4-4
   Apparent Authority 4-5
   Ratification 4-5
Implications of Agency 4-6
Agent Obligations 4-7
   Obligations to the Product Carrier 4-7
   Obligation of Loyalty 4-8
   Obligation to Avoid Conflicts of Interest 4-8
   Obligation to Follow Principals' Instructions 4-9
   Obligation of Careful Solicitation 4-9
   Obligation to Perform with Skill and Care 4-10
   Obligation of Full Disclosure of Information 4-10
   Obligation of Business Transaction Execution 4-10
   Obligation to Account for Premiums 4-11
   Fiduciary Obligation to Carrier and Possible Abuses 4-12
Legal Relationship of Broker and Insurance Carrier 4-13
Revisiting Compliance and Ethics 4-14
   Compliance Needs Ethics 4-15
   Undermining Ethics with Compliance Dependency 4-16
   Compliance and the Letter of the Law 4-16
   Acting to Avoid Punishment 4-16
   Compliance As Reactive Rather Than Proactive 4-17
   Compliance and Professionalism 4-18
Summary 4-19
Chapter 4 Review Questions 4-21

The Concept of Agency

An extremely important legal concept that governs the ethical behavior of financial advisors is that of agency. An agent has a primary responsibility to act in the best interest of a principal.

Financial services professionals are subjected to the general legal requirements of an agency relationship.

One needs to ask the question: on whose behalf is an agent acting? Legally, an agent acts on behalf of a company, but in the financial services area, agents are required by their codes of conduct to act in the best interests of their clients.

Thus, the concept of agency is particularly pertinent in spelling out the relationship between financial professionals and their carrier and the relationship between a financial services professional and his or her clients.

Agency involves two basic concepts—power and authority. An authorized agent has the power and authority to act on behalf of another.

What is an Agent?

The NAIC Model Agents and Brokers Licensing Act defines an insurance agent as "...an individual, partnership or corporation appointed by an insurer to solicit applications for a policy of insurance or to negotiate a policy of insurance *on its behalf.*" This appointment is usually evidenced by a written and signed contract between the insurance agent and the carrier. As part of the process, the agent must normally be licensed in the state in which the contracts are to be solicited. Under this definition, the professional is an agent for the company.

Agency Principles

An agency relationship between an insurance professional and an insurance carrier gives the agent the power to sell insurance on behalf of carriers through their agency agreements. Through the agency agreement, the insurance professional is given the power to contractually bind the carrier. The principle of power is fairly broad and has been used by the courts to extend the express authority granted an insurance agent by a carrier.

Agents also derive their authority from the agency contract. Typically, the agency contract specifically authorizes the agent to solicit insurance applications, describe coverage, and provide service to the company's policyowners. The agency contract may also authorize the insurance agent to collect premiums.

The power and authority granted by the agency agreement should not be confused with obtaining a state license. For example, an agent may be licensed to sell both life and health insurance in a particular state. The carrier, however, may only be involved in the life side of the insurance business. The agent under the agency agreement would only have the power and authority to solicit life insurance, not health insurance, for this particular carrier.

Types of Agent Authority

An agency relationship that binds the carrier can, however, be created in several ways including

- express authority
- implied authority
- apparent authority
- ratification

Express Authority

This type of authority is specifically spelled out and granted to the agent in the agency contract. An example of this type of express authority is the authority of the insurance professional to solicit applications for the type of insurance sold by the carrier.

Very few legal questions arise in regard to express authority. This is the type of authority that is actually held by the agent. It can be clearly identified from the terms of the agency contract. Life and health insurance agents, for example, have the express authority to solicit insurance applications.

Implied Authority

Express authority is not the only type of authority that may be actually held by the agent. An agent has actual authority to act on the principal's behalf when he or she reasonably believes that such authority has been given.

For example, the express authority given to an insurance agent to act on behalf of a carrier will not necessarily spell out every detail of the authority given to the agent. This is where the concept of implied authority comes into play. It is the type of authority a carrier intends an insurance agent to have but does not put into writing.

Usually, the agent is given implied authority to act in accordance with the general customs of business. It is implied that the agent can use all reasonable means to carry out the purpose of the agency agreement. For example, as part of their express authority to solicit business, agents have the implied authority to explain the terms of whole life insurance policies to prospects.

Apparent Authority

This is the type of authority that gets insurance agents and their companies into the most legal trouble. In general, Party A is not legally responsible for the acts of Party B simply because B says he was acting on A's behalf. However, A will be responsible if A has created the reasonable appearance of authority in B.

For example, Agent Burke has worked for AAA Life Insurance Company for several months. Due to poor production, Agent Burke's contract is terminated. Agent Burke retains her rate book and business cards. She sells a policy to Client Charles. Charles relies on the apparent authority placed in Burke by AAA Life Insurance Company.

Situations of apparent authority can also involve insurance agents who are under contract but go beyond the terms of the agency agreement. For example, an insurance agent may make credible statements regarding the terms of a health policy. Because the agent represents the insurer in the eyes of the client, the company becomes bound for benefits beyond the terms of the contract.

Ratification

If an insurance professional sells a product that he or she is not licensed to sell, the company is not obligated to honor the insurance professional's acts. If the company, however, issues the policy, it validates or ratifies the agent's act. Ratification, in other words, is the validation of an unauthorized act by the person or entity on whose behalf the action purportedly took place.

What Type of Authority?

Client Clara Johnson:

"Jack, I don't understand what this policy covers."

Agent Jack Jensen:

"Let me explain. . . ."

Is this the way you would respond? Under what type of authority is Jack operating? Is this type of authority expressly spelled out in his contract? Is it implied?

Log your answer in the space below.

Implications of Agency

The agency contract between an agent and an insurer carries with it the following primary legal implications:

- The insurance agent represents the interests of the carrier. This means the agent's prime legal responsibilities and obligations are to the insurer, not to a potential client.
- The agent is given power to act on behalf of the insurer. This power includes the power to enter into legal contracts on behalf of the insurer. For example, the agent can bind the carrier. In other words, the agent can create legal liability for the carrier under the insurance contract. The agent can also create legal rights for the carrier under the insurance contract.
- The acts of the insurance agent are considered acts of the insurer. For example, collection of insurance premiums by a debit agent is considered collection by the carrier.
- Knowledge of the insurance agent is considered to be knowledge of the insurer. For example, if the agent has knowledge of health matters pertinent to the issuance of insurance, it is assumed that this information is also available to the carrier.

Legal but Ethical?

Client Edith Spinster:

"I've always been single. I'm not really close to my nieces and nephews. Are you sure this is the right product for me?"

Agent Cliff Morris:

"Sure it is, you can afford the premium on the policy, and it offers tax-favored cash build-ups."

This approach may be legal but is it ethical? Would an annuity paying a lower commission be more appropriate in light of Edith's lack of dependents? Would an investment other than life insurance be more appropriate?

Log your answer in the space below.

Agent Obligations

Obligations to the Product Carrier

Where the financial services professional is an agent of a company, certain obligations obtain to that company.

The agency agreement spells out the contractual obligations of agents to their carriers. An agent's duties to the carrier, however, go beyond the strictly delineated terms of the agency agreement. The agency agreement establishes a fiduciary relationship between an insurance agent and the insurer. This entails a high level of trust and the obligation to act according to high ethical standards of conduct. The agent as fiduciary must act in the best interests of the carrier.

Credibility

The word *credible* is the key to whether or not the notion of apparent authority will bind an insurer. If a statement is credible, it will generally be binding. If a statement is obviously outlandish, it will not.

Obligation of Loyalty

Agents owe a duty of loyalty to their carriers. In other words, agents must act solely for the benefit of their carriers in all matters connected with their agency agreement. Agents must display the utmost good faith and integrity in dealing with their carriers and must be scrupulously honest in handling all affairs dealing with respect to their carriers.

Obligation to Avoid Conflicts of Interest

Closely related to an agent's obligation of loyalty is his or her obligation to avoid conflicts of interest. This has slightly different meanings depending upon whether or not the agent is a captive agent or an independent agent.

Generally speaking, captive agents are held to a stricter standard in this regard. For example, captive agents cannot serve two carriers that sell competing products at the same time. It may be possible, however, for captive agents to sell products not offered by their own carriers but sold through other carriers.

The wise course of action in this situation is for a captive agent to inform his or her carrier of the complete facts. In this way, the agent's carrier can determine whether or not there is a conflict of interest. This procedure also indicates the agent's adherence to strict ethical standards and serves to enhance and protect his or her reputation.

Captive agents solicit business on behalf of insurance carriers. Brokers act on behalf of individual clients in order to secure products. True consultants provide advice on the type of products to be obtained. For this they are paid a fee and are not dependent upon commissions. In this section, particular attention will be paid to the captive agent and broker roles.

Financial services professionals have three potential roles under the law of agency:

- captive agents
- brokers
- consultants

Independent agents represent both carriers and clients at different points in the transaction. The client is represented during the selection process. Once a determination has been made in regard to the coverage to be selected, loyalty is owed to the carrier during the application, underwriting, and record-keeping process.

Obligation to Follow Principals' Instructions

Agents have an obligation to follow their carriers' lawful and reasonable instructions. This obligation is of particular importance in today's litigious environment. Many carriers already provide strict instructions about the solicitation of business and client communication. These instructions often limit the type of illustrations that may be used or the type of letters that may be sent to prospects.

Review Item

Literary Critic

Agent Edward Unger:

"This company-provided letter sounds stilted to me. I'll just change a few words. What an improvement!"

Do you see any possible problems arising here? If so, explain. Why do companies specify the language to be included in client communications?

Log your answer in the space below.

Obligation of Careful Solicitation

Agents' jobs involve seeking out profitable business for their carriers. This involves the selection of who are fit for the product. It also involves the selection of prospects who can reasonably pay both the initial premium and future premiums. In this manner, life insurers obtain the benefits of good mortality statistics and low policy lapse ratios.

Review Item

Confusing New Product?

Agent Jim Scully:

"This looks like a situation for our new Roth IRA. Should I tell the client? I'm still uncertain about all those rules."

What would you do? Would you ignore the need? Would you risk giving inaccurate advice?

Log your answer in the space below.

Obligation to Perform with Skill and Care

Insurance agents have the obligation to carry out their duties with reasonable care. Agents must execute these duties with the level of skill ordinarily possessed by individuals engaged in the same type of business. Agents are obligated not to engage in business they are not capable of performing. In other words, if you are dealing in an area with which you are not familiar, bring in a specialist. Alternatively, learn the area. One way to do this is through quality continuing education.

Seeking Competent Advice

Agent Adams deals with personal life insurance on a day-to-day basis. One of his clients, Bruce, owns a small business—The Corner Confectionery, Inc. Bruce has heard about pension plans and wants to install one. Adams has never worked in this area before.

In order to provide his client with proper service and execute his duties under his agency contract, he calls in David Doit, the home office pension expert.

Obligation of Full Disclosure of Information

An agent has the obligation to make full disclosure of all pertinent information that bears on the placement of an insurance policy to the insurer. In other words, part of the agent's duty is to alert the carrier of facts known to the agent. The type of facts includes those that the carrier needs to know in order to protect itself and profitably underwrite business.

The obligation of full disclosure first becomes significant during the application process, and second, during the claims process.

For example, an agent is obligated to reveal accurate information about a prospect's smoker status even if the prospect says "no" while answering health-related questions on the application.

The point is that the insurer has entrusted the agent to act on the carrier's behalf in seeking out information to make valid underwriting judgments. Not questioning suspect information is a willful omission. It is, in effect, unethical behavior.

Obligation of Business Transaction Execution

An agent is obligated to process or follow through on business transactions within a reasonable amount of time. This obligation arises most frequently in relation to premium payments and the submission of completed insurance applications.

If a premium is not transmitted within a reasonable time period, a policy may lapse. This places the client in a position of risk. However, it also opens the carrier to charges that it is obligated to honor any claims due to the negligent behavior of its agent.

Is the Carrier Bound?

Agent Brian Turner:

"Your new policy will cover your medical expenses up to one million dollars."

Client Marion Miller:

"That's reassuring. I hate to read the fine print of these documents. I find it so confusing."

What if the policy only covers three quarters of a million dollars? Do you see any ethical problems arising? Do you think the carrier might be bound by Agent Turner's statements?

Log your answer in the space below.

The carrier is also placed into a situation of risk if an insurance application is not submitted on a timely basis. In some cases, a binding receipt has been issued. This makes the carrier liable for a claim on even a poor risk until the application has been formally rejected. Without the application in hand, the carrier is unable to issue the rejection and protect itself from liability.

Obligation to Account for Premiums

Agents have the fiduciary duty to account for all of the funds in their possession that have been received on behalf of their carriers. Many agents are authorized by their carriers to collect initial premium payments in order to facilitate the application and underwriting process. Some agents are also authorized to collect subsequent premium payments. Payment made to an agent is considered payment to the agent's carrier. Any funds collected are considered to be held in trust.

The obvious point to remember is that funds must not be pocketed for personal use. It is also important to keep in mind that most states have laws making it illegal to commingle premium dollars with personal funds. Many agents have lost their licenses because they commingled insurer and personal funds.

Fiduciary Obligation to Carrier and Possible Abuses

Agents may sometimes be confused about the nature of their fiduciary duties to their carriers. This confusion can lead to unintentional abuses of fiduciary obligations to the carrier. This, in turn, can present you with career difficulties.

The following are some general guidelines that should help avoid such confusion:

- Agents represent their insurer when insurance is being placed.
- Agents represent their insurer in maintaining policyholder records
- Agents represent their insurer when delivering insurance policies.
- Finally, agents represent their insurer when premiums are collected.

8 Obligations

Agents' fiduciary obligations to their carriers as it extends to eight areas of responsibilities and concerns:

- loyalty
- avoidance of conflicts of interest
- obedience
- careful solicitation
- performance with skill and care
- full disclosure of information
- business transaction execution
- accountability for premiums

Review Item

No Need to Compare

Agent Ian Wilkerson:
"Our company is offering a new type of coverage. I'm sure it would be cheaper than your old policy."

Client Helen Norris:
"What should I do with my old policy? Should I just drop it?"

How would you suggest Agent Wilkerson answer? Should he take any steps before replacing the old policy?

Log your answer in the space below.

Legal Relationship
of Broker and Insurance Carrier

The role of a broker differs from that of an insurance agent. The NAIC Model Agents and Brokers Licensing Act defines the term broker as follows:

Any individual, partnership or corporation who, for compensation, not being a licensed agent for the company in which a policy of insurance is placed, acts or aides in any manner in negotiating contracts for insurance or placing risk or effecting insurance for a party other than himself or herself.

The definition clearly indicates the importance for an insurance professional to determine his or her exact role in a given situation. Is the insurance professional a captive agent, an agent licensed with several companies, or a true broker? Fiduciary responsibility and liability is determined on the basis of the answer to this question.

A true broker is in the business of bringing insurance buyers and sellers together. A broker acts in the interest of the *insurance applicant* with regard to the procuring of insurance and the making of the insurance application. On the other hand, a broker acts on behalf of the carrier with regard to the collection of premiums and the policy delivery.

The role of a true broker is different from that of an agent licensed with several companies. In most instances, these individuals owe their prime fiduciary responsibilities to the carriers. Legally, most of these insurance professionals are actually agents of each carrier rather than brokers.

And, remember, the role of a broker is substantially different from that of a captive agent who clearly acts in a fiduciary capacity for his or her carrier.

Knowing your role is important from a professional risk standpoint. If you are an agent but lead the client to believe you are providing special services, you are likely to be held to higher fiduciary obligations toward the client.

Many courts have blurred the differences between agent and broker in favor of client claims of agent negligence and/or misconduct. If you want to limit your liability toward the client and are under an agency contract, be sure to act as an agent and not as a broker.

Revisiting Compliance and Ethics

George Washington, Benjamin Franklin, Thomas Jefferson and the other founding fathers of the United States were not inclined to comply with the law unless they had good reasons to do so. Those reasons were not provided by authoritarian declarations but by appeals to sound ethical principles. As we learned from the American Revolution, a demand for compliance without accompanying good reasons can create resentment.

Compliance also has its good side. It is necessary when the internal controls or mores that provide for an orderly and just society have lost their effect.

When ethical expectations are not met, society calls upon legal remedies, which, unlike appeals to morality, can impose sanctions and penalize undesirable behavior in the here and now. However, because laws impose sanctions, they use fear as a motivator: "Obey me or pay the price." It is, therefore, the laws and regulations, although necessary, that will be resented for the compliance they require because they restrict liberty and appeal to fear.

As we know all too well, breakdowns in ethical behavior on the part of some members of the insurance and financial services industry required the introduction of legal remedies, the end result of which was the emphasis (some would say overemphasis) on compliance. While the goal of compliance—to establish or reestablish ethical behavior—is laudable, the resulting new emphasis on compliance and compliance training leaves a lot to be desired.

Compliance Needs Ethics

Even though the goal of compliance is to help improve ethical behavior, simply concerning ourselves with being in compliance and satisfying the letter of the law will not improve ethical behavior by itself; being in compliance with the law is not the equivalent of being ethical. To equate following the law with being ethical is a mistaken view.

To illustrate how being ethical demands that we go beyond the law, let's review one of the great moral stories of Western culture—the story of the good Samaritan. A man traveling the road from Jerusalem to Jericho is attacked by robbers and left to die on the side of the road. A priest and Levite pass the man by, and it is only a Samaritan—the supposed enemy of the man—who stops to help him. It is clear that when the priest and the Levite passed by the wounded man, they did nothing illegal. But there has been near universal agreement that the priest and Levite were morally irresponsible and that the real moral hero is the Samaritan who, in spite of his fear and hatred of Jews in the abstract, was led by sympathy for his wounded fellow man. Therefore, although a legal judgment of the priest and Levite would find nothing illegal, a moral judgment would find them morally deficient. This story reveals why going beyond the law is morally required. Ethics calls on us to do more than just obey the law.

Clarence Walton, the first chairholder in ethics at The American College, posits a Law of Social Motivation which asserts "...that in

---

Avoiding Ethical Dilemmas

Many ethically related problems can be avoided if an agent follows the following simple steps:

- Always act in good faith when dealing with your carrier.

- Read your agency contract. Become familiar with its terms. Don't toss it into a file cabinet to collect dust! Its terms will provide the answers to many of your questions regarding the extent of your authority.

- Use reasonable skill and care when soliciting and placing business. If you need additional help, call upon your home office experts.

- Know your carrier's underwriting guidelines before you solicit business. These guidelines will point you in the direction of proper client solicitation.

- Make sure any application submitted to your carrier is complete and the prospective insured has answered all questions. Never sign an application on behalf of a prospective insured.

- Disclose all material facts surrounding the case to your carrier. Err, if necessary, on the side of full disclosure. This enables your carrier to make a proper determination as to whether or not the proposed insured is an acceptable risk.

---

advanced industrial affluent and democratic societies, people demand that consideration of the common welfare be borne in mind by large private associations—even when the law is silent on such demands." In short, neither individuals nor companies meet their full ethical responsibilities when they simply aim to stay in compliance.

Undermining Ethics with Compliance Dependency

Beyond the realization that to be ethical we need to go beyond compliance, it is interesting to note that if companies rely solely on appeals to compliance to promote ethical behavior, they may end up undermining the very ethical behavior they seek to encourage.

Compliance and the Letter of the Law

Because compliance is targeted at meeting the basic legal requirements, it emphasizes the letter of the law, rather than addressing the reasons for the law or the spirit of the law. But just as an arrow aimed too low will miss the target, aiming only to meet the basic requirements of compliance—to be in accord with the letter of the law—will fail to hit the target of acting ethically (that is, acting in the spirit of the law).

Simply meeting the demands of compliance does not always make it ethical. For example, consider your disgust when upon purchasing a product on the strength of an advertisement, you discover you aren't getting nearly the bargain you had thought you were getting because you hadn't read the ad's small print. Although the small print in the advertisement meets the legal requirements and puts the company in compliance, it manipulates the customer and fails to live up to the spirit of the law against false advertising.

The spirit of any law for truth in advertising rests on a moral belief that a prospective customer, like you and me, has a right to know what he or she is purchasing (informed consent) and should be able to make that choice freely without being manipulated. Small print violates that spirit. If the small print is there merely so a company can be in compliance, then being in compliance violates the spirit of the law. Thus, by aiming only at being in compliance, we may end up being unethical.

Acting to Avoid Punishment

There are two reasons for obeying the law or being ethical. First, it is the right thing to do. Second, we do not want to get caught and be punished. We often do things because we wish to avoid penalties and punishment. Fear is a very effective motivating tool. Consider what happens, however, when fear of punishment or avoidance of penalties becomes the only reason for acting. If the sole motive for acting in a particular way in certain circumstances is to avoid punishment, then when punishments to avoid in those circumstances no longer exist, the reason for acting in that way is removed. If your only reason for not lying is that you are afraid of the consequences of getting caught, what reason do you have to avoid lying if you know you will not get caught?

Some behavior is prohibited by law because it is viewed as undesirable or unethical. It is not undesirable because it is prohibited. Thus, lying is wrong and, hence, prohibited because other people are being used for individual purposes. It makes no sense to say that the risk of getting caught in a lie is why lying is considered wrong. Of course, when an unethical action is declared illegal and a sanction is attached to it, there is an additional motive for not acting in that way. Nonetheless, the primary reason for not acting unethically is that the action hurts people or is unfair. Excessive or exclusive reliance on compliance to motivate ethical activity puts the cart before the horse, and attempting to modify behavior through fear of sanctions sends the wrong message about why it is unacceptable to treat customers or clients unethically.

Compliance As Reactive Rather Than Proactive

There are those who say sports are a microcosm of life. I think they are correct, at least to the extent that we can learn many lessons about life by observing sports behavior. Assume it is Sunday afternoon and you are watching your favorite NFL team. It is the last quarter of the game. Your team has just scored to go ahead by two points and kicks off to the opposition. Your team goes into a prevent defense. Most of the time it doesn't seem to work. Compliance can be likened to a prevent defense that causes the players to sit back on their heels—to react instead of attack.

It is important to make sure that the compliance mentality permeating the financial services industry is not like a prevent defense. This shows us that acting out of defensiveness or fear is rarely as effective as acting in a more proactive and positive way. Acting defensively, with only compliance as our guide, is being reactive, not proactive. Proactive people and companies are robust and confident, they surge forward and are not afraid to make a mistake. Reactive people and companies are retiring and defensive, moving ever so slowly, preferring to do nothing in order to avoid making a mistake.

A company whose decisions are always constrained by a legalistic, hypercautious approach and whose sole concern is the avoidance of trouble is a company that has lost its self-confidence. Not much new and creative will come from that company. The paradox is that if your only goal is to protect yourself, you probably won't. Rather, you will create many other problems. There is something disconcerting about a multibillion-dollar corporation that deals with its problems in a dictatorial way when the environment calls for a values-based empowerment approach that builds upon integrity and honesty. With such a culture, a company can be more aggressive and build flexibility into the system. It will think of what its customers want and gear the company toward meeting those needs, instead of focusing on how to avoid litigation.

Compliance and Professionalism

Acting out of fear and being governed by fear causes us to be excessively self-absorbed. There is nothing wrong with looking out for our own interests. But it is not certain that extreme risk aversiveness works in the long run for our best interests. To have robust, fulfilled lives, we need to be willing to take the initiative, make commitments, set high goals and expectations, and set out to achieve them.

What makes a financial services professional more than a commodity salesperson is the desire to bring value-added service to others. That turns the role into more than merely a job; it becomes a career. The vast majority of financial advisors are not insensitive individuals with no interest in their clients; they are people who get great satisfaction in helping others solve financial problems. This is why so many of the financial advisors—successful, honest, ambitious people—resent the compliance restraints. They believe those restraints keep them from doing their best, and they assume that the company's motives for restraining agents do not give any indication of faith in the agents' own integrity. It is incumbent upon a company, then, to promote the message that it is committed to an ethical perspective, that the reason for doing something is because it is the right and ethical thing to do. In that way, compliance may be seen as a necessary tool for the short run, but the long-term goal is ethics-based empowerment.

It is quite popular these days for companies to stress the procedural side of ethics through compliance. It is important, however, that companies begin soon to look beyond the mere procedural approach and begin building an ethics-based culture throughout the organization for the future that will rely less and less upon compliance. Successful companies do not prosper at the expense of customers. They prosper because of the value they bring to their customers. If a company has a soul, the surest way to lose it is to view the customer as someone to exploit rather than as someone to serve.

Summary

This chapter has looked at the relationship of ethics and the law. While the law is the public's agency for enforcing moralities, acting legally is not always acting ethically. So we study law because it is a prime step leading us in the direction of ethical behavior. What is legal is usually ethical. However, financial services professionals are subject to both federal and state laws. Laws at both levels impact the products and selling practices of financial services professionals.

Financial services professionals act as agents. Agency is based on the principles of power and authority. Authority may be expressed, implied, or apparent. Unauthorized acts of an insurance agent may be ratified later by a carrier.

Financial services professionals owe fiduciary obligations to their carriers and clients. The extent of these fiduciary obligations depends on whether the professional is acting as an agent or broker. Agent fiduciary obligations include loyalty, careful solicitation, and full disclosure.

Brokers owe their prime fiduciary loyalty to their clients in placing insurance. Brokers do, however, have fiduciary responsibilities toward carriers such as the remission of premium payments. Insurance agents operating as consultants or financial planners owe broad fiduciary responsibilities to their clients. All financial services professionals should pay particular attention to the mandates of state law and licensing requirements.

To ensure as much freedom to its citizens as possible, governments establish laws as a minimum standard, or as Paine phrased it, "moral mediocrity." Many aspire to much higher standards. We could depend on the ethical or moral standards of our society, but there may be disagreement about some of those and how they apply to the specific subcultures to which we belong. Hence, to promulgate desirable modes of behavior, professions and industries have traditionally supplied their practitioners with codes of ethics. For example, the Hippocratic Oath that doctors still abide by goes back to the days of ancient Grecian society.

In conclusion, financial services professionals must take account of the limitations of laws and regulations. They are an important, but not the only, source of guidance. They do not take the place of personal reactions, professional codes, or the moral guidelines. Mere compliance with the law is not enough. One must act as a professional. What is involved in fulfilling the ethical obligations of a profession is covered in the next chapter.

Chapter 4 Review Questions

Answers to Review Questions start on appendix page A-53.

1. Agency involves what two basic concepts?
   (a) law and ethics
   (b) liability and power
   (c) authority and liability
   (d) authority and power

2. One of the implications that the agency contract between an agent and an insurer carries with it is that
   (a) the acts of the insurance carrier are considered acts of the agent
   (b) the acts of the insurance agent are considered the acts of the insurer
   (c) the agent's primary legal obligation is to the state
   (d) the agent's primary legal obligation is to his or her profession

3. Insurance professionals act in what three primary capacities for purposes of the law of agency?
   (a) captive agent, broker, and consultant
   (b) trustee, fiduciary, and administrator
   (c) solicitor, prospector, and administrator
   (d) field underwriter, manager, and general agent

4. Which of the following types of relationships entails a high level of trust and the obligation to act according to high ethical standards of conduct?
   (a) professional relationship
   (b) fiduciary relationship
   (c) business relationship
   (d) working relationship

5. What type of financial services professional solicits business exclusively on behalf of an insurance carrier?
   (a) captive agent
   (b) broker
   (c) consultant
   (d) financial planner

6. Which of the following statements regarding the relationship between compliance and ethics is true?
   (a) Being in compliance with the law is the equivalent of being ethical.
   (b) Being in compliance with the law is not the equivalent of being ethical.
   (c) To equate following the law with being ethical is a mistaken view.
   (d) Being in compliance and satisfying the letter of the law will improve ethical behavior.

7. Which of the following types of agent authority involves the validation of an unauthorized act by the person or entity on whose behalf the action purportedly took place?
   (a) express authority
   (b) implied authority
   (c) apparent authority
   (d) ratification

8. The agency contract specifically authorizes the agent to do all of the following activities EXCEPT
   (a) solicit insurance applications
   (b) describe coverage
   (c) provide service to the company's policyowners
   (d) commingle premiums

9. All of the following are general guidelines that should help agents avoid confusion about the nature of their fiduciary duties to their carriers EXCEPT
   (a) Agents represent their insurer when insurance is being placed.
   (b) Agents represent their insurer in maintaining policyholder records.
   (c) Agents represent themselves when delivering insurance policies.
   (d) Agents represent their insurer when premiums are collected.

10. All of the following are obligations that an insurance agent has to his or her carrier EXCEPT
    (a) an obligation of loyalty
    (b) an obligation to perform with skill and care
    (c) an obligation of continuing education
    (d) an obligation of full disclosure of information

5

Professionalism

Learning Objectives

5-1. Identify the four characteristics of being a professional.

5-2. Describe the way the "practice of financial services" meets each of the seven basic requirements for being considered a profession.

5-3. List the ten hallmarks of being a professional.

5-4. List and describe three elements that contribute to the price of professionalism for the financial services professional.

5-5. List seven practical steps that a financial services professional can use in order to avoid legal liability.

5-6. Identify the seven common themes in the codes of ethics applicable to the financial services professional.

5-7. List five professional responsibility guidelines found in the financial services industry's professional codes.

Chapter Outline

The Financial Services Professional

Characteristics of a Professional   5-4
   Requirements for a Profession   5-6
   Behaving Professionally   5-8
Responsibilities of Professionalism   5-11
   Increased Client Service   5-11
   Increased Need to Be Aware of Ethical Issues   5-12
   Increased Risk of Legal Liability   5-13
   Practical Steps to Avoid Legal Liability   5-14
   Attributes of Professional Behavior   5-18
Professional Codes of Ethics   5-19
   Codes Applicable to the Financial Services Professional   5-19
   Common Themes among Professional Codes   5-19
Practical Application   5-22
   Client Education   5-24
   Client-Focused Service   5-25
   Agent of the Client   5-25
Professional Competitive Integrity   5-28
   Summary of Professional Responsibilities   5-29
Chapter 5 Review Questions   5-31

The Financial Services Professional

We have seen that a primary ethical responsibility is to live up to one's commitments. The decision to act as a professional imposes obligations on people. The fact that you are taking this course or the fact that your company or employer requires you to get a professional designation, and that you concur, means that you are making a commitment to act as a professional.

There is a current advertisement used by a financial consulting investment company. It presents a picture of a sales manager entreating his sales force "to unload this dog." In short, he is encouraging salespeople to sell an inferior product to whomever (client) they can persuade to buy it. The advertisement makes it clear that a respectable company does not engage in that kind of behavior. The respectable company looks out for the best interests of the client, handles reliable products, and makes sure the products are suitable for the client. In short, the respectable company expects its sales force, distributors, or agents to act like professionals.

The value of professionalism has a long history in the financial services industry. In 1915, in an address delivered before the annual meetings of Baltimore Life and New York Life Underwriters, Solomon S. Huebner, the founder of The American College, laid out his lifetime dream—to turn the life insurance salesperson into a professional. This dream motivated him to establish The American College in 1927 to educate insurance salespeople and award them a designation, the CLU (Chartered Life Underwriter), which indicated they had achieved a certain level of expertise. The College required, and it still does today, that each designee pledge to serve the best interests of the client. In that way, students of financial services would fulfill the characteristics of a professional, according to Dr. Huebner.

But what exactly does it mean to be a professional, and what responsibilities does being a professional impose upon a person?

Characteristics of a Professional

Using physicians, lawyers, teachers, and others as models of what professionals should be, Dr. Huebner crafted as fine a statement of what it takes to be a professional as any that exists, one that is as valid today as in 1915. He cited four characteristics of the professional.

1. The professional is involved in a vocation that is useful and noble enough to inspire love and enthusiasm in the practitioner.
2. The professional's vocation requires an expert's knowledge in its practice.
3. "In applying that knowledge, the practitioner should abandon the strictly selfish commercial view and ever keep in mind the advantage of the client."
4. The practitioner should possess a spirit of loyalty to fellow practitioners, of helpfulness to the common cause they all profess, and should not allow any unprofessional acts to bring shame upon the entire profession.

It is evident that rendering financial services is a useful occupation, and the fact that financial planning helps people alleviate anxiety and gain security makes it a noble vocation. Thus, involvement in financial services meets Dr. Huebner's first characteristic of a professional.

The second characteristic is expert knowledge. Clearly, the practice of financial services is complicated and requires study to achieve competence and expertise. To stay abreast of the latest developments in financial instruments and to know which products are beneficial for different clients, requires ongoing study.

The third characteristic that Dr. Huebner lists is the most interesting characteristic of the professional for our purposes because it lays out an ethical prescription. It requires the professional to "abandon the strictly selfish commercial view and ever keep in mind the advantage of the client."

The "strictly selfish commercial view" is the view that the *only* concern of business is to make money or increase profit. It is the view of those whose only concern is to sell a product without regard for the needs of the client. It is a view made popular by extreme advocates of the free market system echoing the economist Milton Friedman and others who claim "the primary and *only* responsibility of business is to increase profit."

It is a view that distorts the position of Adam Smith, the father of the capitalistic free-market economy. Smith, the 18th century economist-philosopher, in his book *The Wealth of Nations,* convinced economists that a great deal of good comes from a system that allows people to pursue their own interests. Smith's view became the theoretical foundation and justification of the capitalist free-market economic system. However, according to Smith, this pursuit of self-interest, this strictly selfish commercial pursuit; must be constrained by ethical considerations of justice and fairness. Hence, one should not always look out for one's own interest. There are times when it is ethically necessary to constrain that self-interest in the name of justice or fairness.

Pursuing our own interest is perfectly acceptable. The New Testament of the Bible wisely prescribes that we love our neighbors as ourselves, thereby reminding us that if we don't have a healthy self-love and self-interest, we do both our neighbors and ourselves a disservice. Nevertheless, if we pursue our self-interest at the expense of another, we act unethically.

Because a "strictly selfish commercial view" encourages the pursuit of self-interest with no limits, it is a pursuit that inevitably leads to selfishness. English uses two different words, *self-interest* and *selfishness*, to distinguish between behavior that is perfectly acceptable (self-interested behavior) and behavior that is ethically inappropriate (selfish behavior). To have an ethical world, we need to avoid selfishness and at times sacrifice our own interests for the common good, that is, to abandon the "strictly selfish commercial view." Hence, there are times when the financial services professional, in looking out for the good of the client, might have to abandon a sale if the client does not need the product.

This third characteristic is embodied in the pledge mentioned above that all new CLU and ChFC (Chartered Financial Consultant) designees of The American College must make. "In all my professional relationships, I pledge myself to the following rule of ethical conduct: I shall, in light of all conditions surrounding those I serve, which I shall make every conscientious effort to ascertain and understand, render that service which, in the same circumstances, I would apply to myself."

The pledge is a version of that great moral precept, the Golden Rule, found in every great civilization and religion since the beginning of history. Financial services professionals' concerns may change. Their approaches may change, but the fundamentals of the ethics pledge, and of the ethical obligations of all financial services professionals, do not.

Financial services professionals, whatever their tasks and whatever they are named, must always put their clients' advantages first.

The fourth characteristic of professionalism cited by Dr. Huebner involves a spirit of loyalty to fellow practitioners, helpfulness to the professed common cause and disparagement of unprofessional acts that shame the profession. This means financial services professionals need to view themselves as part of a group, dedicated to serving others that condemns the shameful acts of exploiting customers (such as those acts in the 90s that earned insurance agents such a bad reputation). Part of being a group of professionals means the professions regulate themselves. This occurs with codes of ethics.

This means professional status is a double-edged sword. While it offers financial services professionals added recognition and status, it also means they must act according to professional levels of conduct in their dealings with clients.

Requirements for a Profession

Expanding on Huebner's four basic characteristics of a professional, we can mention additional requirements that a professional group must insist upon in a profession. We will show how the financial services profession meets all of these requirements.

- **Body of Technical Subject Matter**—Any profession has at its core a body of subject matter, which must be sufficiently technical so the average layperson cannot readily understand it. We have seen how sophisticated financial planning has become and how complex financial instruments are.
- **Academic Study**—Entrance into the profession requires mastery of the technical subject matter. Achieving this mastery requires a period of academic study. Those seeking mastery of financial services must involve themselves in a program of academic study. Presentation of this technical subject matter for financial advisors can be found in Life Underwriter Training Council courses and materials prepared by The American College, as well as other educational institutions.
- **Entrance Barrier(s)**—An individual cannot be a self-declared professional. A profession has, as one of its hallmarks, a barrier to entry. This standard frequently involves examinations on the technical subject matter through which the "prospective professional" demonstrates his or her competence and expertise.

Those seeking to sell insurance must first pass state-licensing tests. If variable products and securities are to be sold, these individuals must comply with federally based licensing tests. In addition, those seeking professional designations such as the LUTCF (Life Underwriter Training Council Fellow), CLU, ChFC, and CFP must pass a series of examinations.

- **Independence**—Members of the profession must conduct their affairs in an independent manner. They must reach their judgments objectively. Financial service professionals, through detailed fact finding, apply independent judgment to their recommendations. Moreover, financial services professionals, by the very nature of their work, are dealing with many clients at a time. This ability to generate income from more than one source further assures the independent nature of the advice rendered by the financial services professional.

- **Public Recognition**—There must be public recognition of the profession. Professional designations such as LUTCF, CLU, ChFC, CFP, and other professional designations have gained wide public acceptance. The public has come to rely more and more upon the technical advice of financial services professionals in planning their affairs. This situation is evidenced by the high standards of ethical behavior demanded of financial services professionals and by the judicial system in cases dealing with alleged financial advisor negligence and ethical misconduct.

- **Professional Society(ies)**—A profession needs to be guided by a society of its members. The functions of such a society include monitoring the professional actions and competence of those practicing the particular profession. There are several professional societies in any community, which guide the conduct of the financial services professional. These include NAIFA, Society of Financial Service Professionals, the CFP Board of Standards, and other groups.

- **Code of Ethics**—One way a professional society monitors the behavior of its members is through the promulgation of a code of ethics. Those codes of ethics set standards of conduct for members of a profession. Such standards are set at a level that exceeds the minimum legal requirements in regard to the conduct of professional affairs. Ethical codes have been promulgated by NAIFA and The Society of Financial Service Professionals. The American College has a pledge for its CLU and ChFC and its designees, the LUTC program has the LUTCF Pledge. Other organizations, such as the CFP Board with which a financial service professional may be affiliated, also have ethical codes. These codes set the level of professional behavior far above minimum legal standards.

Behaving Professionally

A client may or may not be familiar with the characteristics of being a professional we have just mentioned. The client, however, looks for the hallmarks of the way to behave professionally when dealing with financial services professionals. What are these hallmarks? We believe there are ten things a client looks for when judging whether or not he or she is dealing with a professional. We can capture these hallmarks of professional behavior by asking these ten questions:

1. **Does the professional listen?** Do you do all the talking? You shouldn't. Good fact finding depends on getting the client to reveal both financial and personal information. Stop and listen. Get to know the client's needs and aspirations. Obtaining this information permits you to custom design a financial program geared to the client's specific needs.

2. **Does the professional answer my questions?** Sometimes a client will ask a question to which the answer is not immediately clear. Don't ignore the question or gloss over it. If you need to research an answer, say so. The client will respect you.

   Sometimes clients should ask obvious questions but they do not. Probe the clients for information. If necessary, ask if they have any questions. This will provide you with feedback on whether or not they understand their needs and the role of financial products in fulfilling those needs.

3. **Is the professional gathering information sufficient to provide good advice?** The answer will be "yes" if you are conducting a thorough fact find. The point is, be sure you have the facts before making a recommendation.

4. **Has the professional educated me about the product?** Some clients understand the intricacies of how a financial product operates, but many do not. Take the time to educate your clients on basics and the range of available products. This way, your clients will understand what they purchased and why they purchased it.

5. **Has the professional taken my ability to deal with risk into consideration in making his or her recommendation?** We know that different clients regard risk differently. Many clients will reject a proposal that makes them feel uneasy because it's outside their financial comfort zone. It is good ethics and good business to find out where a client stands in this regard before making a recommendation. (We will engage in a thorough discussion of risk tolerance later.)

6. **Does the professional tell me about his or her designations and affiliations, and am I really dealing with someone knowledgeable?** Many of your clients are individuals you have known a short time. Many are unfamiliar with your background but want to know more before entrusting you with financial or other highly confidential information. Some clients will ask questions in this regard. Others will remain silent but move on if the unasked question remains unanswered.

   Provide your clients with information regarding your background. Initially, your professional business card introduces you. Don't try to hide behind high-sounding business names such as Michael Princely, President of Princely Financial Services, Ltd. Your clients are smart enough to understand that this doesn't provide them with information regarding your educational background or other qualifications.

   List your designations and other related information that indicates your status as a professional. Tell the client what professional associations you belong to when asked. For example, Michael Princely, LUTCF, CLU, ChFC, CFP tells clients immediately that they are dealing with a knowledgeable individual capable of providing appropriate advice in financial matters.

7. **Does the professional provide me with a sense of steady service or am I meeting with an individual seeking a one-time sale?** Do you return client calls? You should. Both during and after the sale, maintain contact with the client. Explain the role of periodic reviews to the client during the initial sale—then keep your promise and conduct them. Use company-approved literature to keep in touch and provide your client with current information of interest, such as pending legislation. Your client will view you as a professional with whom a business relationship should be developed.

8. **Does the professional handle money matters properly?** Never ask the client to make a check payable to anyone other than the specific financial services company. In simpler terms, never ask the client to make out a check to you for financial products. This invites commingling of funds and represents a violation of most state laws. Keep accurate records of what monies you have collected from clients. Provide clients with the proper receipts. And, don't let checks sit in your briefcase day after day because the necessary paperwork is a hassle.

9. **Does the professional refer to other experts or is he or she intimidated by them?** Financial advisors are not accountants, attorneys, or trust officers. Nor is every financial advisor an expert in all financial-related fields. Clients understand this. If necessary, refer your client to a specialist. One of the most effective methods of doing this is to become part of a professional team.

Review Item

Estate Advice

Client Anne Brandon:
"Will this insurance be part of my estate?"

Agent Brendan Malley:
"Insurance proceeds are received income tax free."

Agent Malley has answered an estate tax question with an income tax answer. Do you think this may cause confusion in the client's mind? Do you think this may lead to future problems if the insurance proceeds are included in Anne Brandon's estate and subject to estate taxes?

Log your answer in the space below.

For example, if your client wishes to implement an estate plan, don't try to draft the documents or provide your client with doctored home-office proformas. Discuss with the client the need to call on the expertise of another professional.

10. **Does the professional seem current in his or her information?** Are you maintaining your professional skills? Many clients can sense when professionals seem out-of-touch with current issues. It's all well and good, for example, to obtain a professional designation, but that designation becomes worthless if your knowledge becomes outdated and irrelevant.

Most states now require a financial advisor to complete a specified number of continuing education hours in order to maintain his or her license. Don't look at this as a burden. Look at these continuing education requirements as an opportunity to maintain and enhance your skills. The more you know, the better able you will be to provide your clients with timely and up-to-date financial advice.

Responsibilities of Professionalism

Being a professional carries a price tag that includes

- increased demands for service by clients
- increased need to be aware of ethical issues
- increased risk of legal liability

Increased Client Service

The financial services professional finds, as he or she gains knowledge and experience, that clients demand service. Frequently, this service involves broad-based advice on technical subjects such as retirement planning and business taxation. This means that the financial services professional must constantly seek and absorb technical knowledge.

---

10 Hallmarks of a Professional

- Does the professional listen?
- Does the professional answer my questions?
- Is the professional gathering information sufficient to provide good advice?
- Has the professional educated me about the product?
- Has the professional taken my ability to deal with risk into consideration in making his or her recommendation?
- Does the professional tell me about his or her designations and affiliations, and am I dealing with someone knowledgeable?
- Does the professional provide me with a sense of steady service or am I meeting with an individual seeking a one-time sale?
- Does the professional handle money matters properly?
- Does the professional refer to other experts or is he or she intimidated by them?
- Does the professional seem up-to-date in his or her information?

For example, many financial services professionals engage in estate planning. In order to competently render advice about how life insurance should be owned, financial services professionals must be aware, among other things, of tax codes, trusts, and probate laws. Much of this knowledge is interrelated to the discipline of law. And herein lies a danger for financial services professionals.

In seeking to provide clients with superior information and service, an advisor could *inadvertently engage in the unauthorized practice of law*. Avoid the temptation to bypass the attorney. The unauthorized practice of law opens the financial services professional, in turn, to charges of ethical misconduct. This presents a dilemma for the financial services professional, namely, how to balance the demand of increased technical levels of service from clients without violating ethical codes by delving into other professional disciplines.

Here is a course of action:

- If you must give technical advice to a client, present it as much as you can in general terms.
- If you must give specific advice, cite sources of common knowledge. Stick to situations where the law is black and white, such as the nondeductibility of life insurance premiums on an individual 1040 tax return. If the law is open to interpretation, say so and refer the client to a legal expert for an opinion. *Never draft legal documents.* If you do, you are leaving a paper trail of evidence showing ethical violations.
- Where possible, work as a member of a professional team. This team should draw professionals from a variety of disciplines. For example, a team might consist of a financial services professional, a lawyer, and an accountant.

Increased Need to Be Aware of Ethical Issues

A salesperson merely sells. A professional only sells when it is in the best interest of the client. Being a professional involves a high level of trust. Clients trust you to provide the best advice for their particular situation and to look out for their best interests. These rules of trust go back to the Middle Ages. In a time period, where few could read or write, clients had to rely on the ethical behavior of lawyers to draft legal documents that carried out their wishes. This ethical behavior was expected and it was enforced.

These same rules regarding professional conduct apply today. Financial services professionals must constantly bear in mind the ethical implications of their actions. Financial services professionals, in effect, must objectively judge their actions through the eyes of an unrelated third party. The prime criterion by which an action is judged is whether or not the financial services professional has acted for the welfare and benefit of the client (public) or has acted on behalf of his or her own self-interest.

Increased Risk of Legal Liability

Professional status confers additional responsibility in the eyes of the law. Simply stated, professionals are held to higher standards in the execution of their business duties. They are expected to have expertise and act accordingly.

They are expected to have knowledge of the law and to comply with its dictates. They are expected to place the interests of clients above their own. Under the law of torts, professionals have historically been held by the courts to higher standards of expertise and behavior than nonprofessionals.

This expectation places many financial services professionals in a situation where they face greater legal liability than previously. The recent rash of lawsuits against the insurance industry exemplifies what can happen if financial advisors fail to act in an ethical manner. It also exemplifies what can happen to advisors even if they are innocent.

Review Item
Bothersome Paperwork
Agent Jessica Landers:
"These home office rules are silly. Why should we bother keeping all these reports and illustrations? Who's going to want to look at this information years from now anyway?"
How would you respond to Agent Landers?
Log your answer in the space below.

Lawsuits can damage reputations. They take considerable time and emotional energy. They can result in fewer leads, less selling time, and shattered careers. They can also result in high legal costs, stiff fines, and financial ruin. If you are accused of unethical and/or illegal behavior and cannot adequately support your innocence, a court may find in favor of a dissatisfied client.

The key is to maximize the rewards offered by professional status and to minimize the risks of legal liability.

Practical Steps to Avoid Legal Liability

There are seven practical steps you can follow in order to enhance your reputation as a professional and to avoid legal pitfalls. They are as follows:

1. **Conduct a Compliance Audit of Written Sales Materials—** Have you been in the business 20 years? 10 years? Even if you've been in the business 5 years, you've witnessed many changes in the way financial advisors are expected to conduct their business. Yet, how often have you reviewed the written materials you are presenting to clients? In some cases, the materials are comfortable and do the job—or so you think.

   Changing company rules and client expectations are just two of the reasons for you to take the time to review your sales materials. If your company provides sales materials, make sure you are using the current versions. If you have previously developed materials, send them to your company compliance department for review before further use. Many home offices look for creative ideas and try hard to find ways of reworking materials, if necessary, so they are acceptable from a compliance standpoint.

   If you are selling variable products, pay close attention to your company guidelines regarding the materials that must be provided to the client (for example, prospectus) as well as the type of materials that you are permitted to use. For example, you may have materials in your files that are acceptable for use in the sale of a term insurance policy but that require approval by your broker/dealer for use in the context of a variable life sale.

   Be careful not to discard too much. The NASD (National Association of Securities Dealers) requires that sales materials be maintained for 3 years. Don't be tempted to throw away valuable records just to save space. Remember that problems often arise many years after a sale has taken place. If you know what type of sales materials were presented to a client, you have an indication of the potential problems that could arise. You may also have a more clear recollection of why the client made the purchase. And you're more likely to know how to go about defusing any client dissatisfaction.

2. **Conduct a Compliance Audit of Your Sales Presentations**— How do you approach a prospect? What do you say once you are in front of a prospect? Do you collect data about the client? If so, what type of materials do you use? Do you send a letter after an interview? What type of materials do you bring to a follow-up interview? Do you use illustrations? Do you follow up a sale with a letter? If so, what do you say?

   These are the types of questions you should ask yourself as you review your approach, sales, and post-sale techniques. Develop a standardized system of what you say and do. Write it down. This will provide you with documentation should problems arise at a later date.

   For example, the first item in your sales presentation system may be the use of a telephone track. Gather those telephone tracks. Make sure they are up-to-date and have the necessary company approvals.

3. **Review Licensing Requirements**—This may sound like a given. Most of you are licensed to sell insurance. Take a closer look, however, at your client list. Have a number of your key accounts moved to other states? Are you still servicing their business and selling those individuals more insurance? If so, you should investigate the licensing requirements of that second state. Generally, the address to which premium notices and other communications are sent is the determining factor in deciding which state rules apply.

   Given the high mobility of our society, many of you are forced to maintain licensing in several states. State insurance departments often recognize this and allow for reciprocity. In other words, you don't have to sit for a second or third examination, but you do have to apply for licensing and pay the necessary fees.

   Ethical issues can unintentionally arise in this area. For example, a former resident of your state calls you. Like many early retirees from your area, she's moved to a particular mountain state. She's a long-time client and wants to obtain insurance. She needs the insurance now—not tomorrow. You stretch the residency facts as a favor and write the case. A review of the files would probably have avoided the situation. The necessary licensing in the client's new home state could have been obtained before the call.

A second type of licensing must also be considered. Has your product portfolio broadened? Are you selling variable annuities? Are you selling variable life insurance? Perhaps you've added mutual funds. If so, have you kept your licensing up-to-date? Are you processing the business through another financial advisor who is licensed but never sees the client? Do you justify this action because the review courses are too time-consuming? Do you feel the exam is too hard?

The point here is that if you are selling variable products or mutual funds, you'll need to comply with NASD rules and sit for the appropriate examinations. Selling these types of products without the proper licensing is both unethical and illegal. Also keep in mind that NASD actions are widely publicized. In other words, a tarnished reputation, due to a NASD violation will be apparent to both present and potential clients.

4. **Pursue Continuing Education (CE)**—Sales techniques evolve and change over time—so do the laws that apply to financial products. For example, a few years ago the tax rules regarding withdrawals from annuities were tightened. Currently, there are open questions about various split-dollar plans.

Continuing education is an excellent way to keep your knowledge base current and maintain your professional expertise. If you do not, you may inadvertently give the wrong advice to a client.

Most agents must complete a specified number of hours of CE in order to renew their state insurance license(s). Those selling variable products must also comply with tightened NASD rules in this regard. Don't make this a travesty by rushing through a self-study course or sleeping through a seminar. Think carefully about what you hope to learn, what topics would broaden your abilities and where you need cutting-edge data to maintain your skills. Plot out your own tailored curriculum. This is good career planning. It will enhance your ability to provide clients with the best advice. And, it will add to your reputation as a true professional within your community.

5. **Don't Overlook Documentation**—Many of us hate paperwork. That's one reason we gravitate toward sales and people skills. Unfortunately, it's no excuse when dealing with a client complaint or a lawsuit. Take the time to document your activities. Build on our audit suggestions. Once you have reviewed both the written materials you use and the sales practices you employ, set up a system that makes it easy to pinpoint your actions.

    For example, this documentation should include placing a signed copy of the illustration used to sell a policy in each client's file. It might also include the drafting and retention of a follow-up letter outlining what was sold and for what purpose(s). Documentation can also help your sales effort by making you more cognizant of what you are doing and why.

6. **Maintain Errors and Omissions (E&O) Coverage**—Are client complaints always justified? Is the plaintiff in a lawsuit always the aggrieved party? Simply stated, the answer is an emphatic "No!" Even the most scrupulous financial advisor can run into difficulties. The complexities of today's products, coupled with the rapid changes in our economy, mean that even the soundest recommendation can turn sour. An insurance product or mutual fund can fail to perform as expected. A client, despite education and periodic servicing, may choose to forget what he or she was told.

    Consequently, all agents should maintain E&O coverage. This coverage typically provides excellent legal counsel and helps to defray the costs involved in defending your actions and reputation in a lawsuit. Without E&O coverage, you risk both your property and your career.

    E&O coverage has its limitations. For example, it will not protect you in situations of intentional deceit and fraud. It will, however, enable you to properly present your side of a case. Coupled with our other suggestions, E&O coverage enables you to launch a defense, which demonstrates that you have behaved in both a legal and an ethical manner.

    Many of you already maintain E&O coverage. It is provided to you through your company or may be available through your professional association. Examine the terms of the policy.

They'll provide you with additional guidance in the conduct of your career.

For example, your company-provided policy might cover you only in sales situations involving in-house products. If you're a captive agent and outside sales are not permitted, the terms of the policy serve as a further warning of your obligation to live by the terms of your contract. If you're permitted to sell or broker other products, the terms of your current policy may indicate a need to obtain supplementary coverage. The risks are too great to your family, your property, and your career to conduct any sale without the protection of E&O coverage. Take a few minutes to determine if you are covered, and the extent to which you are covered.

7. **Provide Clients with Good Service**—It's easier to avoid a problem than to solve a problem. This statement is particularly true when it comes to issues of ethics and marketplace practices. Providing your clients with good service at the time of the initial sale is a big step in the right direction. Periodic reviews (a process that continues this good service) are crucial in preventing trouble.

Satisfied clients do not engage in litigation. They don't file complaints with state insurance departments. Furthermore, they don't damage reputations—they enhance them. Financial advisors who perform needs selling, who maintain regular contact, and who keep their clients fully informed about product performance are taking three key steps to prevent ethics-related problems before they arise.

Attributes of Professional Behavior

We can conclude that a professional is an individual with a high level of knowledge and expertise on a technical subject, who needs to adhere to high ethical standards in the application of this knowledge and expertise.

Although this criteria may sound like an onerous burden, it is not, when one considers the gains. The financial services professional has achieved a role as a member of the professions. This creates opportunity for increased service. It also provides increased business rewards. *Once again, good ethics and good business go hand in hand.*

Professional Codes of Ethics

Professionals take the law seriously, but they also take the law as a starting point in guiding their actions. Between the positive law and the unwritten ethical laws are codes of ethics.

The fourth criteria of Dr. Huebner was a spirit of loyalty to other professionals, helpfulness to the common cause, and the forbiddance of unprofessional acts to shame the profession. The most useful guide in their enterprise are codes of ethics.

Halfway between ethics and the positive law are codes of ethics. Codes of ethics have been developed to provide professionals with ethical rules and working guidelines that go beyond the law. These codes offer a series of guidelines for work-related decision making. The codes also serve to standardize public and professional expectations. Finally, codes of ethics aid professionals in reaching the level of trust that the public has come to expect.

Codes Applicable to the Financial Services Professional

Financial services professionals are fortunate in that they have a variety of organizations dedicated to their professional needs. These organizations are aware of the increasing ethical pressures on their members. In response, they have drafted professional pledges and codes of conduct. Among the pledges and codes applicable to the financial services professional are the following:

- LUTCF Pledge
- NAIFA Code of Ethics
- The American College Code of Ethics
- Society of Financial Service Professionals Code of Ethics
- The Million Dollar Round Table Code of Ethics
- The CFP® Code of Ethics

Applicable portions of these codes are reproduced within the appendix at the end of this text.

Common Themes among Professional Codes

There is no need to feel overwhelmed by the number of pledges and ethical codes that apply to them. They should be looked on as reference devices. Relying on a number of sources, rather than relying on just one, is a means of assurance. Most codes rest on ethical common sense and share seven common themes:

- Every code calls on professionals to look out for the best interests of the client.
- Most of the codes in one way or another ask the professionals to conduct themselves with fairness, objectivity, honesty, and integrity.
- Each code requires the professionals to protect the confidential information of the clients.
- Most codes require that the professional present enough information to allow the client to make an informed decision.
- Each of these codes requires the professionals to continue the learning process throughout their careers.
- Each code asks professionals to conduct themselves in such a way as to bring honor to themselves and to their professions.
- Most of the codes specify that the financial services professionals should comply with the law.

These common themes and sentiments should strike you as common sense. You are urged to study these codes and take them seriously. They will serve as strong guideposts to your professional development and achievement.

Knowledge of the codes and their common themes can enable you to better deal with the complexities of today's marketplace. They can provide a barometer of what is expected of you by your profession and by the public. They are not a substitute for the law. They are meant to act as a supplement.

They often go beyond the law in providing guidelines for ethical behavior, guidelines that, in turn, translate into sound business practices.

1. First and foremost in each code is the requirement to look out for the best interest of the client. The Million Dollar Round Table Code states that members shall always place the best interests of their clients above their own direct or indirect interests. Your role is to serve your client even if that means setting aside your interests. For many, this is simply the application of the Golden Rule.
2. The codes also insist on fairness, honesty, objectivity and integrity. The NAIFA code calls for the agent "to present

accurately and honestly all facts essential to the client's decisions." The code of the Society of Financial Service Professionals has canons that deal with "fairness" and "integrity." *Fairness* means giving everyone their due, and *integrity* means being honest and true to oneself. *Objectivity* means that habit of mind that allows one to step back from a situation in order to make a judgment from a disinterested perspective. It involves avoiding conflicts of interest or conflicting interests, in particular, avoiding giving in to the financial advisor's self-interest, and giving the client's interest due weight. These characteristics are the basic virtues of the ethical person.

3. The third provision found in each code lays out the requirement of confidentiality. The NAIFA code puts it succinctly. It is the professional's responsibility "to maintain the client's confidences."

4. The fourth provision, found in several codes, is the requirement to disclose the information necessary for the client to make an informed decision. The MDRT code states that members shall "make full and adequate disclosures of all facts necessary to enable their clients to make informed decisions." The NAIFA code cites the responsibility "to present accurately and honestly all facts essential to clients' decisions."

5. The next provision deals with competence and continuing education. The American College Code in Canon IV calls on the professional "to continue your studies throughout your working life so as to maintain a high level of professional competence." NAIFA's code calls on the financial advisor "to perfect skills and increase knowledge through continuing education," while MDRT insists members shall "maintain the highest standards of competence . . . and improve professional knowledge, skills, and competence."

Clients expect sound and accurate recommendations. Clients can be harmed by incompetent advice. Agents can be harmed when they provide it. These factors demonstrate the need for financial services professionals to keep abreast of changes in their field. The NAIC has long recognized this need and has strongly backed continuing education requirements.

You have a responsibility as a professional to continue your education. Further, if you wish to expand your area, you need to get education in those new areas.

1. An important way to maintain competence is to admit your lack of expertise in an area where you lack such expertise. If you are involved in a case that requires expertise that you lack, call on an expert. The client will respect you and appreciate the expert advice.

2. All the codes require behavior that brings honor to individuals and the profession. NAIFA cites a responsibility "to address professional standards of conduct . . . to help raise the professional standards." The MDRT requires a member to "maintain personal conduct which will reflect favorably . . . on the industry."

3. The codes specify that the professional should comply with the law. The MDRT code puts it this way, "abide by and conform to all provisions of the laws and regulations in the jurisdictions in which they do business." As we have seen, it is an important ethical obligation to abide by all just laws, because the laws are society's rule to help achieve the common good.

Those guidelines constitute the most basic requirements of the industry's codes.

The Code of Ethics and Professional Responsibility adopted by the Certified Financial Planner Board of Standards presents these provisions in a slightly different way. They offer seven principles that cite character traits the CFP should possess—integrity, objectivity, competence, fairness, confidentiality, professionalism, and diligence. What the seven principles require is that the CFP designee offer services with integrity and honesty, not misrepresenting products and treating all stakeholders fairly. The service should be competent and diligent, that is, prompt and thorough. Decisions should be made with objectivity, which requires putting the client's needs to the forefront and in a professional manner, always respecting the client's confidentiality.

Practical Application

What do these codes mean in terms of daily professional practice? The American College pledge says "I shall . . .render that service which. . . I would apply to myself." The Society's code calls for putting the client's interest before one's own, and the CFP code calls for the practitioner to act "in the interest of the client." Though not identical, all mandate something like the Golden Rule, "Do unto others as you would have them do unto you."

To offer a client the same thorough attention to detail that a financial services professional would apply to an investment for himself or herself is no small requirement. Think about the kind of service a planner would give to himself or herself and to close relatives or friends. The planner would make absolutely certain to understand all the apparent and hidden costs. The planner would want to know how much it would cost now and whether the cost over the life of the product would be fixed or variable. The planner would want to clearly understand the potential risks of the investment or insurance policy. So much for the shady selling of derivatives, the needless churning or the replacements we have witnessed lately. If it is an interest-sensitive product, is the financial advisor (or the client) able to regularly monitor the financial stability of the product? What are the costs of withdrawal? Does the financial advisor understand the potential benefits of the product in the short term, as well as in the long term? Does he or she know exactly how to maximize those benefits or what actions to take to reduce the potential harms? The professional would not go into an investment or insurance policy purchase without making use of as much knowledge about the product as he or she was able to responsibly acquire.

The professional may believe that the client has a particularly strong interest in knowing all the professional details, however, some clients simply are not interested in all those details. One of the benefits of being in the financial services business is that the planner has access to information and knowledge that the general public does not have. But the advisor relationship requires that he or she make that knowledge available to help the client make better-informed investment decisions.

Rendering that service to clients that he or she would expect for himself requires the professional's responsibility to present the information in a way that clients can understand and use in their decision making.

Of course, a professional cannot force someone to understand something, and a client may not even want to know all the details. Nonetheless, it is definitely the planner's obligation to provide the client with the needed information and to present this information in a manner that the client can understand. The professional should help the client understand why he or she needs the information about the product and what its financial effect will be in the short and long term. This brings us to the important area of client education.

Client Education

The professional wants the client to make an informed decision. The best way to do that is to educate the client. If clients understand the type of product they are buying and how it operates, they will have insight into the risks involved and can best decide whether to purchase it.

Review Item

Understanding Interest Rate Swings

Client Della Davis:
"It looks like I have to increase the amount of my premiums. Interest rates have gone down so much. I'm glad you explained how this universal policy worked when I bought it. Would it be possible for me to budget these extra dollars?"

Agent Clara Cleary:
"Paying monthly through automatic checking account withdrawals may be an option you would like to consider."

Does it sound like Agent Cleary educated her client about the operation of a universal life policy? Do you think this education has paid off for Agent Cleary? For Client Davis?

Log your answer in the space below.

For example, if a client understands how interest rates affect the cash build-up within a universal policy, he or she is less likely to complain if a premium has to be raised. In fact, a sufficiently educated client may approach the financial services professional about needed premium readjustments.

Education is also one of the best ways to promote sales. Many people simply refuse to buy what they don't understand, and many individuals don't understand financial products. Educate your prospects and watch your client list grow.

For example, if you are selling life insurance, a first step-in client education can be provided by a financial advisor, using the *Life Insurance*

Buyer's Guide. Use it to alert clients about how a particular policy works. Explain any available riders or options to the client.

Explain the function of illustrations to the client. Mention they will serve as an illustration (example) of what will happen if certain factors actually take place.

Explain what is guaranteed and what is not guaranteed on the illustration. This educational process will help to avoid client dissatisfaction if results differ from those illustrated.

Client-Focused Service

Most codes also stipulate that the financial services professional take into account the conditions surrounding the client and, as The American College pledge requires, "shall make every conscientious effort to ascertain and understand" such conditions. This means one cannot simply "sell off" products and be a salesperson. There must be "consultative" or "client-focused" planning or selling. Such an approach requires the financial advisor to gather as much information as possible from the client about needs, goals, interests, and assets in order to put together an investment or insurance package that will best meet the client's needs. (We'll discuss what this involves in chapter 6.)

The sale of products is essentially client driven. The financial advisor must approach the client with a willingness to listen carefully. The client can best provide the information regarding his or her own needs and goals. The client may also think that he or she knows what product best fits those goals, but the advisor should keep the client focused on articulating needs and goals so the planner can then find the best product to match those goals.

Agent of the Client

Consultative financial advising or selling is a sound approach to building good relationships with clients and selling life insurance and other financial products. It is also an ethical requirement because of the nature of the client-professional relationship. In a previous chapter, we looked at the financial services professional as an agent of a company. But the role of the professional is more complicated that that. The professional usually has the dual role of agent for a financial services company and agent for the client. As the agent of the company, he or she is expected to accurately represent the products or services sold by the company and their costs and benefits to the client, and to act on behalf of the company. Not many life insurance companies still have exclusive relationships with financial advisors, so while financial advisors' loyalty is a concern, the financial planner who is a life insurance agent is usually not required to sell only the policies of one or two companies. Most financial services professionals, who deal primarily with the products of one company, feel that their obligation to the company is to consider those products first to meet client needs and then go outside only if an appropriate policy or investment is not available within that company.

This traditional approach serves several purposes. First, the advisor is able to gain in-depth knowledge of the products of one or two companies, which would be nearly impossible if a person tried to cover all the products on the market. This knowledge enables the professional to serve the client better. Second, it saves the financial services professional extensive research time to be able to work from a body of familiar products. Of course, in some instances this could be detrimental to a client who needs more extensive research to find just the right product. It is important for the professional to honestly inform the client of his or her primary relationship with a particular company. The client should understand that these products are the ones the planner will research and present in most cases. It is deceptive and clearly unethical to fail to disclose that primary relationship.

Review Item

Professional Puffery

Agent Albert is licensed to sell traditional life and health products. His company offers variable products, but he has not applied for his NASD Series 6 license. His company also offers mutual funds, but Agent Albert has chosen not to learn about the products featured in the company's sales brochures.

Consider Agent Albert's situation. Do you have any comments? Does this present any ethical, licensing or legal issues?

Log your answer in the space below.

The financial services professional is also an agent for the client. The client trusts the agent with confidential information. In spite of what was said in chapter 4 about agency, it is important to note that courts have increasingly found that the common law understanding of the word *agent* is "agent of the client." Courts have held that when a financial services professional induces reliance on his or her expertise, that person incurs liability for decisions made on the basis of the expertise. When a financial advisor says to a client, "I am your agent," the planner does indeed take on the responsibilities and liabilities of an agent of the client.

Many educators, speakers, and managers stress the importance of selling a financial service or product solely on the basis of client need. Selling on any other basis, such as the needs and interests of the salesperson, the sales manager, or the company, makes no sense in the long term. The salesperson may be persuasive enough to make fast sales in order to meet a bonus deadline, or the company may be promoting a particular product with higher commission rates. But unless the product really meets the needs of the client over the long term, that client will not keep up the payments, which eventually costs the company money. Clients who feel they were sold products that did not meet their needs are not likely to become repeat customers.

Review Item
Professional?   **Agent Hennessy:** "Well . . . I just passed my last exam for my LUTCF designation. No more school work or studying for me!"   *What do you think of the agent's attitude? Does it exemplify the attitude of a true professional?*   Log your answer in the space below.

A client will not refer friends and relatives to a salesperson if the client does not believe in the salesperson's ability to listen carefully and respond. So, while the short-term sales may look good, the long-term financial position of the salesperson, the selling agency, and the selling company are hurt by any sales that do not meet client needs. The same arguments, of course, support continuing attention to the changing needs of clients over time.

In summary, it is both ethically required and financially wise for the financial services professional to thoroughly understand the client's needs and act to fulfill those needs as much as possible. This approach is further corroborated by the Code of Ethics of the Society of Financial Service Professionals.

Professional Competitive Integrity

We have mentioned that each code requires personal conduct that brings honor to the profession. That involves treating other professionals with respect. The link of the financial services professional to the industry as a whole is of particular importance when speaking of competing companies and financial advisors. Too often advisors have separated themselves from the industry. They speak of their products and their company as if these elements were totally separate and apart from the industry. They do not see the link between company bashing and industry bashing.

For example, a financial advisor might refer to Competitors A and C as being financially unsound. The advisor says that his or her company is financially sound. Unfortunately, the seeds of doubt have been placed into the client's mind about the entire industry.

The rule here is to avoid company bashing. Not only is it poor ethics, it may be illegal. Many state insurance regulations prohibit the use, for example, of impaired financial status of a competitor as a tool to make new sales. Be very careful in making comparisons between your product and the product of another company. Use the marketing literature and information supplied by your company. If necessary, get help from the competitive unit at your home office in preparing a comparison.

Here is one final note of caution. Many financial services professionals work for more than one carrier over the course of a career. They become familiar with each company's products and operations. They develop their own opinions as to where each company is superior. Sometimes these opinions can lead to ethical and legal troubles. Be sure to review the agency agreements you have signed with your prior carrier(s) and your current carrier. Be careful not to violate any provisions regarding the transfer of business from a prior carrier.

Don't move clients from one carrier to another unless it is clearly in their best interests. No client likes to think he or she bought the wrong product. If you place doubt in a client's mind about a prior decision, you are likely to place doubt in the client's mind as to the wisdom of your current recommendation.

Summary of Professional Responsibilities

Insurance and financial advisors are increasingly gaining public recognition as professionals. With this recognition comes both status and additional responsibility. Advisors now face higher standards of behavior and service. They face increased liability. They also face far greater opportunities.

Become aware of the laws that apply to your practice. Ignorance of them is no defense. Assume responsibility for your career growth. Do not rely solely on company training to provide you with the newest ideas or the freshest techniques. Participate in recognized continuing education programs.

Follow the guidelines found in the industry's professional codes. They will encourage integrity, disclosure, and honest dealings with your clients.

Review Item

Striving for Professionalism?

Agent Jenny Mayfair:
"I've just completed my licensing. What more should I do to become a financial services professional?"

How would you answer Agent Mayfair's question?

Log your answer in the space below.

Educate your clients about your products. Make sure they understand the type of product(s) they are buying and the reasons behind their purchase(s).

Conduct periodic reviews. They will serve to reeducate your clients on the reasons for their purchases as well as on the process to uncover new needs.

Document your activities. The documentation may protect you in the case of legal action. The documentation will also help to make you more cognizant of what you are doing and why.

Refer to other professionals when needed. Do not attempt to feign knowledge or expertise. Become part of the client's advisory team. Leverage the influence of other professionals to bring the client to closure.

Strive to create and maintain a positive public image in your community not only of yourself, but of the industry. Doing all of these things is both good ethics and good business.

Financial services advisors have achieved public recognition as professionals. People want to deal with ethical individuals. They want to trust those with whom they conduct business. Those who engage in deceitful practices may close sales in the short run, but it is ethical financial advisors who ultimately build practices.

Chapter 5 Review Questions

Answers to Review Questions start on appendix page A-53.

1. Which of the following is one of the seven basic requirements for a discipline to be considered a profession?
   (a) Members of the profession must earn above a standard minimum level of income.
   (b) Members of the profession cannot be self-declared as professionals.
   (c) Members of the profession must hold a postgraduate degree from an accredited university.
   (d) Members of the profession cannot enter the profession prior to a completion of a 7-year apprenticeship and successful completion of written examinations.

2. The text advises that financial services professionals must be aware of knowledge that is interrelated to the discipline of law. Therefore,
   (a) an insured financial advisor is exempt from rules regarding the unauthorized practice of law.
   (b) attorneys are covered by rules forbidding the unauthorized practice of insurance-related advice.
   (c) technical advice to clients should be specific in nature.
   (d) technical advice to clients should be given in general terms.

3. Under the law of torts, professionals
   (a) are exempt from actions regarding bodily harm
   (b) are exempt from standards of expertise due to their certified credentials
   (c) have historically been held to higher standards of expertise and behavior than nonprofessionals
   (d) have historically been held to lower standards of expertise and behavior than nonprofessionals

4. How does the text suggest you handle requests from clients for specific tax advice or legal matters?
   (a) Refer your client to the appropriate specialist.
   (b) First try to draft the requested documents yourself.
   (c) Provide your client with doctored home-office prototype documents.
   (d) Do not let the client call on the expertise of another professional.

5. A code of ethics establishes which of the following for members of a profession?
   (a) rules of law
   (b) statutes of behavior
   (c) standards of conduct
   (d) rules of etiquette

6. All of the following are requirements of a profession EXCEPT
   (a) Any profession has at its core a body of subject matter.
   (b) Entrance into the profession requires mastery of the technical subject matter.
   (c) A profession has as one of its hallmarks no barriers to entry.
   (d) Members of the profession must conduct their affairs in an independent manner.

7. All of the following are among the codes of ethics applicable to the financial services professional EXCEPT
   (a) The NAIC Code of Ethics
   (b) The American College Code of Ethics
   (c) the Society of Financial Service Professionals Code of Ethics
   (d) the CFP® Code of Ethics

8. All of the following are practical steps that financial services professionals can use to avoid legal liability EXCEPT
   (a) Conduct a compliance audit of written sales materials.
   (b) Conduct a compliance audit of your sales presentations.
   (c) Overlook unnecessary documentation.
   (d) Review licensing requirements.

9. As stated in the text, being a professional carries with it all of the following added responsibilities EXCEPT
    (a) increased demands for service by clients
    (b) increased risk of legal liability
    (c) increased paperwork
    (d) increased need to be aware of ethical issues

10. Clients ask themselves each of the following questions when judging whether or not they are dealing with a professional EXCEPT
    (a) Does the professional listen?
    (b) Does the professional ask me questions?
    (c) Has the professional educated me about the product?
    (d) Does the professional handle money matters properly?

6

Fair Dealing and Suitability in Financial Products Marketing

Learning Objectives
6-1. Explain the role of the NAIC in the field of ethics.
6-2. Describe the NASD Conduct Rules
6-3. Identify a six-step procedure financial services professionals can use to implement the NASD Rules of Fair Dealing into their practices.
6-4. Identify the factors that a prospective investor should consider before investing.
6-5. List and explain the four types of risks.
6-6. Explain the concept of risk tolerance and risk tolerance assessment techniques.
6-7. Describe the categories of investments.
6-8. Identify the characteristics of investment diversification within the context of risk management.

Chapter Outline

Why Ethical Marketing Practices Are Important
Ethical Behavior 6-3
Fair Dealing 6-5
  Understand the Client's Current Financial Condition 6-5
  Understand the Client's Investment Objectives 6-6
Applying Professional Expertise to Facts to Develop Strategies 6-7
  Determining Suitability 6-7
Investment Risk 6-11
  Overview of Investment Considerations 6-11
  Seven Investment Decision Factors 6-11
  Types of Investment Risk 6-14
Risk Tolerance 6-16
  Defining Risk Tolerance 6-16
  Risk Spectrum 6-17
  Categories of Investments 6-17
  Risk Tolerance Assessment Techniques 6-19
Risk Management 6-22
Judging the Client's Situation 6-23
  Continuing Service 6-23
  Practical Aids for Determining Suitability and Finding Facts 6-23
  Fact-Finder Format and Compliance Considerations 6-25
  Supplementary Information 6-26
Regulation of Financial Planning Professionals 6-27
  NASD Conduct Rules 6-27
Chapter 6 Review Questions 6-32

Why Ethical Marketing Practices Are Important

Ethical Behavior

How should a financial services professional behave? Which practices should be followed and which avoided? Is rebating OK? When is replacement of an insurance policy acceptable? What are the limits on how one should advertise? The purpose of this chapter is to examine various practices of financial services professionals to determine which are acceptable and which are not.

Ethical behavior is important, because clients' viewpoints of the financial services industry are shaped by their experiences with an individual financial planner or insurance agent. Positive experiences lead to a respect for the professional and the industry. Negative experiences do great harm to the planner's and the industry's reputation.

Dissatisfied clients speak to friends, neighbors, and acquaintances about their poor experiences thus spreading the negative image of the industry. Dissatisfied clients can also bring the situation to the attention of the Securities and Exchange Commission or state insurance commissioners. A poor public image of a profession creates difficulties for its participants.

Dissatisfied clients don't welcome financial services professionals warmly. Recommendations of products are met with an air of skepticism. Regulatory authorities respond by tightening current rules or imposing new ones. The financial services industry then loses flexibility in doing business. An individual responsible for client dissatisfaction is likely to lose the dissatisfied client's business. There may be a charge back against commission income. Referrals are lost, the professional's reputation is tarnished, and future career opportunities may be closed. Poor marketing ethics hurt the agent, the company, and the industry.

Recent malpractice suits make it clear that there are two areas in which agents are held accountable—suitability (providing suitable products) and disclosure (failure to give sufficient disclosure). The professional pledge taken by CLUs to "look out for the best interest of the client" obliges the agent to find a suitable policy to fill the needs of the client. This requires that the agent has the competence to ascertain which policies or products best suit the client's needs as well as the willpower or moral fiber to overcome the lure of recommending a less suitable policy that pays a higher commission. Meeting the suitability requirement also necessitates that agents "learn enough to maintain their level of competence."

We will discuss the practices that a financial services professional needs to observe in the processes of dealing fairly with clients. We will use NAIC model laws and NASD conduct rules as our guide in determining what is required.

In the chapter on the legal framework we saw there are two sources that articulate proper conduct for financial services professionals—the NAIC model laws and the NASD conduct rules. The NAIC sets out the objective of fair, just, and equitable treatment of policyowners and claimants. As part of its work, the NAIC drafts model laws in the fields of life and health insurance. Today, there are approximately 200 model laws and regulations. Five of these model laws are of particular interest in determining which practices financial services professionals should follow. These models are the

- rules governing the advertising of life insurance
- life insurance and annuities replacement model regulation
- life insurance illustrations model regulation
- life insurance disclosure model regulation
- unfair trade practices act

These five models, broadly adopted by the states, establish marketing and disclosure standards for insurance agents. They prohibit defamation and false advertising. The models give insurance commissioners substantial powers to investigate both carriers and agents suspected of violations. Punishments for violations include fines as well as license suspension and revocation. These regulations provide guidelines for the appropriate practice of financial services professionals. They can be supplemented by the set of guidelines for ethical practice found in the National Association of Securities Dealers Rules of Conduct. (Cf. NASD Manual Section on Conduct Rules. (2000-3410))

Fair Dealing

The essence of ethical conduct for the NASD is fair dealing.

Fair dealing requires several things:

1. There must be an effort to clearly understand the client's current financial condition.
2. There must be an effort to understand the client's investment objectives. In some cases, this involves educating a client and helping the client clarify his or her needs.
3. There must be an application of the professional's expertise to develop strategies to meet those needs and goals. Sometimes there will be one clear strategy. In many situations, however, more than one strategy is possible. It then becomes the job of the representative to explain to and, if necessary, educate the client on the pros and cons of the various proposed alternatives.
4. There must be a consideration of the suitability of the various strategies to meet the client's needs. Determining suitable products to accommodate needs is extremely important.
5. Professionals should only recommend or sell products the client needs. For example, a high-risk strategy of funding college tuition for a newborn might be suitable for a young marketing director but might involve too much risk for a middle-aged engineer who is starting a second family.
6. Finally, there must be periodic reviews, because client's needs do not remain static.

The first four of these professional obligations have to do with suitability requirements, which we will examine more thoroughly. The fifth has to do with ethical sales of products, which we will look at presently. To begin then, it is clear that if a professional is to look out for the client's best interests he should determine which products are suitable for a client, starting with ascertaining the client's current financial condition.

Understand the Client's Current Financial Condition

To ascertain the client's current financial condition, it is necessary to introduce a fact-finding process. This involves asking questions such as:

How much household income is being earned? If the client is married, do both spouses work? How much income does each spouse earn? Are there substantial liabilities such as a home mortgage? Are there smaller credit card debts leading to recurring monthly bills? Are there other sources of income? For example, does the client own rental property? Has the client received an inheritance that has been invested?

Fact-finding involves more than just multiplying an annual salary by a predetermined number of years. It is more than looking at a "guesstimated" set of expenses, extrapolating them against future income, and rounding out a shortfall on a yellow pad. Fact-finding should be thorough. It must take into consideration both financial and nonfinancial information. It should also take into consideration other financial needs aside from life insurance. For example, a thorough fact-find might uncover deficiencies in a client's disability income protection. Fact-finding is also critical when dealing with businessowners.

Other key financial factors that will be uncovered through fact-finding include ownership of life insurance and investment experience. Has the client ever purchased life insurance before? If so, when and what type? Does the client understand and appreciate the various insurance products being offered in the marketplace? Has the client previously made investment in individual stocks or mutual funds? If so, what type of stocks or funds? Were they conservative or aggressive in nature? Did the client select these securities on his or her own initiative, or was the investment based on professional advice? Does the client own shares in a real estate investment trust (REIT) or own real estate as an investment property?

It takes hard work to assemble all pertinent facts about the client. In addition, these factors must be considered for each member of the client's family unit. For example, the client may have substantial assets but have an adult child who suffers from a disability, making future work impossible. Such a situation affects the client's overall financial needs and estate plan.

Understand the Client's Investment Objectives

After determining the client's financial condition, the professional needs to find out what goals the client wishes to accomplish. The fact-finding process should uncover the client's financial goals and investment objectives. Some common financial goals might include a desire to pay off a 30-year mortgage before retirement, save for college tuition, or have the means to opt for early retirement. Lately, some advisors have even begun to investigate the quality of life goals. What else, besides security, is the client interested in? For example, is the client interested in giving to charitable causes?

The fact-finding process should provide you with other pieces of financial information that are important to the development of any financial plan. Key factors would include the client's time horizon. For example, how many years will elapse before the client's child enters college? By early retirement, does the client mean age 50 or age 60? Does the client wish to pay off the mortgage in 5 years, 15 years, or have payoff coincide with a retirement date?

Applying Professional Expertise to Facts to Develop Strategies

A further aspect of fair dealing involves the application of the agent's professional knowledge and expertise to the data to develop strategies that will meet the clients needs. For some prospects, an analysis will indicate that insurance is part of the solution. In other cases, investment vehicles such as annuities or mutual funds will form part of the solution.

Whether your recommendation involves insurance or an investment vehicle, it is important to remember that the product should be appropriate for the particular client. One size does not fit all. The central question is: Does the recommended product meet the client's needs, financial abilities, and personal risk profile?

Determining Suitability

The steps mentioned above are essential in trying to meet the demands of suitability. We need to examine the client's needs and objectives and recommend products and strategies that suit those needs. Determining suitability is difficult. It is the end result of doing the research and fact-finding to determine the client's financial condition, identifying the client's objectives, and developing strategies to meet those objectives. It is determining whether those strategies really fit the objectives and needs. For a more detailed account of suitability, see the box containing NASD Rule 2310. NASD conduct rules require you to make reasonable efforts to obtain information about the customer's financial status, tax status, investment objectives, and other information to be used in making recommendations.

NASD Manual Conduct Rules

2310. Recommendations to Customers (Suitability)

(a) In recommending to a customer the purchase, sale or exchange of any security, a member shall have reasonable grounds for believing that the recommendation is suitable for such customer upon the basis of the facts, if any, disclosed by such customer as to his other security holdings and as to his financial situation and needs.

(b) Prior to the execution of a transaction recommended to a noninstitutional customer, other than transactions with customers where investments are limited to money market mutual funds, a member shall make reasonable efforts to obtain information concerning:

(c) (1) the customer's financial status;
   (2) the customer's tax status;
   (3) the customer's investment objectives; and
   (4) such other information used or considered to be reasonable by such member or registered representative in making recommendations to the customer.

(d) For purposes of this Rule, the term "non-institutional customer" shall mean a customer that does not qualify as an institutional account" under Rule 3110(c)(4).

[Amended May 2, 1990 eff. for accounts opened and recommendations made after Jan. 1, 1991; amended by SR-NASD-95-39 eff. Aug. 20, 1996.]

IM-2310-2. Fair Dealing with Customers

(a)

(1) Implicit in all member and registered representative relationships with customers and others is the fundamental responsibility for fair dealing. Sales efforts must therefore be undertaken only on a basis that can be judged as being within the ethical standards of the Association's Rules, with particular emphasis on the requirement to deal fairly with the public.

(2) This does not mean that legitimate sales efforts in the securities business are to be discouraged by requirements, which do not take into account the variety of circumstances, which can enter into the member-customer relationship. It does mean, however, that sales efforts must be judged on the basis of whether they can be reasonably said to represent fair treatment for the persons to whom the sales efforts are directed, rather than on the argument that they result in profits to customers.

(b) District Business Conduct Committees and the Board of Governors have interpreted the Rules, taken disciplinary action, and imposed penalties in many situations where members' sales efforts have exceeded the reasonable grounds of fair dealing. Some practices that have resulted in disciplinary action and that clearly violate this responsibility for fair dealing are set forth below, as a guide to members:

1. **Recommending Speculative Low-Priced Securities**
   Recommending speculative low-priced securities to customers without knowledge of or attempt to obtain information concerning the customers' other securities holdings, their financial situation and other necessary data. The principle here is that this practice, by its very nature, involves a high probability that the recommendation will not be suitable for at least some of the persons solicited. This has particular application to high-pressure telephone sales campaigns.

2. **Excessive Trading Activity**
   Excessive activity in a customer's account, often referred to as "churning" or "overtrading." There are no specific standards to measure excessiveness of activity in customer accounts because this must be related to the objectives and financial situation of the customer involved.

3. **Trading in Mutual Fund Shares**
   Trading in mutual fund shares, particularly on a short-term basis. It is clear that normally these securities are not proper trading vehicles and such activity on its face may raise the question of Rule violation.

4. **Fraudulent Activity**
   (A) Numerous instances of fraudulent conduct have been acted upon by the Association and have resulted in penalties against members. Among some of these activities are:

   (i)   Fictitious Accounts
   Establishment of fictitious accounts in order to execute transactions which otherwise would be prohibited, such as the purchase of hot issues, or to disguise transactions that are against firm policy.

   (ii)   Discretionary Accounts
   Transactions in discretionary accounts in excess of or without actual authority from customers.

   (iii) Unauthorized Transactions
   Causing the execution of transactions unauthorized by customers, or the sending of confirmations in order to cause customers to accept transactions not actually agreed upon.

   (iv)   Misuse of Customers' Funds or Securities
   Unauthorized use or borrowing of customers' funds or securities.

   (B) In addition, other fraudulent activities, such as forgery, non-disclosure or misstatement of material facts, manipulations and various deceptions, have been found in violation of Association Rules. These same activities are also subject to the civil and criminal laws and sanctions of federal and state governments.

5. **Recommending Purchases Beyond Customer Capability**
   Recommending the purchase of securities or the continuing purchase of securities in amounts inconsistent with the reasonable expectation that the customer has the financial ability to meet such a commitment.

One of the most important aspects of suitability is determining the client's risk tolerance. Is the client aware of his or her risk profile? Is the client aggressive, moderate, or risk-averse (conservative)? Ethical issues can arise if a client is sold a type of product that carries a greater degree of risk than is indicated by the client's risk profile. This means that one of the important obligations of an advisor is to educate the client about risk, risk tolerance, and how to conduct risk management. Let's look at those three factors:

- investment risk
- risk tolerance
- risk management

A financial services professional can typically offer clients greater product selection than was available 20 years ago—or even 5 years ago. A myriad of available products offer everything from term insurance to highly speculative securities.

The broad choice of product offerings permits clients to tailor their programs more than ever before. This variety, however, comes at the price of fewer guarantees. In most cases, a greater proportion of the investment risk inherent in the product is now borne by clients.

More and more the question will be: Was the consumer sold an appropriate or suitable product? Failure to answer this question in the affirmative can be an invitation to a lawsuit. None of us wants to be involved in a lawsuit, and we all want to do the right thing when it comes to providing our clients with service. With increased product choice, we'll have to consider not only how the product meets a client's needs but also how that product matches the client's ability to handle risk.

This raises two questions:

- Does the client understand investment risk?
- How does one determine the client's risk tolerance?

> **Good Ethics**
>
> Good ethics and good marketplace practices indicate that agents assume most clients are risk-averse.

Investment Risk

Overview of Investment Considerations

Individuals have many choices with regard to the investment of their money. In helping your clients achieve their financial goals, it is likely that you will spend some time discussing alternative savings and investment vehicles. As you do, there are seven factors of which you should make your clients aware.

Seven Investment Decision Factors

The seven factors that clients should consider are:

1. **Risk-Reward Trade-Off**—Financial savings and invest-ment vehicles need to be considered in light of both risk and reward. Some investments carry more risk than others. Generally, an investment that offers the potential of greater return carries greater risk. Due to the proliferation of today's sophisticated products, this is a factor that must be considered by clients.

    For example, it is true that cash values may increase at a faster rate within a variable product if the stock market soars—ultimately equating to fewer premium payments and/or greater coverage. However, it is also true that poor stock market results may cause more premiums to be paid at higher rates in comparison to a traditional life insurance product.

2. **Timing of Return**—The dates of some investment returns are easier to pinpoint than others. For example, it's relatively easy to pinpoint when interest will be paid in a certificate of deposit. In general, the easier it is to pinpoint the date of return, the lower the investment risk. And in general, the lower the investment risk, the lower the potential reward.

    For example, a real estate investment might offer the potential of substantial appreciation, but the exact amount and timing of this appreciation is not easily determined. Applying this to an insurance product, we can see that a traditional product offers far more predictability with regard to what is due (premiums) and what will be paid (face value).

---

3. **Tax Consequences**—Some investments offer tax benefits; others do not. For example, interest earned on a certificate of deposit is taxed at regular income tax rates. Appreciation realized on a long-term real estate investment would, in contrast, be eligible for more favorable capital gains rates.

   Similarly, most clients need to be made aware of preferred tax treatment of life insurance. While not the main benefit of the product, tax deferral offers the opportunity for capital accumulation at a more accelerated rate than would otherwise be possible.

4. **Liquidity**—Some investments can be more like cash than others. If one needs quick access to money, liquidity becomes an important factor. For example, a money market account is a highly liquid investment. In many cases, an individual can write a check against these savings without notifying anyone or waiting for any sale of underlying investments.

5. **Marketability**—Some assets can be sold and converted into cash more easily than others. Like liquidity, this becomes an important factor for any client who believes he or she will need to tap their investments quickly to satisfy potential liabilities. For example, stock can be sold relatively quickly through the operation of the exchanges that match buyers and sellers. Dollars can be received within a matter of days. A real estate investment, on the other hand, might take months or years to convert to cash.

   Marketability is an important factor in developing client financial plans. If clients hold assets that are relatively illiquid and/or for which there is a limited market (for example, a small business), life insurance can provide needed dollars to enable the family to avoid a low-priced fire sale.

6. **Required Management and Supervision**—Some investments require relatively little management or supervision and clients remain fairly passive, merely waiting for their returns. A certificate of deposit or mutual fund are two such examples. Other investments require far more hands-on management and supervision.

   For example, rental real estate might require the investors to obtain tenants, make repairs, and personally collect rents. Some clients have the time and expertise needed to make such an enterprise successful; others do not. Even those clients who have the time and expertise may not wish to devote them to a particular project.

It is important to remember that not all investments require your client to devote the same amount of time or to have the same level of expertise. In general, more risky investments offering potentially greater returns require more management and supervision. With regard to insurance, think of these factors in terms of a potential product mix.

For example, older clients who several years ago purchased a variable universal life policy may become concerned if premium dollars are fully allocated into aggressive subaccounts. These clients may choose to reduce their risk exposure by electing a more conservative subaccount mix—an example of management and policy supervision.

7. **Diversification**—In reviewing any financial plan, it is important to consider the role of diversification. Simply stated, clients should not have all of their money in the same place. Clients should spread their risk by spreading money over various investments. With regard to an insurance plan, consider the situation of a highly leveraged client with one or two investment assets. This may sound far-fetched, but how many of your clients carry heavy mortgages on their major asset(s)? Insurance can help to even out this situation by reducing risk in the event of premature death. In other words, a forced sale can be averted because the funds will be there. (We will discuss diversification more thoroughly later in this chapter.)

Consider referencing these seven factors any time you design a plan. They are one way of introducing the concept of investment risk and the need for planning. Some clients— usually those who would consider themselves the most conservative—have difficulty realizing that all financial plans carry an element of risk. Recognizing risk is the first step in determining how to manage it. Alerting your clients to these factors is both an example of good ethics and good business practices.

Types of Investment Risk

What is investment risk? Many people equate investment risk with loss of principal. The seven investment consideration factors can be used to show your client that investment risk involves more than just the loss of principal. There are four major categories of investment risk that your clients should consider: market risk, interest rate risk, inflation risk (purchasing power risk), and default risk.

Market Risk—This involves the loss of money due to a general downward business cycle. For example, clients who invested in publicly traded stock in 1987 suffered losses as the market crashed. It was not just the stock of one company that suffered but stocks across the entire board. Those who invested in the early and late 1990s faced similar losses. These were counter-balanced, however, by subsequent stock market gains, only to experience sharp market declines beginning in April of 2000 and continuing for the next few years. It is important to educate clients on market risk because so many of today's insurance products are based on separate accounts that reflect market gains and losses and so many of our clients invest in mutual funds.

Clients who understand the concept of market risk are able to anticipate the fact that a bull market can become a bear market. They have a better appreciation of the role played by traditional products that offer guaranteed returns, and of your role as a financial services professional.

Interest Rate Risk—This reflects the fact that an investment with a fixed interest rate is worth less if interest rates rise above the guaranteed amount. For example, an individual who purchases a 10-year bond issued by the federal government at 6 percent will suffer a loss if he or she must sell that bond before the maturity date when current interest rates are at 8 percent. The reverse is also true. An investment with a guaranteed rate rises in value as current interest rates fall.

Many of your clients may not have bond holdings, but they may be familiar with the concept of interest rate risk through their adjustable rate mortgages. If rates fall, their mortgage payments fall. On the other hand,

---

Investment Brew

A recipe for an "Investment Brew" includes:

- Risk-Reward Trade-Off
- Timing of Return
- Tax Consequences
- Liquidity
- Marketability
- Required Management and Supervision
- Diversification

---

if rates rise, their mortgage payments ratchet up. Uncovering this type of information as part of your fact-finding will enable you to better advise your clients.

Inflation Risk—The next major category of risk to which your clients should be alerted is inflation risk. Sometimes this is termed purchasing-power risk. It is the risk that a dollar held today will buy fewer goods tomorrow. Many of your clients have had personal experience with purchasing power risk as they tried to save for tuition, homes, and cars. Month by month they watched prices jump. Inflation impacts not just savings accounts. It impacts other types of investments and also our clients' insurance programs. For example, high inflation tends to have a negative impact on financial assets such as bank accounts. Tangible assets such as real estate and collectibles tend to rise in value during periods of high inflation.

Inflation can substantially change a client's insurance needs. For example, wage boosts due solely to inflation can cause a client's disability income coverage to become outdated. The amount of life insurance may need to be increased simply to cover the increased dollar figure of liabilities owed or to preserve the survivor's standard of living. Inflation is one reason a periodic review of insurance needs is so important. Even a low rate of inflation can impact a client's needs. For example, even at a 3 percent inflation level, a client's insurance coverage will be worth one-third less in purchasing power in just a decade.

Default Risk—This involves the loss of principal. It can occur when the organization in which an investment is made goes bankrupt or is otherwise unable to pay off its obligations because of financial strains.

Due to the insolvency crisis of the early 1990s and 2000s, our clients became concerned about the default risk involved in taking out an insurance policy. They wonder if the funds be there when promised. One way to deal with these concerns is to provide your clients with the reports of two or three insurance company credit reporting companies such as A.M. Best, S&P, Moody's, or Duff & Phelps.

Others—There are other types of investment risk that you may wish to discuss with your clients, depending on their individual situations. These include legislative risk, call risk, and additional commitment risk.

Legislative risk involves the possibility that the law that provides a favorable environment for an investment may change. For example, the

> **Investment Risk**
>
> The types of investment risk are:
>
> - market risk
>
> - interest rate risk
>
> - inflation (purchasing power) risk
>
> - default risk

1986 Tax Reform Act cut down the appeal of many highly leveraged oil and gas tax shelters.

Call risk involves the possibility that a client may invest in a high-yield debt instrument only to have the debtor repay the debt prior to its due date. In other words, the investor gets less interest than initially anticipated. This sometimes happens with corporate bonds in a falling interest rate environment. The debt is usually refinanced at a lower rate and the original investors paid off.

Additional commitment risk involves the need to put more funds into an investment. In today's environment, you will be involved in a great deal of fact-finding that will touch upon broad investment discussions. You will have a familiarity with the type of assets held by your clients and the type of risks typically associated with those assets. On the other side of the ledger, you will have familiarity with the liabilities owed by your clients and the risks they assume along with those debts. You will be asked to help fit the client's insurance program into this context.

Remind clients that

- through their day-to-day living patterns, most individuals have assumed an element of risk.
- there is generally a trade-off between risk and reward. The more risk assumed, the greater the expected return. Stated another way, lower returns are associated with lower risk.

Risk Tolerance

Your experience has already taught you that some of your clients can accept risk more easily than others.

Defining Risk Tolerance

The degree to which one is willing to accept risk can be defined as one's risk tolerance. You see this every day in property and casualty policies as some clients opt for very low deductibles while others choose very high deductibles. Those who opt for the higher deductibles take the risk of eventual greater out-of-pocket costs at the time of a loss in return for lower current premiums.

Risk Spectrum

One can make an analogy to a scale when measuring risk. For simplicity's sake, let's assume this risk measurement scale ranges from zero to 100. Some of your clients will stand at zero, others at 100, but most will fall somewhere in between. Those who stand at zero are extremely risk-averse. The closer one moves to 100, the greater degree of risk tolerance. Those who stand at 100 could be viewed not only as completely tolerant of risk but as risk seekers. Those who stand somewhere in between can be considered risk tolerant in various degrees.

Clients need to understand where they stand on the scale. As an advisor, you need to understand both the scale and the fact that different clients have different degrees of risk tolerance. Some recommendations are appropriate for those who are willing to accept risk but inappropriate for those who are risk-averse. Prudent marketplace practice dictates that advisors should assume that most clients are risk-averse. This assumption automatically adds a level of caution to any recommendation.

Assessing risk tolerance often begins with client education. Before clients can fully appreciate the risk involved in any recommendation, they must have some basic knowledge of the different types of investments and the risks associated with them.

Categories of Investments

There are four basic categories of investments that clients should understand so you are able to gauge their risk tolerance. These four investment categories are grouped from lower to higher risk levels as follows:

1. **Cash Equivalents**—These are investments that are highly liquid and have either a nonspecified maturity date or a maturity date of less than one year into the future. Short-term certificates of deposit and money market funds are examples. Cash equivalents are considered to be very low-risk investments. Typically, they offer relatively low rates of return.

2. **Longer-Term Debt Instruments**—Large corporations, local jurisdictions, and the federal government all issue debt instruments to cover expenses. These debt instruments are typically issued in the form of bonds whose repayment safety is judged by rating agencies such as S&P and Moody's. Their maturity dates are greater than one year. For example, investors typically hold federal government bonds with durations of 5 and 10 years.

Longer-term debt instruments contain a greater degree of risk than cash equivalents. Default and interest rate risk are the types of risks typically associated with these investments. As a general rule, the longer the term of the debt, the greater the degree of risk. These instruments, for example, are susceptible to a drop in value when inflation rises. Typically, longer-term debt instruments offer higher rates of return when compared to cash equivalents. In effect, there is added payment for the greater degree of risk assumed.

3. **Equity Investments**—Common stock, preferred stock, and mutual funds are equity-type investments. They represent ownership in a business. If the business prospers, the value of the stock rises. If the business fails, the stock becomes worthless. As a general rule, in most business cycles, the equity-type investments offer greater opportunity for higher returns than do cash equivalents or debt instruments. Not only do stocks appreciate, but also company profits may be distributed in the form of dividends.

   Clients need to understand that equity-type investments carry substantial risk. Profits don't always increase. The business cycle does not always expand. In a poor business climate, dividends may be stopped as the stock falls in value.

4. **Direct Investments**—Clients sometimes invest their money directly in various business ventures. Typical examples of direct investment are rental real estate or a small business. Direct investments offer various degrees of risk and potential return, depending upon individual circumstances. They typically require far more direct management than do other types of investments. They also offer the potential for substantial returns but typically carry substantial risk.

   For example, clients may be small-business owners. The decision they face is whether or not to reinvest earnings from the business back into the business. If the business flourishes, the returns can far exceed those offered by other opportunities. If the business fails, however, not only will the source of annual income be lost, but excess earnings will be depleted as well. Many owners prefer to lower their risks by placing a portion of their savings in assets unrelated to their business ventures and legally shielded from business liabilities.

Risk Tolerance Assessment Techniques

Given the importance of a client's tolerance toward risk, how does one make an assessment? While there is no one absolute way, we offer three suggested methods to gauge a client's risk tolerance:

- an investment philosophy test
- an examination of investment history
- a review of investment objectives

Investment Philosophy Test—The investment philosophy test aims at uncovering a client's risk tolerance through a series of questions. The test usually takes the form of a questionnaire, with a scoring device that quantifies a client's preference for a conservative, moderate, or aggressive investment strategy.

Examination of Investment History—The past is often considered the prologue to the future. One way to gauge a client's risk tolerance is to examine the type of investments the client made in the past. For example, clients who placed their savings solely in certificates of deposit would, in all likelihood, have a very low level of risk tolerance.

Review of Investment Objectives—Another way of gauging risk tolerance is to ask clients about their financial objectives with follow-up questions designed to uncover the client's feelings about various topics related to risk. These follow-up questions would typically concern safety of principal, tax reduction, and asset appreciation strategies. Other follow-up questions would probe the client's feelings regarding the need for liquidity, generation of current income, and inflation. The client's answers to both the financial objective(s) and follow-up questions provide the agent with a source of information from which the client's risk-tolerance level can be inferred.

See pages 6-20–6-21 for the Investment Philosophy Test questionnaire
and instructions on how to score the test.
Information on the meaning of the scores is on page 6-22.

Investment Philosophy Test

Every investment, without exception, involves some risk. Even if you keep your money in an FDIC-insured account, you risk the loss of future buying power because of the erosion caused by inflation and taxes.

But there are many degrees of risk. As a rule, the higher the return you seek, the higher the risk you must take. Many individuals establish their investment programs using one of the three strategies, either alone or in combination:

*   A *conservative* strategy attempts to minimize the risk to investment capital, even though this may mean accepting potentially lower returns.
*   A *moderate* strategy accepts some risk to get potentially higher returns.
*   An *aggressive* strategy stresses greater growth and potentially higher returns, but at a higher degree of risk than either of the other strategies.

This self-test can help clarify savings and investment goals and determine your investment strategy.

Part I: Your Financial Considerations
Check the answer that describes your client's situation.

1. How many years from now do you expect to begin using the money in your savings and investment plan?

   A. _____ More than 20   C. _____ 6–9
   B. _____ 10–19   D. _____ Less than 5

2. Taking all your savings and investments into account—stocks, CDs, savings accounts, IRAs, other annuities, and so on—what percentage of your total retirement nest egg will your investment with this program represent?

   A. _____ Less than 25 percent   C. _____ 51–75 percent
   B. _____ 25–50 percent   D. _____ More than 75 percent

3. How much annual income do you estimate you will need in retirement as measured by the current buying power of the dollar?

   A. _____ Over $60,000   C. _____ $35,000–$40,000
   B. _____ $40,000–$60,000   D. _____ Less than $25,000

4. How many other people other than yourself do you expect will depend on you financially after you retire?

   A. _____ 0–1   C. _____ 4–5
   B. _____ 2–3   D. _____ 6 or more

Part II: Your Investment Philosophy

Check the statement that most closely expresses your viewpoint. There are no "right" or "wrong" answers. Your score will help you make the right investment choices based on your personal needs.

5. I believe that you have to take risks to make money.

   A. _____ Agree strongly   C. _____ Disagree mostly
   B. _____ Agree mostly   D. _____ Disagree strongly

6. I don't mind accepting short-term losses to achieve long-term growth.

   A. _____ Agree strongly   C. _____ Disagree mostly
   B. _____ Agree mostly   D. _____ Disagree strongly

7. It doesn't bother me if the total value of my holdings fluctuates from month to month.

   A. _____ Agree strongly   C. _____ Disagree mostly
   B. _____ Agree mostly   D. _____ Disagree strongly

8. I would be willing to risk losing a substantial amount of money if I had a reasonably good chance for large gains.

   A. _____ Agree strongly   C. _____ Disagree mostly
   B. _____ Agree mostly   D. _____ Disagree strongly

9. I have full confidence in the ability of professionals to choose investments that will make my money grow.

   A. _____ Agree strongly   C. _____ Disagree mostly
   B. _____ Agree mostly   D. _____ Disagree strongly

10. I am positive about the economy and the potential for growth between now and when I retire.

    A. _____ Agree strongly   C. _____ Disagree mostly
    B. _____ Agree mostly   D. _____ Disagree strongly

How to Score

Give yourself :

   4 points for each A answer
   3 points for each B answer
   2 points for each C answer
   1 point for each D answer

Risk Management

Risk management seeks to balance the risks of an individual's various investment decisions one against the other. One of the best ways of managing risk is through financial diversification. Risk management through diversification offers an opportunity for the clients with low risk tolerances to balance loss of principal concerns against needs for capital appreciation. Risk management through diversification also offers clients with higher risk tolerance the opportunity to balance growth investments with sources of steady return.

For example, a client might balance a decision to place money in a CD against a decision to purchase an aggressive mutual fund offered by your company. While the fund may soar up and down, the CD provides a steady return. While the savings in the CD risk loss of purchasing power, the amount put into the aggressive fund offers the opportunity to achieve returns substantially above the inflation level.

There are a variety of ways to manage risk through diversification. A client can diversify investment decisions by holding a variety of assets such as stocks, bonds, and real estate. A client can diversify within an asset category. For example, a client can buy several mutual funds with different objectives. A client can also diversify the timing of financial decisions. For example, CDs can be scheduled to mature over a period of years, allowing an adjustment mechanism for varying rates of interest.

The role of risk management through diversification is an important issue for an agent to take into consideration in developing a client's financial plans.

Judging the Client's Situation

No single approach can be effectively used with all clients. Nor will a single solution apply to all clients. Client risk profiles vary, client needs vary, and client objectives vary.

Continuing Service

A recommendation made today may not be valid tomorrow. The financial and personal needs and goals of individuals change over time. For example, a young couple may need mortgage protection at age 30, college accumulation at age 40, and estate planning at age 55. In some instances, your recommendations and the product selection may take these evolving needs into consideration. In other instances, this is not possible. For example, the death of a spouse followed by remarriage can substantially alter a client's needs and goals.

This is why it is important to establish the practice of periodically reviewing a client's needs. In addition, this periodic review helps to cement the relationship between the insurance professional and his or her client. The financial services professional becomes part of an ongoing monitoring of the client's needs and the solutions to those needs. Record keeping becomes an important part of this process. All of us would like to think that each of our clients is special and that we retain the details of their plans in a mental notebook. Operating on such a basis, however, invites confusion and by necessity downplays the very details that often differentiate one client's situation from that of another. Insurance professionals should, therefore, make it a practice to conduct their periodic reviews with the help of fact-finding aids. Detailed notes should be taken and kept with the client's other records. This provides the insurance professional with a clear method of refreshing his or her memory as to the particulars of each client situation.

Practical Aids for Determining Suitability and Finding Facts

We have seen that fact-finding and suitability are important. There are aids available to help determine suitability and uncover the appropriate facts.

Organized Fact-Finders—Some agents try to uncover information simply through the interview process without the use of any guiding aid. In today's ethics-sensitive environment this is not a recommended process. Simply put, it has too many opportunities for error and provides little documentation. Some needed information may not be acquired. Other information may be forgotten. Prudence suggests the use of an organized fact-finder.

Most companies make such fact-finders available. Some fact-finders are relatively simple, others more detailed. The selection of a particular fact-finder will depend in part on your comfort level and expertise with the type of questions presented and, in part, on the relative complexity involved in the particular client situation.

Government Tax Form(s) as Fact-Finder—In addition to company or commercially developed fact-finders, agents may wish to use government forms. For example, reviewing the 1040 income tax return with a client can pinpoint many issues from the possible redirection of tax dollars to the need for greater retirement savings. Agents involved in estate planning may find that the estate tax Form 706 is a useful tool. Form 706 not only serves as a source of third-party influence as to the impact of estate taxes, it also requires the assembly of comprehensive information for proper completion.

Dialogue of Key Questions as Fact-Finder—Some planners are very comfortable using the typical fill-in-the-figure type fact-finders. Other agents are more comfortable using a suggested dialogue of questions designed to elicit pertinent information from the client. Many of these questions are purposefully designed to be disturbing. In other words, they provide a track for an agent to follow that causes the client to stop and think about his or her current situation. Some agents use a combination of both tools.

Multiple Purpose Form—A fact-finder serves more than one purpose. The most obvious purpose is the organized guidance it provides an agent in assembling the pertinent information about a client. The nature of a fact-finder establishes a professional pattern for the agent. Its use ensures that each client is treated in a similar and proper fashion.

A fact-finder also serves as an important reference tool. Initially, the fact-finder may be used to sort through information. It is a relatively easy way, for example, to pinpoint information inconsistencies. It's a way to test a new plan to see if the agent's proposal meets the client's needs.

Review Item

Jumping the Gun

Agent Scully:

"So, you're a fan of Clint Eastwood and drive a sports car. I have just the product for you."

Is the agent jumping to conclusions about his client's risk-tolerance level? What steps would you suggest to the agent before he makes an inappropriate product recommendation?

Write your answer in the space below.

The fact-finder will eventually serve as a reference for historical information that can be used to conduct periodic reviews. What type of assets did the client own 5 years ago? Has the client's net worth increased or decreased? Have new family members entered into the situation? Have intervening deaths altered the client's initial objectives? In other words, the fact-finder serves as a useful reference tool in conducting periodic reviews.

From a compliance standpoint, fact-finders can serve as evidence of ethical conduct and appropriate agent recommendations should questions arise at a future date about why an action was taken.

Fact-Finder Format and Compliance Considerations

Some fact-finders limit their format to information gathering. Other fact-finders provide additional information that can be used to educate the client or stimulate need. Marketplace practice issues may arise depending on how a fact-finder that contains additional information is used during the sales process. If the fact-finder is being used solely as part of the interview process, few marketplace practice issues arise. The added

---

information could be considered cues and prompts for the agent as he or she conducts the information gathering.

On the other hand, marketplace practice issues can arise if a fact-finder that goes beyond mere information gathering is left with a client to complete. For example, a fact-finder might contain prohibited language implying that a comprehensive financial and investment plan would occur as a result of the form completion. The inclusion of such language in a fact-finding packet delivered to a client for self-completion would be inappropriate if the agent was not a registered investment advisor (RIA). In addition, under NASD compliance rules, agents who are RIAs must be certain that the fact-finders used in their practices have been reviewed by their broker-dealer(s) prior to use. If you are unsure as to whether or not you are using an approved form, call your home office for verification. It is far better to err on the side of caution than to open yourself to charges of improper business practices that could result in a ruined reputation.

Supplementary Information

We've already seen that life underwriters are dealing in an environment where many securities-type standards are being applied. We've also indicated that this should not be an onerous burden for agents. In fact, many of these standards offer agents a road map of protection in instances of legal action as well as increased sales opportunities brought about through greater client services. Many securities representatives apply business-type financial planning concepts to their client dealings.

With this fact in mind, financial services professionals should seriously consider incorporating simplified financial statements into the fact-finding process. A net worth statement would be typical of this type of information. A cash flow or budget statement may also prove helpful in developing a client's financial profile. In some cases, the client is able to prepare these statements. In other cases, these statements will be prepared through the joint work of the agent and his or her client(s). In still other cases, the client's accountant will supply this information.

Fact-Finders

The following are examples of fact-finders:

- net worth statement—a client's financial history
- annual budget and cash flow statement
- client budget—estimates vs. actual dollars

Regulation of Financial Planning Professionals

Most of this chapter has been devoted to spelling out the obligations of financial services professionals who deal with insurance and related products. If you are engaged as a financial planner, be aware that a broader scope of ethical responsibility is involved, and that there is federal monitoring of your behavior.

Your ethical responsibility is that of a fiduciary acting on behalf of your clients. Your services are likely to fall under the jurisdiction of the Securities and Exchange Commission (SEC). Your behavior should be guided by the dictates of the Investment Advisers Act of 1940. This requires you to register as an investment advisor with the SEC and agree to abide by strict standards of ethical conduct. In addition, many states are moving toward stricter regulation of financial planners.

As an investment advisor, you are governed by the NASD Rules of Conduct.

NASD Rules of Conduct

Under the 1934 act, the NASD must promulgate rules designed to

- prevent fraudulent practices and promote equitable principles of trade
- safeguard against unreasonable profits, commissions, or other charge
- prevent unfair discrimination between customers, issuers, or broker-dealers
- provide for appropriate discipline for the violation of its rules (for example, censure, suspension, and expulsion)

The NASD Rules of Conduct require that member broker-dealers and associated persons of broker-dealers observe high standards of commercial honor and just and equitable principles of trade. The rules regulate a wide range of activity relating to such areas as the sale of securities, suitability of such sales, confirmation of transactions, and supervision.

The rules of conduct govern (1) the supervision of the salespersons, (2) private securities transactions, (3) outside business activities of associated persons, (4) suitability and fair dealing with customers, (5) influencing or rewarding employees of other broker-dealers and finders fees, and (6) sales literature, advertising and communications with the public. Some of these rules are considered in the paragraphs that immediately follow.

1. **Supervision**—A broker-dealer must establish and maintain a system of specified written oversight and review procedures to supervise the activities of each registered representative.

2. **Private Securities Transactions**—This area involves any securities transactions beyond the regular scope of an associated person's relationship with a broker-dealer such as new offerings of securities, which are not registered with the SEC. Thus, it is incumbent upon the broker-dealer to train and continually remind its registered representatives (including its life insurance agents) that the definition of a security is very broad and any activity even remotely resembling a securities transaction should be brought to the brokers-dealer's attention for approval.

3. **Outside Business Activities of Associated Persons**—Article III, Sec. 43 of the NASD Rules prohibits an associated person of a broker-dealer from accepting employment or compensation concerning any business activity outside the scope of the broker-dealer employment relationship unless the person provides the broker-dealer with prompt written notice.

   For our purposes, the most important regulation is that of suitability and fair dealing which we have already mentioned. To reiterate:

4. **Suitability and Fair Dealing with Customers,** Article III, Section 2 of the NASD Rules provides that in recommending to a customer the purchase or sale of any security, a member shall have reasonable grounds for believing that the recommendation is suitable for such customer upon the basis of the facts, if any, disclosed by such customer as to his other securities holdings and as to his financial situation and needs.

   In recommending a product, a registered representative must have reasonable grounds to believe that the product being recommended is suitable for his or her customer. Such determination should be based on customer disclosures as to income, net worth, securities holdings, life insurance, real estate holdings, customer financial sophistication, investment objectives, and financial needs. Registered principals of the broker-dealer make the final determination as to suitability and the acceptance of the transaction.

   It should be noted that, in a variation on the suitability theme, the SEC recognizes a broker-dealer obligation of fair dealing under the general antifraud provisions of the federal securities laws. The commission maintains that a violation of the suitability doctrine may constitute a violation of Rule 10b-5 under the Securities Exchange Act of 1934, which is the SEC's general antifraud rule under the act. This position is predicated on the theory that when a broker-dealer holds itself out as a broker-dealer (solicits business), it implicitly represents that it will recommend securities only when it has a reasonable basis that such are suited to the customer's needs.

Judicial decisions have contributed to the development of suitability as a fraud concept outside the antifraud provisions of the federal securities laws. In Anderson v. Knox, for example, a federal Court of Appeals held that an insurance agent who had induced a client to buy excessive amounts of bank-financed insurance was liable for damages for common law fraud since the policies were unsuitable for the policyowner's needs. Judicial thinking, scholarly works, and regulatory attitudes suggest that criminal and civil liabilities attendant to the suitability and fair-dealing concepts set forth in the NASD rules have yet to reach their full potential.

5. **Sales Literature, Advertising, and Communications with the Public**—A series of SEC and NASD rules and guidelines has evolved to govern advertising, sales literature, and communications with the public concerning the distribution of equity products.

6. **Communications with the Public**—Article III, Sec. 35 of the NASD Rules of Conduct mandates that every item of advertising and sales literature (the definition of which is quite broad) be approved by a registered principal of the broker-dealer prior to its use. Furthermore, such material must contain a broker-dealer's name, the identity of the preparer of the material, and the date first published. Advertisements and sales literature must also be filed with the NASD within 10 days of their first use. Such materials can be disapproved for failure to meet NASD guidelines.

On the Insurance Side—The NASD has established a Variable Life Insurance Marketing Guide. Prior to 1990, NASD policy emphasized that the primary attribute of a variable life insurance (VLI) policy is its death benefit even though VLI also contains an important investment aspect in its cash value. The NASD opined, however, that VLI should not be described as an investment. With the advent of single-premium VLI policies, the NASD revised its position to permit broker-dealers to give more weight to the investment element of policies or contracts. By 1990, the NASD further relaxed its position and moved to imposing no absolute requirement that broker-dealers maintain a "balance" in describing the insurance and investment elements of a VLI policy. However, communications should describe both elements.

By early 1994, the NASD had in place SEC-approved guidelines covering variable products to govern the preparation of and communication with the public through advertising and sales literature. The primary thrust of such guidelines is to prohibit referring to variable products as mutual funds. The guidelines require that communications concerning variable products clearly identify the product as either a variable life insurance policy or a variable annuity contract; avoid implying that the underlying product is a mutual fund (since there are significant differences between mutual funds and variable contracts); avoid presenting variable products as short-term liquid investments; disclose the impact of early withdrawal such as sales loads, tax penalties, and potential loss of principal in references to liquidity; and avoid suggestion that guarantees apply to investment returns. Also by mid-1994, the SEC approved a new set of NASD guidelines limiting the use of rankings by mutual funds and other investment companies (including separate accounts underlying variable insurance products) in advertising and marketing materials.

With respect to illustrations, the methodology and format of hypothetical illustrations must be patterned after the required illustrations used in the variable life insurance prospectus approved by the SEC. Illustrations must reflect the maximum guaranteed mortality and expense charges associated with the policy for each assumed rate of return. Current charges may also be illustrated in addition to the maximum charges. Also, an illustration may utilize any combination of investment returns up to and including a gross rate of 12 percent if one of the returns illustrated is a 0 percent gross rate. However, even though the maximum rate of 12 percent may be acceptable, the NASD does require that the broker-dealer confirm that such maximum rate illustrated is reasonable in light of market conditions and available investment options. Mandating the illustration of a 0 percent rate of return demonstrates how the absence of growth in the underlying investment account can affect policy values and reinforces the hypothetical nature of the illustration. NASD guidelines also permit comparisons between variable life insurance contracts and other financial instruments based on actual experience, not assumed hypothetical performance. Performance comparisons must be fair, balanced, and complete and must comply with NASD rules governing communications with the public. In addition, the SEC has imposed performance-comparison advertising rules, including standardized computation of performance data in advertising and sales literature for mutual funds and variable annuities.

As indicated previously, the format of any personalized variable life insurance illustration must be filed with and its use must be approved in advance by the Advertising Department of the NASD. The sale of variable life insurance and the use of personalized illustrations can be conducted only by salespersons registered with the NASD. NASD rules mandate that each broker-dealer review, supervise, and store all sales materials including illustrations.

Chapter 6 Review Questions

Answers to Review Questions start on appendix page A-53.

1. After agent Smith has conducted a thorough fact-finding with client Jones, agent Smith should
   (a) retain these records for use in future periodic reviews
   (b) discard these records as quickly as possible to eradicate all documentation of the sales process
   (c) archive the records for 6 months before destroying
   (d) forward all records to the client for documentation

2. The NASD Conduct Rules
   (a) constitute an undue and illegal hardship on financial advisors selling variable products
   (b) emphasize the need to provide proper client service including disclosure of confidential information regarding your company's investment philosophy and trading positions
   (c) are statutorily inapplicable to insurance agents
   (d) emphasize the need to provide proper client service, including efforts made to understand a client's current financial condition

3. Which of the following statements is true concerning model legislation promulgated by the National Association of Insurance Commissioners (NAIC)?
   (a) NAIC model legislation applies only to agents, not to home offices.
   (b) NAIC model legislation is designed to cover only home office marketing practices.
   (c) NAIC model legislation is designed for implementation by the federal government.
   (d) NAIC model legislation gives state insurance commissioners substantial powers to investigate both carriers and agents suspected of violating the law.

4. Which of the following is an example of an equity investment?
   (a) a federal government bond with a 30-year duration
   (b) a short-term certificate of deposit
   (c) a local jurisdiction bond with a 5-year duration
   (d) common stock

5. Which of the following statements regarding risk tolerance is true?
   (a) All clients maintain the same level of risk tolerance.
   (b) Some clients can accept risk more easily than others.
   (c) Risk tolerance is inapplicable to an agent's insurance practice.
   (d) Risk tolerance is applicable to property and casualty and inapplicable to an agent's life insurance practice.

6. Agents should assume that most clients are
   (a) risk-averse
   (b) risk seekers
   (c) tolerant of moderate levels of risk
   (d) tolerant of high levels of risk

7. Legislative risk involves
   (a) the possibility that the law, which currently provides a favorable environment for an investment, may change
   (b) the possibility that the law, which currently provides a hostile environment for an investment, may change
   (c) exposure to investment default
   (d) exposure to investment appreciation

8. A client's risk tolerance will
   (a) remain static over time
   (b) typically evolve over time
   (c) be generally lowered due to media and cultural influences
   (d) be generally unaffected by media and cultural influences

9. All of the following are suggested methods of assessing a client's tolerance towards risk EXCEPT
   (a) the investment philosophy test
   (b) the 80/20 analysis
   (c) the examination of investment history
   (d) the review of investment objectives

10. All of the following are major categories of investment risk EXCEPT
    (a) purchasing power risk
    (b) market risk
    (c) default risk
    (d) fluctuation risk

7

Marketing Financial Products: Ethical Sales and Full Disclosure

Learning Objectives
7-1. List the steps involved in the ethical sales process.
7-2. Describe misrepresentation and false advertising as ethical missteps within the sales process.
7-3. Explain the principles and benefits of full disclosure.
7-4. List and describe the four keys to full disclosure.

Chapter Outline

Ethical Sales   7-3
The Sales Presentation   7-3
Client Education   7-4
   Client Education Is Selling   7-4
   Client Learning Styles   7-5
   Tools for Educating Clients   7-5
Two Ethical Missteps   7-6
   Misrepresentation   7-6
   False Advertising   7-9

Full Disclosure   7-11
Case Study: A Trip to Aruba   7-13
Benefit(s) of Full Disclosure   7-15
Documenting Full Disclosure   7-17
   What to Document   7-18
   Disclosure in the Application   7-20
   Postsale Disclosure   7-20

Chapter 7 Review Questions   7-22

Ethical Sales

The Sales Presentation

In this chapter, we will cover a variety of marketing practices that financial services professionals (particularly those engaged in selling insurance) should avoid, including false advertising, misrepresentation, lack of full disclosure.

After determining the needs of the client and the suitability of the planning strategies, you come to a point where you need to recommend or sell a product. In that case, you are involved in a sales presentation. Let's define a sales presentation as that part of the process that follows an agent's fact-finding and determination of client objectives. A sales presentation occurs when an agent presents recommendations designed to solve a client's needs and objectives. The presentation can be thought of as a five-part process; the first two steps take place before the actual presentation.

- The agent reviews the data obtained and considers various solutions based on his or her expertise and experience that might solve the client's needs and objectives. This might involve consideration of just one solution, but far more likely three or four of them.
- The agent selects one or two recommendations that best serve the client's needs.
- The agent meets with his or her client and makes the recommendation(s).
- The agent explains to the client the reasons behind the recommendation(s).
- The agent uses his or her sales skills to bring closure by having the client take action on the recommendation(s).

Making a Presentation

Agent Smith:

"Your policy has guaranteed and nonguaranteed elements. . . ."

Client Jones (thinking):

He's been talking for half an hour. If only he'd show me how this policy works!

How should the agent present the information to the client? What is the client's likely learning style?

Log your answer in the space below.

Client Education

Information may not be enough. The client may not comprehend what you are saying without knowledge of how financial products work and, thus, may need to be educated. How do you know whether or not a client needs to be educated? Ask the client questions. The answers to your questions will indicate whether or not more explanation is necessary. The answers will also provide an indication of whether or not the client is misinterpreting what you are saying.

Client Education Is Selling

Client education is not just teaching. Client education is selling. If a client does not understand what you are saying, the chances are that he or she will not understand why he or she should buy your product(s). The client simply won't comprehend the need. Client education and quizzing will provide you with feedback. If a client initially doesn't understand something, you'll know and have an opportunity to present the same concept in a different way.

Client Learning Styles

Keep in mind that some of us learn better by hearing, some by seeing, others by quietly sitting and reading. A one-page chart, for example, might be the best way to convey the need for a funded buy-sell agreement to a visual learner. The second business partner may learn best by hearing. In that case, a lecture type presentation might be the best way to convey basically the same information. A written proposal might work best for a third reading-oriented partner.

Tools for Educating Clients

Professionals engaged in selling life insurance should be aware of two excellent sources that can be used to educate clients in the basics of life insurance: the *Life Insurance Buyer's Guide* and *What You Should Know about Buying Life Insurance* (see the appendix). The *Life Insurance Buyer's Guide* contains a concise explanation of life insurance products. Many states have regulations that require that the guide be provided along with a policy summary to prospective life insurance consumers. The guide is an excellent way to educate your clients and help them understand the different insurance options available to them. This knowledge makes them active participants in the buying process. Many companies have tailored versions of the *Life Insurance Buyer's Guide* for distribution to clients.

Review Item

Proper Documentation

Agent McLean:

"I'll remember to jot down a few notes on her request over the weekend."

Will he remember? Is this a good example of proper documentation?

Log your answer in the space below.

What You Should Know about Buying Life Insurance has been developed by the American Council of Life Insurance (ACLI). It provides readers with basics about life insurance in addition to information about choosing an agent and purchasing insurance. What You Should Know about Buying Life Insurance has been endorsed by the National Association of Insurance and Financial Advisors (NAIFA) and the Life and Health Insurance Foundation for Education (LIFE). The booklet serves as an excellent third-party influence piece that will support other information you provide to your clients.

Two Ethical Missteps

Up to this point we have covered the rules of fair practice and outlined what a proper approach to presenting and selling products would involve. Throughout these processes, the professional must avoid two missteps: misrepresentation and/or false advertising. We examine these two issues below.

Misrepresentation

Periodically, in an effort to make a sale, a professional might be tempted to make the product look better than it is, or suggest that it can perform in a way that it cannot in the belief that if the client believes it, he or she will buy the product. This is misrepresentation. It is a form of lying and, because of that, it is wrong. That lying is wrong is obvious, but it will be helpful at this point to examine what takes place when one lies to see exactly what's wrong with it.

Some people believe that the essence of lying is saying something false. But simply saying something false is not always lying. For example, sometimes people just make a mistake and misspeak. Telling a lie involves more than simply getting things wrong and not telling the truth. The essence of lying is found in its purpose. Lying is attempting, usually by speech (but at times with gestures or looks), to get another person to act in a certain way. So we can define lying as a deceptive activity meant to evoke a certain response that would not have occurred if the truth were told. Simply put, we lie and deceive others to get our way without concern for the other person.

This becomes clear if we think about children who are notorious liars (it takes some growing up for them to develop into honest people). Mostly they lie to avoid punishment. A child draws on the wall with crayons. She is asked if she did it. She says no. Why? Simply to avoid being punished, that is, to bring about behavior in the parent or supervisor other than punishing behavior. So the child lies to elicit desired behavior that she thinks would not occur if the truth were known.

How does this work in the case of deceptive sales? From this perspective, a deceptive sale is an activity whose goal is to get the buyer to do what the seller thinks he or she probably would not do if the truth were known. The financial advisor tells the client the insurance policy is a savings plan. From an economic point of view, such a procedure violates the ideal market principle of perfect information. But more important from a moral point of view, in getting the buyer to do something he or she probably never intended, the seller takes away the buyer's real choice in the situation and thereby uses the buyer for his or her own purposes. Such use is unjust, immoral, exploitative, and manipulative.

Quite often we hear it said that we shouldn't lie, because if we do people will not trust us. That is true. But it is also a somewhat self-centered reason for not lying. From a moral perspective, the primary reason for not lying is that it subordinates another to your wishes without another's consent and for your benefit, without concern for another's benefit. It violates a version of the Golden Rule, which says: "Don't do to others what you wouldn't have done to you." You want to know what you are getting when you buy something. So does everyone else.

Financial services professionals must convey accurate information to clients. This rule applies not only to written information but also to oral statements. Obviously to misrepresent a product to a client is wrong. The client has the right to make his or her own decision based on accurate information.

It may be that most professionals do not intentionally make misrepresentations to clients and believe what they are telling clients is true. In such a case, the financial advisor is guilty of ignorance. Unfortunately, from the viewpoint of agent liability, this is not a valid defense. Many states have laws that specifically penalize financial advisors for misrepresentation. These laws are based on the premise that financial advisors have an ethical duty to know what they are selling and to present policies in a truthful manner.

Below are some examples of situations in which misrepresentation may take place.

- **Policy Terms and Conditions**—During a sales presentation you tell a prospect not to worry about prior ill health. The client has had a serious bout with colon cancer within the past 2 years. You go on, unwittingly confusing the terms of your company's annuity with its whole life insurance policy.

- **Dividend Sales**—During a sales presentation, you indicate that dividends are guaranteed to be paid no matter what the financial results of the company are.
- **Financial Condition of the Company**—Your client is a middle-aged widow applying for her first insurance policy. She is concerned about risking principal. You assure her that your company has the highest rating. In fact, its rating is mid-tier in most reporting services.

Review Item

Hidden Health Condition

Prospect Marvin Young:

"The life insurance coverage is important to my family. Two years ago I had a colon cancer scare, and it changed my outlook. "

Agent Steve Collins:

"Don't worry, that's not the type of information that affects the issuance of this type of policy."

Does it sound like Agent Collins is confusing life insurance with annuity underwriting? Is his statement likely to cause confusion about the terms and conditions of the life insurance policy being applied for?

Log your answer in the space below.

You have an obligation to know the products you promote. The more you know about the company you represent and the products you sell, the less likely that you will inadvertently make misrepresentations to clients. If necessary, set aside time to review your product portfolio. This information will not only enable you to act legally and ethically, it will also provide you with ideas and information to facilitate sales.

False Advertising

Another area of marketing in which a misstep can occur is advertising. Insurance professionals and other financial services professionals must make sure that the materials they use to advertise, sell their products, and portray themselves are true and clearly comprehensible. Advertising that contains untrue, unclear, incomplete, or deceptive statements is unethical. Furthermore, state laws often specifically prohibit such advertising. The application of these laws not only applies to home office material but also to agency-prepared material or material created by the financial advisor.

Insurance departments are particularly concerned about advertisements that confuse life insurance with a savings plan or investment. Calling premiums "deposits" is unacceptable. Referring to life insurance as a "tax shelter" also invites regulator criticism. As a matter of fact, most codes of ethics suggest that to sell life insurance primarily as a tax shelter is wrong if it has little other benefit as insurance.

For example, when you are using advertising literature in the sales process, be sure it emphasizes the death benefit protection offered by life insurance. While the savings element of life insurance can be an important factor, it is essential that the protection element of life insurance is discussed.

Review Item

Bait and Switch

Agent Rock Pushkin:

"This permanent product is what you really need."

Client Michael Meeker:

"When you called for this appointment, you said you would show me your competitive term policy —one with lower rates than other carriers. But now you're recommending this more costly plan."

Do you see any ethical issues raised in this situation?

Log your answer in the space below.

If you prepare customized materials for your clients, recognize that these materials are subject to regulatory oversight. Many companies and home offices have established special units to review these materials. They realize that many creative ideas come from the field, and they are willing to help you satisfy state codes and regulations. Be sure not to bypass the process.

The following are some additional pointers regarding advertising:

- **Testimonials**—Don't use your imagination. Testimonials must be true. Approach satisfied clients about providing you with statements.
- **Insurance**—Don't hide the product you are selling. If you are selling life insurance, this must be clearly stated and not just implied.
- **Statistics**—Don't make up numbers. Base your presentation on facts.
- **Products**—Don't bait and switch. That is, be prepared to sell the product described in your advertising pieces. If you have stressed the economical nature of term, be ready to sell it. Don't retract the letter that opened the door.
- **Type Size**—Don't try to hide the facts in small type. This invites both regulatory and client suspicion. If something is important, say it clearly.
- **Exceptions**—Don't forget the exceptions. If there are exceptions to a policy's coverage, let the client know this in advance. To do otherwise is to invite ethical troubles. Your client may be the very person to whom the exception applies at a critical time.
- **Title**—Don't use a title to indicate that you are something you are not. If you advertise yourself as a financial planner, act accordingly. Remember, financial planners are usually compensated on a fee structure. They must comply with additional levels of regulations and licensing requirements. If you do not intend to do anything but sell insurance, make sure it is reflected on your card.

One final point about false advertising. Be honest and straightforward in presenting yourself and your credentials. Don't portray yourself as an investment advisor if you are not. Don't portray yourself as an expert in fields where you have no expertise. In short, fit the products to the clients' needs, educate the clients, and convince them that these products fit those needs. If they don't, you are wrong to try to sell the products.

Full Disclosure

One of the most important ethical obligations of a financial services professional before and during a sales presentation is full disclosure. Full disclosure means presenting the facts about a product accurately and thoroughly so a client can make a valid informed purchase decision.

This is a particular problem for insurance agents because they have not only an ethical obligation, but also a legal obligation to their clients due in great part to the nature of an insurance contract. Unlike other contracts, a life insurance contract is not negotiated. It is a *contract of adhesion*. This means that a life insurance contract is drawn up by one of the parties (the insurer) and either accepted or rejected by the other party (the policyowner).

Because the insurer draws up the contract, the courts have ruled that the insurer bears the burden of making things clear to the policyowner. Because the agent represents the insurance company to the policyowner, he or she must educate the client.

> **Full Disclosure**
>
> Full disclosure frequently involves client education. Simply put, the client may not comprehend what you are saying without a basic knowledge of how insurance works.

From an ethical point of view, disclosure is a complicated issue for the financial services professional who sells products. How much is the agent ethically obliged to disclose? It is an accepted principle in effective salesmanship (not to be confused with ethical salesmanship) not to say anything negative about the product one is selling and certainly not to disclose shortcomings unnecessarily. For example, if you are selling your home, is it necessary to point out all the defects that only you know? If you do, you probably will succeed in discouraging every prospect from buying it. During a job interview, should you point out the flaws you have to your prospective employer? I know of no job counselor who suggests that. So two questions arise: How much does one need to disclose, and to what extent can failure to disclose be construed as market misconduct? To answer those questions, reflect for a moment on two points: first, reflect on how selling is a market transaction, and second, reflect on how lack of disclosure is similar to lying.

Selling insurance and other financial products is, among other things, a market transaction. In the ideal market transaction, two people decide to exchange goods because they hope the exchange will benefit both of them. That is the genius of the free market system. Freedom of exchange leads to the overall improvement of the traders' lot. In a market exchange, nothing new has been produced, but both people are better off because of the trade. Ideally, there is perfect information about the worth of what is being given and gotten in return. Such a trade, freely entered into with full information, should maximize satisfaction on both sides.

However, if one of the parties is misled into believing a product is not what it is because it is misrepresented, the effect of both sides being better off and satisfied is undermined. Deception leads to the deceived party's getting something different and less valuable than what is expected. The deceived party most likely would not have entered into the exchange had he or she known the full truth about the product. So the conditions for an ideal trade include the freedom or autonomy of the participants and full knowledge of the pertinent details of the product, both of which are required if we are to have what is often called informed consent. Consent cannot be presumed to be given if one is either forced into an exchange or lacks adequate knowledge of the product one is bargaining for. A choice based on inadequate information is not a choice at all.

We talked earlier about misrepresentation being a lie. Is failure to disclose also a lie? Some would say, "Not disclosing isn't lying, it's just not telling." But that misses the point. Deliberately withholding information to get another to act contrary to the way he or she would have acted with the information has the same deceptive structure and consequence as the overt lie. It doesn't allow an informed choice.

Still another question occurs: Must one disclose everything? Certainly some failure to disclose is wrong, but how much must we disclose? The characterization of lying we gave above should help us decide. Whenever you are tempted not to disclose something, ask yourself why you are not disclosing. Withholding information because you fear losing the sale if the consumer or client knows the whole story is manipulating. You might object, saying there are times when one doesn't benefit from not disclosing, such as on social occasions. For example, when your friend asks how you are, you don't have to disclose that you feel miserable. Your friend probably doesn't want to hear it. Or when your friend asks how he looks, you don't have to say, "Like you just got out of bed." That kind of social nondisclosure is acceptable because in those cases one is not trying to change the behavior of another to personally benefit from it. Hence, if one lies for some other reason than manipulating the behavior of the one lied to, that kind of lie may not be wrong. Having said that though, we should introduce a caveat: In such social situations there may be a great deal of paternalism involved, and a great many assumptions being made about what the other wants or needs. It is not clear that it is a totally harmless activity.

It is the case that in some situations it might be hard to decide how much to disclose. Let's consider a brief scenario.

---

*Case Study**

A Trip to Aruba

Brock Roberts, CLU and Cosmic Life agent, needs one more sale to qualify for membership in Cosmic Life's top production club and win a trip to Aruba. Marie, a client who buys all of her insurance from Brock, has a clearly established need for additional insurance. She asks Brock for three proposals from companies with equal credit ratings. Brock presents illustrations from Cosmic Life, Stable Life, and Exciting Life. He accurately demonstrates that all three policies will fill Marie's need. If she chooses Cosmic, Brock will win the trip. Exciting Life pays a first-year commission that is much higher than that paid by the other two carriers, and of the three companies Stable Life has the strongest long-term financial performance history. These facts are unknown to the client. Marie asks Brock to recommend the best of the three. Brock recommends Cosmic to Marie and that is what she buys.

Marie has no inkling that Brock is on the verge of winning a trip to Aruba. Should she know this? Why or why not?

* This case originally appeared in the July 1991 "Strictly Speaking" column by Burke A. Christensen, *Journal of the American Society of CLU & ChFC*; © 1991 The Society of Financial Service Professionals.

As you can imagine, sometimes there is vehement disagreement about whether Brock should disclose the trip. Some say that even if Brock thinks Cosmic is as good a buy as Stable or Exciting, and even if he feels comfortable recommending it, he should disclose the information about the trip. There are others who will disagree and argue that he need not disclose it.

In discussion of this case, any number of reasons are given for not disclosing. "No one does it." "It's not necessary." "The client trusts me." "Clients don't need all that information, they'll just get confused." "It's no business of the client's." Are these reasonable defenses of the behavior, or are they rationalizations? How is one to decide? In the face of such disagreement, I would suggest adopting the following method: Ask yourself why you would be reluctant to disclose the trip.

If you are reluctant because you think telling the client about the trip will affect the sale, shouldn't you disclose it to give the client that option? If you are reluctant because you think telling the client won't affect the sale because the client trusts you implicitly to do the best for her, then why be reluctant to disclose? If you are reluctant because you think too much disclosure gives too much information and will confuse the client, aren't you putting yourself in the position of deciding how much information the client can handle? How do you determine how much information that is? In withholding possibly relevant information, aren't you creating a questionable paternalistic relationship? Why not just give the client the information and let her decide? As an added consideration, contemplate what would happen if the client buys Cosmic Life on Brock's recommendation and it doesn't perform as well as Stable or Exciting. Later Marie finds out the sale of Cosmic was tied to an all-expense-paid vacation. How will that look? Admittedly, bad consequences to oneself do not constitute the primary reason to disclose, but they do provide a consideration to keep in mind

---

Review Item

Risk Alert

Agent Robert Naples:

"There are risks with this type of product. Are you comfortable living with market ups and downs?"

What's your opinion of the way Agent Naples is conducting this presentation?

Log your answer in the space below.

Let's sum up the method that tests when disclosure is necessary. If you are reluctant to tell the client you are selling insurance, ask yourself why? Perhaps you don't think an insurance policy best fits the needs of the client. In that case, you should disclose because you are putting your interest before the best interest of the client. Perhaps you think the client doesn't want insurance so much as a straightforward mutual fund program. In that case you should disclose, again for the same reason. Are you glossing over the nonguaranteed aspect of cash value projections in variable products? Why? Perhaps you think that if the client realizes the growth promises are not guaranteed, he or she will look for another product. Once again, if that is so, it seems clear you are putting your interests above those of the client and using the client to further your own goals. That violates the central ethical tenet of "Do unto others what you would have done unto you." Such nondisclosure fails to respect the other and treats him or her merely as a means or instrument to be used for your own gratification.

However we resolve the issue now, the question of how much disclosure is necessary in order to avoid manipulation of a client, and whether commissions and other costs should be disclosed, is being talked about and will continue to be talked about intensely for the next few years. Consumers will demand to know what they are buying and financial advisors will be pressured into disclosing more and more. Old practices will be reviewed and reformed. That's how ethics usually solves these issues. For now, the safest and most ethical road is the following: ***When in doubt, disclose!***

Benefit(s) of Full Disclosure

Aside from being the right thing to do, full disclosure helps to avoid legal problems, particularly where a financial advisor has taken the time to maintain records documenting the disclosure. For example, a financial advisor might retain a copy of a letter explaining his or her recommendation to a client, together with a signed copy of the illustration used in the sales presentation.

However, beyond the avoidance of legal difficulties, full disclosure enables clients to anticipate how the products they bought will perform. For example, if the client purchases term insurance, he or she will not be surprised when premiums rise. If a client has purchased universal life, the client will know what to expect as interest rates vary from year to year. Full disclosure provides the client, in effect, with ownership of, and participation in, the buying decision. Unpleasant surprises are avoided, policies are retained, and referrals are made. Full disclosure helps to create a sense of trust and cement sales by generating client satisfaction.

Keys to Full Disclosure

Full disclosure involves providing your client with four key pieces of information. Typically, this information is provided during the presentation portion of the sales process.

1. **Provide your client with information about the product.**

   Tell the client exactly what the product will do for the client and what it won't do.

2. **Provide your client with information about the company that is offering the product.**

   Make the client aware of the company's history and ratings. Many home offices will readily supply you with this information for distribution to your clients. Provide your client with information about the type of product being purchased. The difference between whole life and term may seem obvious to you, but to many clients this is new information. Don't overlook the basics.

3. **Provide your clients with information about the illustration used in your sales presentation.**

   Be sure to review the difference between guaranteed and nonguaranteed values.

4. **Provide your client with information as to the role of the insurance application.**

   Explain how it's used in the underwriting process and the importance of providing the company with accurate information. If you feel it is appropriate, point out to the client that supplying inaccurate information may ease the individual underwriting process but may later result in the denial of a claim.

Remember to provide clients with information about their options. If more than one product will fulfill their current needs, tell them. Also inform clients about both the short-term and long-term aspects of each of the presented options. For example, you might explain to a 40-year-old that a term policy is cheaper today but, in the long run, is likely to prove more expensive than a permanent policy.

Marketing Financial Products: Ethical Sales and Full Disclosure

Retirement Specialist

Client Stephanie Dunn:

"I thought you specialized in retirement planning. That's what your card says. Why are we still discussing life insurance? You haven't even mentioned IRAs."

Agent Loretta Vincent:

"I do specialize in retirement planning but with life insurance."

Does it appear that Agent Vincent has confused the client about her role and the nature of the product she sells? If so, does this raise an ethical issue?

Log your answer in the space below.

Documenting Full Disclosure

We've already mentioned that full disclosure enhances client satisfaction and lessens the chance of legal liability. We now need to point out the importance of documenting full disclosure. Why is documentation so important? The answer rests in the fact that when problems arise, they often occur many years after the sale. For example, litigation may occur following the death of a client. Questions may arise about the amount of insurance purchased. Heirs may squabble over the selection of the beneficiary designation. A wife may complain about the continued payment of premiums for a disabled husband, asserting that a disability premium waiver was surely chosen.

In other words, you may not be dealing with a satisfied client but with an irate heir or third-party executor of an estate. In these instances, you no longer have the word of a satisfied client to support you. You are dependent on your recollection and the records that you have maintained.

In other cases, the client may choose to forget what was said at the time of a sale. The uninsurable client may forget that an additional term rider was suggested and rejected at the time an underlying policy was purchased. Once again, you are dependent on your recollection and the records that you have maintained. If a legal action ensues, your contemporaneous written records will be an important part of your defense. (In other words, write down what is happening in your practice now—it may serve a useful compliance purpose later.) In fact, the existence of such records may discourage unfounded lawsuits from even beginning. Remember, even unfounded lawsuits cost you time and money.

Review Item

Office Sweep

Agent Daniels:

"These files need to be cleaned out. I wonder how long I should keep these papers about last year's sales."

What should this agent do?

Log your answer in the space below.

Document Your Disclosure Statements—You not only need to disclose, you also need to document your work. Financial services professionals should use disclosure statements for any aspect of a sale that they believe is best explained and documented.

For example, some clients may insist on buying insufficient coverage. In this case, you may wish to document the fact that additional coverage was discussed with the client. Asking the client to sign a compliance-approved statement to that effect provides you with evidence of the thoroughness of your work. Asking the client to sign such a statement may also encourage the client to obtain the needed coverage.

What to Document
You should document three elements of every sale—namely, the reason for the product recommendation, the illustration used as basis of the sale, and a disclosure statement.

- **The Reason for the Product Recommendation**—Your records should provide a written trail of the reasons why a particular product was recommended. This will involve retention of records showing that you performed adequate fact-finding on which to base the recommended product choice. These records will also show that you took into consideration the client's needs as well as his or her ability to pay the premiums to support the recommended product. If a variable product is being sold, we recommend that records be maintained that provide evidence of the client's risk tolerance.
- **The Illustration Used As Basis of Sale**—We recommend that you prepare three copies of the illustration used to close a sale. Have the client sign both copies and be sure to retain one in your records. (Illustrations are discussed in the next section.)
- **A Disclosure Statement**—Prepare a separate disclosure statement reviewing the type of policy being purchased and how it functions. Review its features, benefits, and costs. Provide a brief explanation of how the policy will meet the client's needs. Have the client sign off on the disclosure statement, and be sure to retain a signed copy for your records.

In the case of insurance, a state insurance department may already have rules regarding what to furnish and retain. Your state may have adopted the Life Insurance Illustrations Model Regulation drafted by the National Association of Insurance Commissioners (NAIC). Among other aspects, the model regulation seeks to protect consumers by establishing stringent guidelines for the illustration of insurance policy elements that are not guaranteed. The disclosure statement should also make reference to the illustration and the fact that both its guaranteed and nonguaranteed elements have been reviewed with the client. The disclosure statement should also verify that the difference between guaranteed and nonguaranteed elements has been explained by the financial advisor and is understood by the client.

How long should you keep these disclosure records? Your state insurance departments have rules regarding retention. We suggest that you keep your records in accordance with the rules of the state in which you do your business.

Disclosure in the Application

One more area that can be a source of confusion is the insurance application itself. Some clients are reluctant to share information with others, whether it be their banker or broker. They have particular difficulty in understanding why financial services professionals need to know so much. This is where your skills as a professional come to bear. The client must understand the importance of providing accurate information on the insurance application so proper underwriting can take place and, likewise, must understand the serious consequences of providing inaccurate information.

Financial services professionals must keep in mind their obligation for full disclosure not only to the client but also to the carrier. It is their job to bring about an open exchange of complete and accurate information so that the client and the company can reach valid decisions about accepting or declining an insurance risk.

Postsale Disclosure

The need for disclosure does not end with the closing of the sale and the delivery of the insurance policy. Good ethics and good business practice dictate that financial advisors maintain contact with their clients until policies mature or are terminated. Annual reviews and updates keep policyowners informed of both contract performance and their insurance needs. This makes active decision makers of your clients and can help to avoid difficulties when economic and market conditions change.

For example, if policyowners understand how to read and use annual policy statements, they will understand the impact of higher or lower interest rates on the performance of universal life plans. Similarly, if clients have purchased variable policies, they will understand the impact of rising or falling stock market values on policy performance.

Educating policyowners and revisiting policies on a periodic basis plants seeds for future business. Policyowners will anticipate the possibility of a need for additional coverage. They will view you as a true professional advisor and will feel comfortable about providing your name to friends and associates seeking insurance.

Postsale disclosure also serves to reduce your legal risks. Clients view you as a professional, not a mere representative of deep pockets to be tapped at the first sign of any trouble. In summary, postsale disclosure facilitates the development of clients, future repeat business, referred leads, and reduced legal liability.

Full disclosure means honesty and leads to informed consent. Misrepresentation and false advertising lead a client to make a decision that might not be made if a more honest picture of the product being considered is presented.

Chapter 7 Review Questions

Answers to Review Questions start on appendix page A-53.

1. Which of the following is a benefit of full disclosure?
   (a) It provides unlimited avoidance of potential legal problems.
   (b) It includes state-mandated bonus commission structures.
   (c) It results in a waiver of state licensing fees.
   (d) It limits legal liability and cements sales.

2. Client education is
   (a) a function of the home office underwriting department
   (b) a function of the agency manager
   (c) limited to teaching
   (d) part of the sales function

3. State insurance department "false advertising" laws typically apply to
   (a) home office-prepared materials but exempt agency- and agent-prepared materials
   (b) home office- and company-prepared materials but exempt agent-prepared materials
   (c) home-office, agency-, and agent-prepared materials
   (d) agency- and agent-prepared materials but exempt home office-prepared materials

4. The obligation that an insurance professional must convey accurate information to a client applies
   (a) only to written information supplied to a client
   (b) only to oral statements made as part of a sales presentation to a client
   (c) both to oral statements and written information intentionally or unintentionally made or supplied to a client
   (d) both to oral statements and written information intentionally made or supplied to a client

Marketing Financial Products: Ethical Sales and Full Disclosure

5. The two ethical missteps referred to in chapter 7 of the text are
    (a) replacement and rebating
    (b) failure to fully disclose information and lying
    (c) misrepresentation and false advertising
    (d) forgery and fraud

6. The text states that an insurance professional's full disclosure duties will
    (a) not include providing full and accurate application information to the carrier
    (b) be limited to providing the applicant with an Insurance Buyer's Guide
    (c) end with the closing of the sale and the delivery of the insurance policy
    (d) dictate that contact be maintained with the client until the policy matures or is terminated

7. The text states that marketing practices that financial services professionals (particularly those engaged in selling life insurance) should avoid include all of the following EXCEPT
    (a) false advertising
    (b) lack of full disclosure
    (c) the use of illustrations
    (d) unnecessary replacement

8. Financial services professionals should document each of the following elements of every sale EXCEPT
    (a) the reason for the product recommendation
    (b) the illustration used as the basis of the sale
    (c) the discovery agreement
    (d) a disclosure statement

9. Each of the following are among the keys to full disclosure EXCEPT
    (a) Provide your client with information about the product.
    (b) Provide your client with information about the company that is offering the product.
    (c) Provide your client with information about the illustration used in your sales presentation.
    (d) Provide your client with information regarding your role in the sales process.

10. The text states that all of the following are steps in the sales presentation process EXCEPT
    (a) The agent selects one or two recommendations that best serve the client's needs.
    (b) The agent meets with his or her client and makes the recommendation(s).
    (c) The agent explains to the client the reasons behind the recommendation(s).
    (d) The agent allows the client time to think over the recommendation(s).

8

Illustrations, Replacement, and Rebating

Learning Objectives
8-1. Identify the necessary steps for the proper use of computer-generated illustrations within the sales process.
8-2. Describe what circumstances constitute a replacement.
8-3. Explain when replacement is and is not an acceptable practice.
8-4. Describe what constitutes rebating.
8-5. List the key arguments for and against the legal use of rebating.

Chapter Outline

Illustrations 8-3
Illustration History and Evolution 8-3
Illustrations—What Are They? 8-4
Illustration Use 8-5
Model Regulations on Illustrations 8-6
Procedures for using Illustrations in the Sales Process 8-7
   Illustration Questionnaire (IQ) 8-7
   Illustrations and Policy Comparisons 8-8
   Advanced Premium Arrangements or Premium Offset: "The
      Vanishing Premium" 8-8
   Documentation of Illustration Use 8-10
   Regulation of Illustrations for Specialized Policies 8-10
Six Necessary Steps in an Ethically Sound Sales Process 8-12
   1. Gain Client Attention 8-12
   2. Explain Policy Structure 8-12
   3. Illustrate Downside Risk 8-13
   4. Clarify Coverage Components 8-13
   5. Explain Who Bears What Risk 8-13
   6. Comply with Regulations and Mandated Standards 8-13

Replacement and Rebating 8-14
Replacement 8-14
   Replacement versus Twisting 8-15
NAIC Replacement Guidelines 8-15
Examples of Inappropriate Replacement 8-17
Rebating 8-18
Pros and Cons of Laws Prohibiting Rebating 8-18
   Why Rebating Should Not Be Allowed 8-19
   Why Rebating Should Be Allowed 8-20
Current Status of the Regulation of Rebates 8-22
Other Marketplace Practice Issues in Today's Selling Environment 8-23
   Product Identification 8-23
   Dividend Description 8-24
   Guaranty Fund Advertising 8-24
   NASD Endorsement 8-24
   Unauthorized Practice of Law 8-25
Unauthorized Insurance Carrier 8-25

Chapter 8 Review Questions 8-27

Illustrations

In the life insurance industry, one of the prominent examples of misrepresentation and lack of disclosure was found in the blatant misuse of illustrations.

In selling insurance products as well as some other financial products, the professional must provide illustrations of possible future gains or losses. Illustrations are a focal point in the ethics of financial services. Most financial advisors provide their clients with product illustrations prior to the close of a sale. Sales illustrations can be useful tools to demonstrate how a product works. They can help a client make an informed decision. They can, however, be a source of ethical conflict. Rather than serving as a disclosure vehicle, illustrations can be improperly used as a vehicle that entices a client to buy, by distorting and misrepresenting the future operation of the financial product. Remind your clients that illustrations are not exact predictions of how a particular product's values will look in the future. Only guaranteed values are guaranteed.

Illustration History and Evolution

In the life insurance industry, policy illustrations were fairly bland and standardized for many years. Illustrations were prepared by home office units. They showed estimated cash values and dividends on traditional whole life policies. The illustrations were fairly straightforward and represented a close approximation of what actually developed in future years.

Illustrations began to change in the 1980s. Technology became more sophisticated and facilitated the illustration of a greater range of variables. At the same time, the product portfolio began to change dramatically with the introduction of universal life insurance. Life insurance was viewed more as an investment product consisting of mortality and side-fund components.

Illustrations followed suit and used historically high double-digit interest rates as the basis for projected values. These values were far in excess of policy guarantees. As long as interest rates remained high, no one seemed to notice the difference between what was projected and what was guaranteed. However, when interest rates began to fall, projected values did not hold up. Policyowners began receiving notices telling them of the need for increased or continued premiums. Consumers have used illustrations produced in the early 1980s, for example, as the basis of complaints that policies did not perform as expected. Agents began receiving angry letters from clients and their attorneys. Charges of unethical behavior were made. Both individual agents and the insurers suffered tarnished reputations. Insurers spent billions of dollars to satisfy the claims of disgruntled policyowners.

Review Item

Time Crunch

Agent Myra Jones:

"Joe, may I ask you a question?"

Client Joe Dunkirk:

"I have no time. Just get me some coverage."

How would you respond?

Log your answer in the space below.

Illustrations—What Are They?

A clearer understanding of what an illustration is and what it is meant to accomplish is one way of avoiding future consumer dissatisfaction. This is why it is so important for financial advisors to explain the role and limitation of the insurance illustration to a client both before and after a sale is made.

An illustration starts as a ledger sheet of numbers provided by an insurance company. Some of the figures on the ledger sheet are guaranteed by the issuing company, other figures are not guaranteed. An illustration is like a snapshot. It shows how a particular policy would operate at a particular time if all the underlying variables were to occur exactly as planned.

People in a snapshot do not remain static after the picture is taken and neither do the figures in a ledger sheet. Variables can and do change, sometimes to the benefit of the client and sometimes to the client's detriment.

We need to explain the variables behind policy illustrations to our clients. Dividend scales, credited interest rates, and mortality charges are among the variables that should be discussed.

For example, a client must understand whether or not a company reserves the right to change mortality charges. The client must further understand the possible implications of such a change. If a world-wide flu epidemic such as the one of 1918 should occur with numerous ensuing deaths, policy mortality charges would likely rise. On the other hand, if the population continues to enjoy increased longevity, policy mortality charges are likely to remain stable or fall.

Clients who understand that an illustration is just that—an illustration—are less likely to file complaints or feel that they have made a wrong purchase decision. These clients also spread the word—insurance is a wise purchase. Such talk is good for the industry and good for our careers. In other words, by explaining the role of the illustration to a client, we are practicing good ethics that translates into good business.

Illustration Use

Agents who historically have sold insurance on the basis of illustrations alone are engaged in an unwise practice. Because of recent bad publicity, some financial services professionals have simply decided not to use illustrations as part of the sales process. However, the NAIC Model Illustration Act requires that an insured receive an illustration at some point in the life insurance purchasing process.

While sympathizing with the financial services professional's concerns over using illustrations, we recommend their use. Properly presented, illustrations are legitimate sales tools that help agents provide clients with full disclosure about the products being considered. Illustrations also provide agents with a documentation mechanism.

Agents who choose not to use illustrations as part of the sales process close off two avenues that facilitate good marketplace practices.

- Without an illustration, an agent runs the risk of forgetting to disclose important information. For example, a client may not realize that there are guaranteed and nonguaranteed elements involved in policy performance. Several years after the sale, the client may discover this on his or her own and become dissatisfied.
- An agent who sells without an illustration loses an opportunity to obtain important documentation of good marketplace practices for his or her files. If there is no illustration used during the presentation, there is no illustration for the client to sign and no file indicating exactly what was shown or discussed.

We wish to offer one caveat before concluding this section. Although we recommend the use of illustrations in the sales process, we want to reemphasize our belief that a decision to purchase a financial product cannot be made by simply reviewing the numbers on a ledger. There must be a need for the product. Before a final purchase decision is made, today's client will seek information regarding the company who sells the product. In other words, you should be prepared to provide your clients with information regarding the history of your company and its financial strength from two or three independent rating services.

Model Regulations on Illustrations

The National Association of Insurance Commissioners (NAIC) has taken an active interest in illustrations. It has recently promulgated model regulations on this subject. These regulations basically call for clients to be supplied with illustrations showing current assumptions together with more conservative assumptions developed under the technical aspects of the Model's guidelines and the Actuarial Standards Board.

Until your state adopts these new NAIC regulations, it is probably prudent to provide your client with illustrations showing the following:

- guaranteed values
- current return values
- current return values minus one percent—or, to be even more conservative, 2 percent (This guideline applies to newer-type interest or investment-sensitive policies.)

The NAIC Life Insurance Illustrations Model Regulation provides that the insurer's illustrated scale be used with the nonguaranteed element, reduced as follows:

- dividends at 50 percent of the current dividends contained in the illustrated scale used
- nonguaranteed credited interest at rates that are the average of the guaranteed rates and the current rates contained in the illustrated scale used
- all nonguaranteed charges, including but not limited to, term insurance charges and mortality and expense charges, at rates that are the average of the guaranteed rates and the current rates contained in the illustrated scale used

This takes time to explain. However, this type of client education pays off. Clients begin to anticipate how changes in interest rates can affect their cash values and premiums. If an unscrupulous agent follows you illustrating exaggerated returns, your clients will be able to spot the difference and your business is far more likely to remain on the books.

Procedures for Using Illustrations in the Sales Process

Illustration Questionnaire (IQ)

One disclosure tool with which all agents should be familiar is the *Illustration Questionnaire,* commonly referred to as the *IQ.* The *IQ* was developed by the Society of Financial Service Professionals. It is a set of questions designed to obtain information from an insurance company regarding the methods used in the generation of its illustrations— regarding or relating to life insurance proposals.

The purpose of the *IQ* is to help financial advisors obtain the information they need to understand, evaluate, and explain how the nonguaranteed elements of a life insurance policy can impact its future performance. Another purpose it serves is to help an insurance company convey information to its financial advisors. The more a financial advisor understands the product he or she is selling, the better the quality of information he or she is able to convey to the client. In other words, the *IQ* is one more tool in the financial advisor's client education kit.

Those interested in obtaining further information on the *IQ* should contact the Society of Financial Service Professionals in Bryn Mawr, Pennsylvania (800) 392-6900.

In addition to disclosure and adequate illustrations, there are other things necessary for a professional treatment of the sales process.

Illustrations and Policy Comparisons

Some agents try to compare policies based on illustrations. Are such comparisons valid? Probably not. It's like comparing apples and oranges. Such illustrations are designed to show how a particular product of a particular company works. These illustrations are not suitable for comparing the product of one company with the product of another. There are too many variables and the variables are inconsistent from company to company.

Policy selection starts with knowledge of the insurance product and analysis of the assumptions underlying each policy. Policies should be selected on criteria that include each company's financial circumstances and the quality of service. Other factors involved in policy selection include the quality and availability of service offered by the individual financial advisor representing the company.

Advanced Premium Arrangements or Premium Offset: "The Vanishing Premium"

Our discussion of policy illustrations would be incomplete without consideration of the concept known as advanced premium arrangements or premium offset, both of which sometimes referred to in the past as "the vanishing premium."

This premium offset concept is based on the premise that future premiums due after a policy has been in effect for a number of years need no longer be paid out-of-pocket by a policyowner. Instead, after a number of years, policy premiums are to be paid out of the cash value build-up of dividends.

In reality, premiums do not disappear. They are advanced or offset from policy dividends. Therefore, the concept is more accurately described as an advanced premium arrangement or premium offset.

This concept was used in many sales presentations during the 1980s. Typically, the policyowner was told that the premiums would need to be paid for only 8 to 10 years. The projections were based on the high interest rates paid during that decade. Unfortunately, many policyowners did not understand or chose not to understand that continued high rates of return were necessary for the premise to work. With the advent of lower interest rates, many of these clients found that they had to continue to pay premiums in order to keep their policies in force.

Clients claimed that no one explained the fact that the rate of return on which the advanced premium arrangements had been based were not guaranteed. The result was dissatisfied policyowners and a black eye for the reputation of both the individual financial advisor and the company.

Lower interest rates do not invalidate the advanced premium concept. They simply move the target when no additional premiums need to be paid further into the future. The concept still has application. The key to its use is client education and proper disclosure of the concept's premise and parameters. A good place to begin is with an accurate description of the concept. Check with your company for preferred terminology. Avoid the use of the term "vanishing" as it implies that premiums cease, which they do not.

Review Item

Running the Numbers

Client Albert Byron:

"I see these figures are guaranteed. What about those?"

Agent Brian Beck:

"The numbers in that column. . . ."

How would you respond if you were Agent Beck?

Log your answer in the space below.

Good ethics and good business practice dictate that our illustrations show both guaranteed and nonguaranteed values. The difference must be clearly explained to the client. It is also important that an illustration show not only the concept based on current assumptions but also the amount of premiums necessary to maintain the original death benefit of a policy until maturity based on guarantees.

Use an illustration format provided by your carrier for the specific product involved if one is available. Do not use the premium offset concept if it is not approved by your carrier or allowed under state regulations.

Documentation of Illustration Use

You need to document your illustration work. We recommend that you use the company's illustration formats. In addition, we recommend that you take (to the policy delivery) three copies of the illustration used to close the sale. At that point, you and the client should sign all three illustration copies. Give one signed copy to the client. Retain one signed copy for your records. Finally, use one signed copy as a disclosure statement to be turned into the insurance carrier. The policyowner would acknowledge having read the policy illustration and noting the nonguaranteed elements. Agents verify that they have explained both the guaranteed and nonguaranteed elements of the policy. As more and more states adopt the NAIC Life Insurance Illustrations Model Regulation, this final step will become a mandatory element of the selling process.

These steps provide evidence of the illustration specifically used for the insurance policy should any questions arise in the future. They stress to the client the importance of understanding just what an illustration is and what it is not.

Regulation of Illustrations for Specialized Policies

Many insurance professionals meet client needs with a variety of specialized products. These include blended policies, second-to-die policies, and senior citizen policies. The illustrations prepared for these policies require particular attention to client education and ethical concerns. What follows are some suggestions about the obligations we have in presenting and selling these types of products.

Blended Policies—Blended policies are combinations of permanent insurance and term riders. These policies serve the needs of many individuals who require high amounts of coverage but cannot currently afford to pay permanent insurance rates. The blended policy solves this problem by locking in insurability at an affordable cost. Clients who purchase these policies must be educated as to their components and the implications of those components.

Second-to-Die Policies—These policies are designed to pay a death benefit at the death of the second insured. Clients must be educated to the fact that although both parties may be insured, there is no payment at the first insured's death. Changes that occur in the policies at the first death should also be clarified.

Another sensitive issue involves what happens to the policy in the case of a divorce of insured parties. Clearly explain your company's policies. As we have suggested before, documentation is frequently important to demonstrate the thoroughness of your business practices. Follow up your discussions of these policy provisions with a letter enclosing explanatory materials provided by your company.

Senior Citizen Policies—Some insurance professionals sell policies aimed at the over-age-60 seniors market. These policies frequently limit the level of death benefits during a period following the inception date of the policy. Sometimes these policies are designed so that accumulated premiums exceed policy death benefits during the first 10 years when the policy is in force. If you sell such a policy, be aware that the NAIC model disclosure law specifies that the policyowner must be given a free look of 30 days. This is longer than the ordinary 10-day free-look period. In addition, you are required to provide the senior policyowner with a special insurance guide. NAIC Model Regulations also specify that a policy financial review form be provided to a client.

Universal Life Policies—The NAIC has drafted model legislation that applies to universal life products. The NAIC specifies that purchasers of universal life be supplied with a special statement of policy information. The aim here is to alert the policyowner to the fact that he or she has bought a universal life product and not a traditional whole life product. Whether or not your state has currently adopted the NAIC model legislation, follow its overall dictates and educate your client about the differences between universal life insurance and traditional life insurance.

Annuity Products—The NAIC has endorsed a new Annuity Disclosure Model Regulation. The purpose of this regulation is to provide standards for the disclosure of a certain minimal amount of information about annuity contracts to protect consumers and foster consumer education. The regulation specifies the minimum information that must be disclosed and the method for disclosing it in connection with the sale of annuity contracts. The goal of the regulation is to ensure that purchasers of annuity contracts understand certain basic features of annuity contracts.

You may find compliance with these guidelines cumbersome. Keep in mind, however, that the guidelines protect not only policyowners but also financial services professionals. Financial advisors who follow these guidelines demonstrate and provide proof of ethical behavior.

Six Necessary Steps in an Ethically Sound Sales Process

We conclude this section by outlining what is required for an ethically sound sales process.

1. Gain Client Attention

Before you start to discuss a product with a client, make sure you gain his or her attention and convey the importance of the information that you are about to relay. Sometimes a client appears to be disinterested. He or she may say that your advice is trustworthy and no further explanation is required. This may be flattering, but it is potentially dangerous to your relationship with the client.

We suggest that you handle such a situation by telling the client that part of your job is to make sure he or she understands what is being proposed. Keep in mind that if there are any future misunderstandings or dissatisfactions with the product, the client or the potential beneficiaries are unlikely to remember their initial disinterest. The responsibility will rest on your shoulders.

Document your efforts through a follow-up letter outlining the proposal and explanation.

2. Explain Policy Structure

Educate your client on the structure of a life insurance policy and how it works. An illustration can help you do this by demonstrating the three key components that your client must understand, namely, the premium, the cash value, and the death benefit. The properly constructed illustration will also help you explain the difference between guaranteed and nonguaranteed cash values and death benefits.

3. Illustrate Downside Risk

Seriously consider the use of more than one illustration to show the downside risk in policy performance. This will help to demonstrate how the recommended policy is expected to perform under various market conditions. It will also help to set realistic performance expectations in the client's mind.

4. Clarify Coverage Components

Sometimes a portion of the insurance coverage is provided by term riders paid for with dividends or excess interest. Dividends and excess interest are not guaranteed elements of a life insurance policy. They change over time as a company's actual experience varies from its original assumptions. Often clients do not understand this. Be sure your clients are not among this group. Fully explain what portion is term and what portion is permanent coverage and how each portion is being funded. Don't let your client be under the assumption that his or her blended policy is just another name for traditional permanent coverage with all its guarantees.

5. Explain Who Bears What Risk

Nearly all insurance coverage sold today contains both a level of guaranteed performance plus enhancements beyond those guarantees. This dual performance system of minimum guarantees combined with potential enhancement is unique to the life insurance product. This is one reason why it is so difficult for many consumers to understand this product. As part of the illustration disclosure process, educate your client on the risks involved. In other words, point out that the insurance company bears the risk on the guaranteed elements in the policy while the client bears the risks on the nonguaranteed elements.

6. Comply with Regulations and Mandated Standards

Most companies now provide their financial advisors and brokers with guidelines regarding the illustrations that will be provided to clients. These guidelines have been drafted for the protection of the client, the company, and you, and failure to follow them puts your career at risk. Failure to follow them could create unrealistic expectations on the part of the client and could leave the carrier open to lawsuits, impeding its ability to operate on a competitive basis. Failure to follow these guidelines can mean limitations in your E&O coverage and can also weaken your legal position should client complaints arise at a future date.

Replacement and Rebating

In addition to misrepresentation, lack of disclosure, and misuse of illustrations, there are two other significant practices that are subject to ethical abuse and need to be examined: replacement and rebating.

Replacement

Replacement is a very broad term. It means more than just substituting one life insurance policy or annuity contract for another one that was issued earlier. It includes situations where existing life insurance policy or annuity benefits are terminated or modified in conjunction with the purchase of a new life insurance policy or annuity, or where existing life policy or annuity values are used to fund a new life policy or annuity. Replacement is usually not in the best interest of a client.

Review Item
Application Information
Client Molly Fenwick:
"Why do you need to know all this information? I like my privacy."
How would you respond?
Log your answer in the space below.

The chief ethical rule is this: Policy replacement should always be focused on the best interest of the client. Careful compliance with state regulations is one way of ensuring that both you and the client have the information necessary to decide whether the replacement is in his or her best interest. The new policy should be based on the client's needs, and it is prudent to document the specific needs satisfied by the new insurance. If replacement is appropriate, the transaction should be done as a tax-free exchange under Section 1035 of the Internal Revenue Code so it remains tax favored.

Replacement versus Twisting

Many financial services professionals are familiar with the term twisting, but twisting and replacement are often confused. Replacement is legal and in many cases ethical. Twisting is not.

Twisting is unnecessary replacement of a product to benefit the financial advisor or the broker. It occurs when a financial advisor induces a client to drop existing coverage without clearly explaining the benefits that will be lost under the old policy. In addition, there is often a failure to reveal the new costs involved with taking out a new policy or the effect of new policy coverage on access to cash values. In other words, twisting can be considered a form of misrepresentation. In most cases, it is motivated by financial advisors seeking commission dollars.

Twisting can be external or internal. Agents may unethically replace policies sold by other companies or replace old policies issued by their own carrier in prior years.

Piggybacking is another type of replacement activity. It is the practice of using existing policy values, whether through a loan, dividend withdrawal, or partial or full cash surrender, to fund a new policy. Like twisting, piggybacking can be illegal and unethical.

NAIC Replacement Guidelines

In recognition of the potential abuses that surround replacements, the NAIC drafted a Life Insurance and Annuities Replacement Model Regulation that most states have adopted.. The model requires a financial advisor who is replacing a product to comply with detailed disclosure rules in order to protect policyowner interests.

The disclosure rules require that the policyowner be provided with enough information to make a comparison between current and proposed coverage. The rules first require the insurance professional to make a determination about whether or not replacement is involved in a particular sales situation. That may sound simple, but replacement is a complex concept.

The NAIC defines replacement as follows:

"Replacement means a transaction in which a new policy or contract is to be purchased, and it is known or should be known to the proposing producer, or to the proposing insurer if there is no producer, that by reason of the transaction, an existing policy or contract has been or is to be:

- lapsed, forfeited, surrendered or partially surrendered, assigned to the replacing insurer or otherwise terminated;

- converted to reduced paid-up insurance, continued as extended term insurance, or otherwise reduced in value by the use of nonforfeiture benefits or other policy values;

- amended so as to effect either reduction in benefits or in the term for which coverage would otherwise remain in force or which benefits would be paid;

- reissued with any reduction in cash value; or

- loans used to finance the purchase of a new policy."

If, in fact, replacement is involved, the financial advisor must provide the policyowner with a special form. This form is called *Notice Regarding Replacement.*

The Notice Regarding Replacement form enables policyowners to obtain up-to-date information on their existing coverage in order to compare it with newly proposed coverage. In addition, the NAIC model regulation provides for notification of the proposed replacement to the existing carrier. Where external replacement is involved, this encourages policyowners to confer with representatives of their current carrier. Where internal replacement is involved, this helps to assure compliance with internal company rules.

The replacement compliance rules protect both the consumer and the financial services professional. If a replacement does, in fact, occur, its reasons and justification will be clearly documented.

Producers should remember that they are vulnerable to legal action for damages should they fail to disclose to the client any material consequences of a replacement transaction, such as a decrease in coverage, loss of cash value, or an increase in premium. Producers should also keep in mind that failure to comply with state insurance laws and regulations can result in fines, license suspension, or termination. Additionally, material misrepresentation or nondisclosure in the context of a replacement transaction involving an equity product, such as a variable life policy, can constitute violation of the securities laws.

Examples of Inappropriate Replacement

No two life insurance clients have the exact same goals or financial needs. Therefore, applying one set of rules to fit all situations is virtually impossible when deciding whether or not to make a replacement. Here, however, are some examples of when replacement may be inappropriate.

- **First-Year Commission**—Your client obtained coverage several years ago from a highly rated company. The policy cash values are building. The client has just broken even between premium dollars and cash values. You can offer a slightly different policy and full commissions will be payable. Cash value that the client has built up will be consumed in meeting initial costs of the new policy. The numbers show the new policy is simply not cost effective in comparison with the established coverage.
- **Suicide and Incontestable Provisions**—Your client has a policy that has been in force for 5 years. Contestability provisions have already been met. Your client's father had a history of severe depression requiring, at one point, institutionalization. This concerns your client. Replacement means starting suicide and contestable periods anew.
- **Declining Health**—Your client took out a policy several years ago at standard rates. Since that time he has had heart surgery. New coverage would come with a high rating.
- **Increasing Age**—Your client took out a policy when she was 30 years old. It is 10 years later and the premium for the same coverage has increased over time.
- **Attractive Loan Rates**—Your client's current coverage provides her with the ability to borrow against cash values at a 5 percent guaranteed loan rate. She has borrowed and repaid loans several times. The face value of the policy, however, is inadequate to meet her needs. Your initial suggestion was to

replace this coverage, but a better solution would be to write new, additional coverage.

- **Adverse Tax Consequences**—Many times a client considers replacing a policy that has large outstanding loans. The law does permit the income-tax-free exchange of one life insurance policy for another.

   However, if a policy loan is not carried over from the old policy to the new one, the loan is not part of the income-tax-free exchange. This can lead to adverse tax consequences. Your client has a large loan outstanding on her policy, which she does not wish to currently repay. Your company will not roll over the loan. Your best course of action is to tell your client to get specific advice on the tax consequences.

To sum up: If you are going to replace a client's policy, make sure it is in the client's best interest. That means you have to evaluate all of the pros and cons of the replacement activity. To replace a life insurance policy, simply to generate commissions for yourself is the height of unethical behavior for the financial services professional.

Rebating

Another practice that comes under fire in the insurance industry is the practice of rebating. Rebating is an effective sales tool in many areas, such as an automobile dealer offering a rebate when selling a car. But the situation is different in selling life nsurance.

In selling life insurance, rebating involves reducing the premium or giving some other valuable consideration not specified in the policy to the buyer as an inducement to purchase the insurance. The classic rebate situation involves a financial advisor giving a portion of his or her commission that reduces the first premium in order to induce the prospect to insure.

Pros and Cons of Laws Prohibiting Rebating

Why would there be opposition to rebating? Financial advisors generally tend to view rebates as unwarranted pressure on their compensation. They also believe that widespread rebating would adversely affect both the insurance-consuming public and insurers in several ways including the following.

Why Rebating Should Not Be Allowed

1. **Rebating Would Be Unfair**—Rebating would result in varying first-year charges to similarly situated policyowners, thereby, fostering unfair discrimination against those consumers not possessing either economic leverage to demand rebates (that is, purchasers of small amounts of coverage) or the knowledge to do so. If forced to make rebates in selected situations to meet the competition, financial advisors would be forced to demand higher commissions from their insurers in order to make a living. Eventually, such increased commissions would work their way back into the cost of the product, which would result in higher premiums across the board for policyowners, many of whom would be unable to demand and obtain rebates.

2. **Rebating Has an Adverse Impact on Companies' Financial Condition**—Further, permitting rebates could lead to the ruinous competition that initiated the bans in the first place nearly 100 years ago. Intense competition through rebates may adversely impact the financial condition of insurers (perhaps to the point of insolvency). This could be rooted in increased early year lapse rates resulting from replacements, thereby preventing insurers from recovering issue expenses normally amortized over several years. Weakened financial conditions also could emerge from the pressure on the insurer to raise commission rates to enable financial advisors to compete even though the insurer might be unable to raise premiums to recover the increased expenses because of competition in the marketplace.

3. **It Leads to Unnecessary Replacements**—Rebates afford a powerful tool for those financial advisors inclined to replace policies. Utilizing the lure of rebates, an agent can more easily encourage a policyowner to replace his or her existing policy, thereby incurring the expensive burden of another set of acquisition costs. In situations where replacement is not warranted in terms of policyowner interest, the availability of rebating exacerbates the replacement problem.

4. **Causes Shortage of Financial Advisors and Adverse Public Effects**—Larger agencies and more established financial advisors tend to be better positioned to offer significant rebates. Consequently, the removal of the ban on rebating would encourage

the concentration of agency forces, would favor the more established financial advisors, and would result in increased turnover of financial advisors, especially new ones who already have a difficult time surviving long enough to develop a viable career. In turn, these impacts could aggravate the shortage of financial advisors in life insurance agencies, thereby reducing the number of financial advisors available to service the public and limiting competition in the marketplace. Furthermore, in view of the generally held axiom that life insurance is sold rather than bought, the fewer the number of financial advisors, the smaller the amount of life insurance sales and, in turn, the greater the underinsurance of this nation's population.

5. **Weakens Quality of Policyowner Decision Making**—The availability of rebates detracts from the likelihood of prospective policyowners making the best decisions for themselves in purchasing long-term contracts of life insurance. Encouraging prospective buyers to focus on the size of the rebates in the first year (a very small portion of the total cost of insurance over the life of the policy) will tend to reduce the quality of buyer discernment in comparing prices. Perhaps the gravest danger posed by rebating is the all-too-real possibility that the buyers will be more influenced by the size of the rebate, that is, by the "deal" they can make, than by the merits of the insurance contract, the total long-range costs, the nature and suitability of the products, and the quality of the financial advisor's counseling and service.

Why Rebating Should Be Allowed

Despite these public policy arguments, the 1980s witnessed increasing agitation for the elimination of the ban against rebating. The critics of antirebate laws maintain the following.

1. **Laws Against Rebating Are Anticompetitive**—The rebate laws are anticompetitive by needlessly sheltering financial advisors from competition, thereby contributing to excessive insurance costs. Consumer opportunity to negotiate between financial advisors for a better price is barred. In contrast, the removal of the ban on rebates will focus on competition for the consumers' business rather than insurers simply competing for financial advisors to market their products. Permitting rebates would contribute to lower costs for at least some consumers.

2. **Rebating Permits Less Competent Financial Advisors to Compete While Consumers Pay More**—In stifling competition between financial advisors, the ban on rebates permits the less competent or inefficient ones to be compensated on a basis equivalent to that of those who are the most knowledgeable and efficient. The absence of competition reduces incentives for providing superior service. The essence of negotiated commissions is the ability of the consumer to purchase the amount and quality of services desired and needed. In contrast, under the fixed-commission system, the consumer may obtain a particular service only by paying for the full range of services the financial advisor offers. Whether the consumer wants, needs, or actually utilizes the financial advisor's services does not affect the price paid.

3. **Rebate-Caused Discrimination is Not Unfair**—Rebating does not give rise to unfair discrimination. The life insurance business is replete with examples of discrimination. (Remember, it is only unfair discrimination that is prohibited.) Economies of size garner better rates. Insurers discriminate in underwriting by allocating policyowners to different rate classifications. Group insurance policyowners enjoy the lower costs associated with the absence of the high first-year commissions paid on individual policy sales. Financial advisors discriminate in selecting their prospects.

4. **The Amount and Quality of Service**—Similarly, buyers should be able to select from among several financial advisors and vary their costs based on the amount and quality of work performed by them. A knowledgeable buyer who needs little prospecting, analysis, or research should not be compelled to pay the same commission as a difficult customer who utilizes far more of the financial advisor's time.

We conclude the discussion of the pros and cons of rebating by quoting Jon Hanson, who says, "It is not the function here to resolve the merits of the dispute over the continued appropriateness of the antirebate laws. However, a wider and better understanding of the pros and cons by those interested in the insurance business should contribute to a better resolution of the issue if and when it comes up for debate in a given state."[1]

---

1. Jon S. Hanson, *Regulation of the Life Insurance Business*, pp. 116–119, © 1996 The American College, Bryn Mawr, PA.

Current Status of the Regulation of Rebates

In 1986, the Florida Supreme Court overturned that state's law prohibiting rebates as a violation of the Florida Constitution's due process clause. In the court's view, the ban on rebating commissions has no legitimate state interest. It bears no reasonable relationship to the health, safety and welfare of the citizens of Florida. For many persons, including courts in other states, the Florida Supreme Court's due process analysis has proven unpersuasive.

While acknowledging that rebating is now legal in California, several life insurers in California have taken the position that it is within their right to refuse to deal with agents who do rebate. The California insurance department moved against insurers who fired an agent who offered his customers commission rebates. An administrative law judge concluded that it is not an unfair business practice for life insurers to do so. Although initially indicating that he would not accept the judge's ruling, the insurance commissioner ultimately concluded that insurers may fire agents who rebate. Proposition 103 repealed the prohibition against rebates. Insurers may fire those financial advisors who engage in such practices if doing so constitutes a violation of their agency contracts with the insurer.

Elsewhere, to date, the arguments and influence of the proponents of the ban against rebating have prevailed in both public policy forums and judicial challenges. Other than in Florida, judicial challenges to the antirebate laws have proven unsuccessful. Only in California has a comparable result been achieved by voter referendum. In the other 48 states, the antirebate laws remain intact. Unless change should be compelled at the federal level, it appears that the antirebate provision will remain the law in the vast majority of states at least for the immediate future. While rebating in Florida and California is legal, the legal climate remains hostile.

Today, the consumer movement and various court decisions have reopened the topic of rebates. Rebating is still both illegal and unethical in almost all jurisdictions. These states recognize that insurance rebating is different from other types of coupons, such as those available in food markets. The same amount of rebate is unlikely to be available to all consumers. In an argument we have seen above, they suggest that rebates can, in effect, result in discrimination between those who have the power and the means to negotiate better net costs and those who don't.

Florida is a notable exception in that it clearly permits rebates. Even in Florida, however, rebates must be offered according to strict guidelines designed to prevent discrimination. The law is currently evolving in California.

If you do business in a state that prohibits rebating, your ethical and legal obligation is to follow the law and not rebate. If you do business in a state where rebating is allowed, be sure to comply with insurance department guidelines. In addition, check with your company. Rebating may be against company policy even in states where it is legal. Violation of company guidelines can lead to termination and permanently jeopardize your career.

Other Marketplace Practice Issues in Today's Selling Environment

Other areas that require careful conduct are

- product identification
- dividend descriptions
- guaranty fund advertising
- NASD endorsement of variable products
- unauthorized practice of law

Product Identification

In our discussion of illustrations, we mentioned the need to clearly identify the particular type of product being sold to a client. In other words, the client should understand not only that he or she is buying life insurance but its generic type, such as a 10-year term. You may use the company's name, whether or not it contains the word "life insurance," to describe a product to a client. For example, you may call the product "Ajax Company Modified Premium Mode," but you must make sure the client understands that this is a whole life insurance policy. If the company's proprietary name does not mention life insurance, you must add this to the information you provide to the client.

Once again, in regard to product identification it is important to emphasize the insurance nature of a life insurance product. It is unethical to try to disguise the life insurance product by emphasizing its tax benefits and accumulation features. Your client must understand that the death benefit is the key feature offered by a life insurance policy. Not only is it unethical, it's illegal to do otherwise.

Dividend Description

It's tempting to link life insurance dividends to stock dividends, but there is a major difference between the two. Life insurance dividends represent a return of premium. They are not interest earned on the cash values, nor are they earnings on life insurance company stock. Stock dividends represent a distribution of corporate profits. Clients should understand this difference. Clients should also understand that life insurance dividends are not guaranteed. Therefore, whether or not they are paid and the amount that is paid may vary over time.

Guaranty Fund Advertising

Individual states establish guaranty funds to protect the life insurance benefits of their residents. These funds received substantial attention in the early 1990s during the insolvency crisis faced by our industry. The fact that your state has a generous level of benefits covered by its guaranty fund or that the policy you are proposing is covered by such a fund are not factors that should be used to influence your client's purchasing decision. In other words, a state guaranty fund cannot be advertised in a manner similar to FDIC insurance.

NASD Endorsement

The NASD works basically in an oversight, information-gathering capacity regarding variable products. It does not endorse the recommendations given by financial advisors who are either registered representatives or registered investment advisors. It does not provide a government guarantee for the products sold by financial advisors who are licensed to sell variable life insurance and annuities. Agents who imply that NASD registration is an endorsement, approval, or guarantee are acting in violation of its rules.

Unauthorized Practice of Law

Today's life insurance agent is increasingly involved in more complex sales as a result of client demands. For example, more clients are interested in estate planning. More clients are concerned about retirement. Many times our clients will ask for our advice as part of our involvement in these complex sales situations. This can inadvertently lead to the unauthorized practice of law. As a rule of thumb, you may provide a client with general advice about these issues.

For example, you may point out that the estate tax law allows an individual a certain amount of credit against the estate tax. However, you must be careful that your advice does not become too specific. For example, you should not redraft your company's model retirement plan agreement nor should you provide your client with a filled-in life insurance trust agreement. Those who practice the law require specific licensing. This is a rule that exists in all states. To practice law without being admitted to the state bar is a violation of the law.

Realize that there are many times when you must be part of the client's professional team. The client's attorney and CPA are likely to be other members of that team. Let them do their jobs. Let them serve as centers of influence for your role as a financial advisor.

One final tip in dealing with attorneys: provide the client's attorney with the model agreements supplied by your company. Let the attorney know you are knowledgeable, but let him or her draft the final document and provide the specific legal advice. It's good ethics…and it's good business!

Unauthorized Insurance Carrier

One final obligation of financial advisors must be addressed. Financial services professionals have an obligation to make sure the carrier they represent is licensed to do business in the state where they solicit the sale of life insurance policies. Each state has laws specifying that only admitted carriers may issue life insurance policies within its boundaries.

Failure to follow this rule can have serious consequences for both the policyowner and the financial advisor. Policyowners are jeopardized because state guaranty funds typically are set aside to cover only losses of admitted carriers. This means that the policyowner may lose all benefits of coverage should the unauthorized carrier run into financial difficulties.

Solvency concerns faced by the insurance industry should serve as a warning to any financial advisor contemplating placing business with an unauthorized insurer. Taking such a step puts both the client and the financial advisor at risk.

This risk may emanate directly from state insurance laws that hold the financial advisor personally liable for any client losses arising out of business placed with an unauthorized carrier. The client may bring additional legal action against the financial advisor based on more generalized concepts of malpractice.

Good ethical and business practice dictates that you investigate the company(ies) you represent. Potentially higher commissions cannot repay you for the risks involved in representing an unauthorized carrier. If you are uncertain about whether or not your company is authorized to conduct business in a state in which you solicit business, call your home office.

Chapter 8 Review Questions

Answers to Chapter Review Questions start on appendix page A-53.

1. Which of the following statements regarding twisting and replacement of life insurance policies is correct?
   - (a) Twisting is legal.
   - (b) Replacement is illegal.
   - (c) Twisting is illegal.
   - (d) Twisting is confined to internal policy transfers.

2. Illustrations should be described as
   - (a) binding legal documents prepared by state insurance departments
   - (b) nonbinding legal documents prepared by state insurance departments
   - (c) ledger sheets of guaranteed numbers prepared by an insurance company
   - (d) ledger sheet of guaranteed and nonguaranteed figures prepared by an insurance company

3. Rebating is legal in which of the following states?
   - (a) Colorado and Florida
   - (b) Connecticut and Florida
   - (c) California and Florida
   - (d) Colorado and Connecticut

4. Which of the following statements best describes the text's definition of rebating?
   - (a) Rebating is the process of reducing the premium from a secondary policy in order to credit another competing policy.
   - (b) Rebating involves reducing the premium or giving some other valuable consideration not specified in the policy to the buyer as an inducement to purchase insurance.
   - (c) Rebating involves reducing a premium or giving some other consideration to the writing agent as commission for a pending sale.
   - (d) Rebating is the process of giving the consumer added dividends from insurance company assets as compensation for poorly performing policies.

5. Universal life policy illustrations
   (a) have increased in accuracy due to the introduction of computer technology in the 1980s
   (b) contractually lock in projections of illustrated cash values
   (c) should be prepared showing guaranteed values, current return values, and current return values reduced according to NAIC guidelines
   (d) should be prepared solely on the basis of historical past returns

6. Failure to follow company illustration guidelines is
   (a) inconsequential because they generally impede a financial advisor's ability to sell in an ethical manner
   (b) likely to create unrealistic expectations on the part of the client.
   (c) immaterial to the legal liability faced by a carrier
   (d) a valid and recognized method of avoiding the conflict-of-interest dilemma between carriers and insurers

7. In light of recent compliance concerns, which of the following statements is correct?
   (a) Financial advisors should discontinue the use of all illustrations.
   (b) Financial advisors should discontinue the use of illustrations that contain nonguaranteed values.
   (c) Financial advisors should use illustrations with due regard for full disclosure.
   (d) Financial advisors should use illustrations as their primary sales tool.

8. The sale of a life insurance policy issued by an unauthorized insurer may
   (a) present no difficulty to policyowners because unauthorized carriers typically self-insure
   (b) jeopardize policyowners because state guaranty funds typically cover losses only of admitted carriers
   (c) be permitted in a jurisdiction in which neither the agent nor the insured maintains legal contacts
   (d) add to unauthorized carrier costs by forcing carriers to contribute to multistate guaranty fund compacts

9. All of the following are "other marketplace practice issues in today's selling environment" that require careful conduct EXCEPT
   (a) product identification
   (b) company ratings
   (c) guaranty fund advertising
   (d) unauthorized practice of law

10. Each of the following circumstances that involves an existing life insurance policy or contract constitutes a replacement EXCEPT
    (a) when a policy is lapsed, forfeited, surrendered or partially surrendered
    (b) when a policy is converted to reduced paid-up insurance
    (c) when a policy is reissued with any reduction in cash value
    (d) when a policy is converted from term insurance to whole life insurance

Appendix

The LUTC Fellow Pledge — A-1

NAIFA Code of Ethics — A-2

The American College Code of Ethics — A-3

Code of Professional Responsibility
of the Society of Financial Service
Professionals — A-8

MDRT Code of Ethics — A-22

Certified Financial Planner Code of
Ethics and Professional Responsibility — A-23

What You Should Know about Buying
Life Insurance — A-43

Answer Key to Review Questions — A-53

The LUTC Fellow Pledge

"As an LUTC Fellow, I recognize that the designation carries with it certain duties and responsibilities. And so, guided by the precepts of the Code of Ethics of the National Association of Life Underwriters, I reaffirm that I believe it to be my responsibility:

To hold my profession in high esteem and strive to enhance its prestige

To fulfill the needs of my clients to the best of my ability

To maintain my clients' confidences

To render exemplary service to my clients and their beneficiaries

To adhere to professional standards of conduct in helping my clients to protect insurable obligations and attain their financial security objectives

To present accurately and honestly all facts essential to my clients' decisions

To perfect my skills and increase my knowledge through continuing education

To conduct my business in such a way that my example might help raise the professional standard of life underwriting

To keep informed with respect to applicable laws and regulations and to observe them in the practice of my profession

To cooperate with others whose services are constructively related to meeting the needs of my clients."

NAIFA Code of Ethics

Preamble

Those engaged in offering insurance and other related financial services occupy the unique position of liaison between the purchasers and the suppliers of insurance and closely related financial products. Inherent in this role is the combination of professional duty to the client and to the company as well. Ethical balance is required to avoid any conflict between these two obligations.

Therefore,

I Believe It To Be My Responsibility:

- To hold my profession in high esteem and strive to enhance its prestige.

- To fulfill the needs of my clients to the best of my ability.

- To maintain my clients' confidences.

- To render exemplary service to my clients and their beneficiaries.

- To adhere to professional standards of conduct in helping my clients to protect insurable obligations and attain their financial security objectives.

- To present accurately and honestly all facts essential to my clients' decisions.

- To perfect my skills and increase my knowledge through continuing education.

- To conduct my business in such a way that my example might help raise the professional standards of those in my profession.

- To keep informed with respect to applicable laws and regulations and to observe them in the practice of my profession.

- To cooperate with others whose services are constructively related to meeting the needs of my clients.

The American College Code of Ethics

Throughout the life span of The American College, education and ethics have been inextricably combined. Dr. Solomon S. Huebner, the pioneering educator who founded the College, seldom spoke of education without also speaking of ethics. To him a professional relationship between agent and client had to be based on sound ethical principles.

At the College, courses and designations have changed over the years, but the ethical emphasis has remained constant and all new students enter a designation program aware that it involves more than just education.

Until recently that has been enough.

Now a new climate surrounds financial services. Institutional lines and prerogatives have become blurred. The role of those who serve the financial needs of the public has changed. Competition has increased. New products and services abound.

In this climate the College feels an imperative to be more forceful in the application of long-standing ethical principles. What was once a matter of persuasion is now a matter of requirement.

RATIONALE FOR THE CODE OF ETHICS

The College's major programs are of two distinct types. Some lead to degrees that are based solely on educational achievement and have no postgraduation ethical requirements. Those that lead to designations, however, have not only educational and experience prerequisites but also ethical requirements that continue beyond graduation and require the maintenance of ongoing standards of conduct. The display of a designation is a continuing representation that the holder will act competently and ethically in all professional relationships.

Before conferring a designation, the College has historically examined the experience as well as the educational and ethical qualifications of candidates for its designations. Unless an individual acted fraudulently to obtain a designation, no postgraduation action to remove a designation was ever taken. However, since the adoption in June 1984 of the College's Code of Ethics, the board of trustees has acted to assure postconferment fidelity to the ethical standards that accompany Huebner School designations.

THE PROFESSIONAL PLEDGE AND THE CANONS

The Code consists of two parts: the Professional Pledge and eight Canons.

The Pledge to which all Huebner School designees subscribe is: "In all my professional relationships, I pledge myself to the following rule of ethical conduct: I shall, in light of all conditions surrounding those I serve, which I shall make every conscientious effort to ascertain and understand, render that service which, in the same circumstances, I would apply to myself."

The eight Canons are:

I.   Conduct yourself at all times with honor and dignity.
II. Avoid practices that would bring dishonor upon your profession or The American College.
III. Publicize your achievement in ways that enhance the integrity of your profession.
IV. Continue your studies throughout your working life so as to maintain a high level of professional competence.
V.   Do your utmost to attain a distinguished record of professional service.
VI. Support the established institutions and organizations concerned with the integrity of your profession.
VII. Participate in building your profession by encouraging and providing appropriate assistance to qualified persons pursuing professional studies.
VIII. Comply with all laws and regulations, particularly as they relate to professional and business activities.

ADMINISTRATION

The certification officer of the College is empowered by the board of trustees to implement the Code by investigating complaints and reports of violations, which may originate with state commissioners of insurance, other public and judicial bodies, individuals, and established institutions or organizations. In certain instances the College itself may initiate action based on an apparent violation.

Violations that may cause the certification officer to begin an investigation include conviction of a misdemeanor or felony, suspension or revocation of a license, or suspension or revocation of membership in an established institution or organization.

Although only actions that occur after October 1, 1984, are subject to the Code, the standards established by the Code apply to students in the CLU and ChFC programs who matriculated on July 1, 1982, or later. All earlier CLU and ChFC matriculants were invited to subscribe to the Code and to accept its mandates voluntarily. Jurisdiction does not extend to pre-1982 matriculants who have not consented to be bound by the Code. The Code of Ethics also applies to students in the RHU and REBC programs who matriculated on January 1, 1996, or later.

PROCEDURES

I. Initiation of Action
    The College, acting through the certification officer, investigates all alleged violations of its Code that are reported by state or federal authorities, individuals, and/or established financial services institutions or organizations.

II. The Certification Officer
    A. The certification officer of the College makes a preliminary appraisal to determine whether
        1. the complaint involves a violation of the Code there is sufficient evidence for presentation to the certification committee
    B. The certification officer determines the facts of the complaint by
        1. reviewing the charges with the complainant(s)
        2. relaying the complaint to the person charged and permitting him or her to respond examining all the facts that appear relevant to the complaint
    C. After completing the above steps the certification officer

1. determines whether to discontinue action or to present the case to the certification committee
2. transmits the determination in writing to all parties involved in the complaint
3. reviews the earlier steps if new information comes to light
4. prepares the file and presents the complaint to the certification committee if the case so warrants

III. The Certification Committee
   A. Membership.
      The certification committee is composed of a chairperson who must be a trustee of the College and three to five members, including one senior administrative officer of the College. (Note: The College's legal counsel may serve in an advisory role.)
   B. Duties
      1. The certification committee reviews the case and requests any additional information that it considers necessary.
      2. After reviewing the case, the certification committee may either dismiss the complaint or decide that the Code has been violated and impose an appropriate sanction.
      3. The decision is conveyed in writing to all parties involved in the complaint.
   C. Action. The certification committee decides to impose a sanction only by unanimous vote.

IV. Sanctions
   A. The certification committee may order suspension or revocation of the right to use the CLU designation, the ChFC designation, the RHU designation, the REBC designation, or a combination of designations. The suspension or revocation notice is sent by registered mail.
   B. If no appeal is received, a copy of the suspension or revocation notice is sent to the complainant(s) and made a part of the College's permanent records.
   C. The College reserves the right to transmit the decision to other parties.

V. Appeals
  A. A suspension or revocation may be appealed by notifying the certification committee chairperson in writing within 30 days of receiving the suspension or revocation notice.
  B. When an appeal is received, the chairperson of the certification committee notifies the chairman of the board of trustees, who appoints a hearing committee composed of no fewer than three members who may be trustees but not College staff members. The members may have no prior connection with the case or with any company with which the appellant has been associated.
  C. The certification officer or a member of the certification committee who voted the sanction presents the case and may answer questions but may not participate in the deliberations.
  D. The appellant may present his or her position, call witnesses, and point to the alleged errors in the decision.
  E. If the appellant is represented by counsel, the hearing committee must also be so represented. Counsel to the committee may be present to clarify issues even if the appellant is not represented.
  F. A recorder who is not a member of the hearing committee keeps minutes of the proceedings.
  G. The hearing committee sets the rules for conduct of the hearing.
  H. A majority vote based on information provided during the hearing is required and is final and binding on the College and the appellant.
  I. The decision and statement of reasons for the decision is sent by the hearing committee chairperson to the College. The certification officer notifies the appellant and the complainant(s) of the committee's decision by registered mail within 15 days of the hearing.

The College reserves the right to convey the decision to other parties.

Code of Professional Responsibility of the Society of Financial Service Professionals

The Code of Professional Responsibility of the Society of Financial Service Professionals is divided into five components, as follows:

- Preamble—a brief introduction to the Code of Professional Responsibility, including its history and purpose.
- Canons—aspirational model standards of exemplary professional conduct.
- Rules—specific standards of a mandatory and enforceable nature.
- Applications—practical examples of how the canons and rules apply in given situations.
- Disciplinary Procedures—the mechanisms for enforcement of the Code of Professional Responsibility.

PREAMBLE

The Society of Financial Service Professionals is dedicated to setting and promoting standards of excellence for professionals in financial services. In fulfillment of this mission, the Society's Board of Directors has adopted this Code of Professional Responsibility. All Society members are automatically bound by its provisions.

The ultimate goal of enacting the Code is to serve the public interest. The path to fulfilling the goal is the fostering of professionalism in financial services. A profession has been defined in the writings of Solomon S. Huebner as possessing four essential traits:

- knowledge or expertise
- service to others
- working with other professionals to enhance the practice and reputation of one who is a member
- self-regulation

Through its Code of Professional Responsibility, the Society strives to improve the level of ethical behavior among its members by articulating standards that are aspirational in nature, that is, by identifying the lofty, altruistic ideals that define a true profession, and by delineating and enforcing minimum standards of ethical conduct.

This Code of Professional Responsibility has its origin in the code of ethics of the American Society of CLU & ChFC, the predecessor organization of the Society of Financial Service Professionals. The members of the Society created and adopted a code of ethics in 1961. With a name change in the fall of 1998, and a broadened membership constituency, it became appropriate to create this new Code of Professional Responsibility.

The Society acknowledges the diversity of its membership...from those that serve the public directly, as advisers, to those that serve indirectly through companies, educational organizations, and the like. Whatever role he or she plays within the financial services industry, it is the responsibility of each Society member to understand and adhere to the Code of Professional Responsibility.

From time to time, a Society member may be unclear about the ethical implications of a given course of action. In such cases, a Society member may request an advisory opinion from the Society; or may seek confidential advice through the Society's Ethics Information Line. Advisory opinions will be unpublished and specific to the inquiring member. However, there may be instances in which the subject matter of the advisory opinion has broad, general application and in such cases, at its discretion, the Society may chose to publish a given opinion for the benefit of all members, preserving the anonymity of those involved.

An alleged violation of the Society's Code of Professional Responsibility will result in an enforcement action, carried out in accordance with the Disciplinary Procedures. The procedures ensure that any member charged with ethical misconduct is afforded appropriate due process. The procedures also provide for appropriate sanctions, such as reprimand, censure, and revocation of membership, should a member be found to have acted in violation of the Code.

True enforcement of ethical behavior must come from the personal conscience of each individual, rather than external forces.

Nevertheless, as an organization that promotes its members' education and expertise to the consumer, the Society believes it is essential that it act in an enforcement capacity.

CANONS

Canon 1—Fairness

A member shall perform services in a manner that respects the interests of all those he/she serves, including clients, principals, partners, employees, and employers. A member shall disclose conflicts of interests in providing such services.

Fairness requires that a professional treat others as he/she would wish to be treated if in the other's position. A professional also strives to avoid unfairness by inflicting no unnecessary harm on others and, when possible, shielding others from harm.

Rules

R1.1 A member shall not engage in behavior involving concealment or misrepresentation of material facts.

Applications for Rule 1.1:

A1.1a. In the sale of financial products, the use of product projections that are more aggressive than the company's current assumptions—without offering alternate illustrations/projections using more conservative assumptions—is a form of misrepresentation. It is best to show a range of assumptions for each product to illustrate the impact of changes on the rate of return and other expenses.

A1.1b. To avoid misrepresentation, the financial services professional is advised to use unbiased historical illustrations, show past performance, and to educate the consumer on the difference between past results and projections, and actual future results.

A1.1c. Improper replacement is a form of misrepresentation. When considering the replacement of one insurance, annuity, or other financial product for another, a thorough comparison of both products, including surrender charges, incontestable clauses, expenses, fees, and tax consequences, should be completed. The Society's Replacement Questionnaire (RQ) provides a tool for the thorough analysis of replacement issues.

A1.1d. Failing to note a preexisting medical condition on an insurance application is a form of concealment.

R1.2. A member shall respect the rights of others.

R1.3. A member shall disclose to the client all information material to the professional relationship, including, but not limited to, all actual or potential conflicts of interest. In a conflict of interest situation, the interest of the client must be paramount.

Applications for Rule 1.3

A1.3a. A potential conflict of interest is inherent in the relationship between the client and the financial service professional when the professional is compensated by commissions on the sale of financial products. In such circumstances, if asked by the client or prospect, the professional should disclose, to the best of his/her knowledge, all forms of compensation, including commissions, expense allowances, bonuses, and any other relevant items.

A1.3b. The potential for a conflict of interest exists when a financial service professional receives fees for referring business to another practitioner. The referring professional should disclose this information.

A1.3c. A member who serves as a director or trustee of an organization/business faces a conflict of interest when competing to provide product or services to this organization for compensation. For example, Jackie Jones, ChFC, a professional money manager, is on the board of XNet Corporation. XNet is currently interviewing candidates to manage its $10 million investment portfolio. If Jackie decides to seek XNet's account, she is in a conflict of interest situation. Under these circumstances, Jackie should disclose the conflict to all relevant parties and have the parties acknowledge and accept the conflict. Additionally, Jackie should consider recessing herself from all discussions and decision-making regarding the selection of Xnet's money manager. She may also consider resigning from the board or taking her name out of consideration for the money manager position.

R1.4. A member shall give proper respect to any relationship that may exist between the member and the companies he or she represents.

Application for Rule 1.4

A1.4a. Society members frequently have contractual relationships with the company whose products they sell. Honoring the terms of these contracts and refraining from negative statements about such companies are examples of giving proper respect to the relationship. Note, however, the need to balance the requirements of Rule 1.4 with the duty to act in the best interest of the client.

R1.5 A member shall make and/or implement only recommendations that are appropriate for the client and consistent with the client's goals.

Applications for Rule 1.5

A1.5a. Compliance with Rule 1.5 requires the financial service professional to use his/her best efforts to (1) understand the client's/prospect's personal and financial background and experience; (2) understand the client's/prospect's risk tolerance; and (3) educate the client about the various options available to meet identified needs and goals. This may include utilizing a fact-finding and/or risk assessment tool, one-on-one educational/counseling sessions, sharing newspaper or magazine articles, etc. In these circumstances, the financial service professional is cautioned against providing advice if he or she is not properly licensed or authorized to do so. See also Rule 2.2 and the Application A2.2a.

A1.5b. Appropriateness of the recommendation to the client's needs must take precedence over any sales incentives available to the financial service professional, such as conventions, trips, bonuses, etc. For example, Bob Bucks needs to sell just one more policy to qualify for MDRT. He knows he can convince his best client to purchase additional insurance coverage even though Bob knows the current coverage is more than adequate. If Bob makes this sale, he has violated Rule 1.5.

R1.6. In the rendering of professional services to a client, a member has the duty to maintain the type and degree of professional independence that (a) is required of practitioners in the member's occupation, or (b) is otherwise in the public interest, given the specific nature of the service being rendered.

Application for Rule 1.6

A1.6a. The requirement of professional independence mandated by Rule 1.6 presents a special challenge for Society members who are contractually bound to sell the products of only one company, or a select group of companies. In such cases, the member must keep paramount his/her ethical duty to act in the best interest of the client, even if this means forgoing a sale.

CANON 2—Competence

A member shall continually improve his/her professional knowledge, skill, and competence.

Professionalism starts with technical competence. The knowledge and skills held by a professional are of a high level, difficult to attain, and, therefore, not held by the general public. Competence not only includes the initial acquisition of this specialized knowledge and skill, but also requires continued learning and practice.

Rules

R2.1. A member shall maintain and advance his/her knowledge in all areas of financial service in which he/she is engaged and shall participate in continuing education programs throughout his/her career.

Application for Rule 2.1

A.2.1a. Compliance with Rule 2.1 requires, at a minimum, meeting the applicable continuing education standards set by state licensing authorities, the Society of Financial Service Professionals, the American College, the CFP Board of Standards, and any other entity with appropriate authority over the member's license(s) or other credentials. For example PACE, the joint CE program of the Society of and the American College requires 30 hours of CE every 2 years. The CFP Board of

Standards also requires 30 hours of continuing education every 2 years for CFP licensees.

R2.2. A member shall refrain from giving advice in areas beyond the member's own expertise.

Applications for Rule 2.2

A2.2a. A member shall not give tax, legal, insurance, accounting, actuarial, investment, or other advice unless the member has professional training and is properly licensed in these areas. For example, to avoid the unauthorized practice of law, the financial service professional will clearly mark specimen documents, such as living or testamentary trusts or buy-sell agreements, as samples and inform the client that the documents must be reviewed by a licensed attorney.

A2.2b. Billy Burke, CFP, has a specialized financial planning practice that focuses on assisting clients with funding college for their children. When Billy's long-time client and friend, Margaret Hamilton, asks for help in managing the distribution of funds from her defined benefit plan, Billy knows this is beyond his area of expertise, but he doesn't want to let his friend down. Billy proceeds to recommend several investment options to Margaret, but neglects to mention the early withdrawal taxes and penalties. Billy has violated Rule 2.2.

Canon 3—Confidentiality

A member shall respect the confidentiality of any information entrusted to, or obtained in the course of, the member's business or professional activities.

A financial service professional often gains access to client records and company information of a sensitive nature. Each Society member must maintain the highest level of confidentiality with regard to this information.

Rules

R3.1. A member shall respect and safeguard the confidentiality of sensitive client information obtained in the course of professional activities. A member shall not divulge such information without specific consent of the client, unless disclosure of such information is required by law or necessary in order to discharge legitimate professional duties.

Application for Rule 3.1

A3.1a. Examples of sensitive client information include, but are not limited to, medical data, information about financial status, Social Security or credit card numbers, information about personal relationships, etc. In determining whether information is sensitive, the Society member should take a cautious approach, and if in doubt, discuss the issue with the client.

R3.2. A member shall respect and safeguard the confidentiality of sensitive company/employer information obtained in the course of professional activities. A member shall not divulge such information without specific consent, unless disclosure of such information is required by law or necessary in order to discharge legitimate professional duties.

R3.3. A member must ensure that confidentiality practices are established and maintained by staff members so that breaches of confidence are not the result of intentional or unintentional acts or omissions.

Application for Rule 3.3

A3.3a. A member who employs others who work with sensitive, confidential client information has the responsibility to train these employees in the handling of such information. These employees must be instructed that they will be held responsible for unauthorized disclosure of confidential data. For example, Judy Parker has set up detailed procedures for her staff to follow in safeguarding confidential client information. On three separate occasions, Judy overheard her office manager gossiping with friends about the size of Client X's investment portfolio. Judy has not taken any action in regard to the office manager's behavior. Judy has violated Rule 3.3.

Canon 4—Integrity

A member shall provide professional services with integrity and shall place the client's interest above his/her own.

Integrity involves honesty and trust. A professional's honesty and candor should not be subordinate to personal gain or advantage. To be dishonest with others is to use them for one's own purposes.

Rules

R4.1. A member shall avoid any conduct or activity that would cause unnecessary harm to others by:

Any act or omission of a dishonest, deceitful, or fraudulent nature.

Pursuit of financial gain or other personal benefits that would interfere with the exercise of sound professional judgments and skills.

R4.2. A member shall establish and maintain dignified and honorable relationships with those he/she serves, with fellow practitioners, and with members of other professions.

Application for Rule 4.2

A4.2a. A member needs to be respectful in all dealings with another financial service professional in competitive engagements and avoid at all costs defamatory remarks to the client or other professionals. This does not mean a member cannot provide impartial factual information about a competitor. For example, in trying to help a friend make a decision about which long-term care policy to purchase, Joe Carter, CLU, reviews the features of each contract and accurately notes that his competitor's policy fails to provide coverage for Home care. Joe recommends that his friend review this information with his agent.

R4.3. A member shall embrace and adhere to the spirit and letter of laws and regulations governing his/her business and professional activities. See also Rule 6.1.

R4.4. A member shall be truthful and candid in his/her professional communications with existing and prospective clients, and with the general public.

Applications for Rule 4.4

A4.4a. Financial service professionals will not use words or make statements in brochures or advertising materials or in any client communication that create false impressions or have the potential to mislead. For example, product salespersons should not refer to themselves as financial/estate planners/consultants, if they do not provide these services. Words such as deposits or contributions should not be used to describe life insurance premiums. Life insurance policies should not be referred to as retirement plans. Discussion of vanishing premiums and guaranteed performance should be avoided. Financial service professionals must avoid creating the impression that they represent a number of companies when they place business with only a few companies. (See also Rule 1.6.)

A4.4b. Candid communication is required when a client is acting or intends to act outside the law. In such cases, the member should terminate the professional relationship and seek the advice of appropriate advisers. For example, Lisa Long, CLU, CFP, an investment adviser, has been asked by her client to effect a transaction based on insider information. Lisa must immediately advise her client that insider trading is a violation of SEC rules and could result in criminal charges. Lisa should also document what has happened; and if, the client plans to proceed with the transaction, Lisa should terminate the relationship. Lisa should also consult her own legal and ethical advisers as to whether she has additional legal obligations under these circumstances. Lisa's legal obligations will impact her ethical obligations.

R4.5. A member shall refrain from using an approved Society designation, degree, or credential in a false or misleading manner.

Application for Rule 4.5

A4.5a. A member must not use Society-recognized professional designations in his/her company name, tagline, or brochures in a manner which would be misleading. For example, John Smith, ChFC, and Associates is acceptable. John Smith and Associates, Chartered Financial Consultants is not because it creates the impression that everyone associated with the firm is a Chartered Financial Consultant. (See Rule 7.7 also.)

Canon 5—Diligence

A member shall act with patience, timeliness, and consistency in the fulfillment of his/her professional duties.

A professional works diligently. Knowledge and skill alone are not adequate. A professional must apply these attributes in a prompt and thorough manner in the service of others.

Rules

R5.1. A member shall act with competence and consistency in promptly discharging his/her responsibilities to clients, employers, principals, purchasers, and other users of the member's services.

R5.2. A member shall make recommendations to clients, whether in writing or orally, only after sufficient professional evaluation and understanding of the client's needs and goals. A member shall support any such recommendations with appropriate research and documentation.

R5.3. A member shall properly supervise subordinates with regard to their role in the delivery of financial services, and shall not condone conduct in violation of the ethical standards set forth in this Code of Professional Responsibility.

Canon 6—Professionalism

A member shall assist in raising professional standards in the financial services industry.

A member's conduct in all matters shall reflect credit upon the financial services profession. A member has an obligation to cooperate with Society members, and other financial service professionals, to enhance and maintain the profession's public image and to work together to improve the quality of services rendered.

Rules

R6.1. A member has the duty to know and abide by the local, state, and national laws and regulations and all legal limitations pertaining to the member's professional activities.

Applications for Rule 6.1

A6.1a. The financial service profession is subject to state and federal laws and regulation in the areas of securities, insurance, banking, and unfair trade practices, among others. Society members must understand these laws and regulations and their applicability to their practices. For example, Susan Short, CLU, just earned her CFP license, and is planning on expanding her practice to include comprehensive financial planning services. Does Susan need to register as an investment adviser? Must she be licensed with the National Association of Securities Dealers? What about state insurance laws? Susan must answer these questions and comply with the appropriate requirements for her business activities.

A6.1b. Jon Planner receives equity commissions throughout the year. As part of a prearranged agreement, he transfers these commissions to the corporation for whom he works. Jon later learns that this is a violation of NASD rules and that commissions cannot be split with corporations. Jon is ethically obligated to correct this situation and to further educate himself on the rules and regulations applying to his business.

R6.2. A member shall support the development, improvement, and enforcement of such laws, regulations, and codes of ethical conduct that foster respect for the financial service professional and benefit the public.

Application for Rule 6.2

A6.2a. Suppose Congress is contemplating a measure that would increase the regulatory burden on financial service professionals by requiring increased documentation of specific client transactions. There is firm evidence that enactment of this measure would substantially reduce the likelihood of client's being misled or confused about such transactions. Rule 6.2 would require Society members to support such a measure.

R6.3. A member shall show respect for other financial service professionals and related occupational groups by engaging in fair and honorable competitive practices; collegiality among members shall not impede enforcement of this Code.

R6.4. A member shall cooperate with regulatory authorities regarding investigations of any alleged violation of laws or regulations by a financial service professional.

Canon 7—Self-Regulation

A member shall assist in maintaining the integrity of the Society's Code of Professional Responsibility and of the professional credentials held by all Society members.

Every professional has a responsibility to regulate itself. As such, every Society member holds a duty of abiding by his/her professional code of ethics. In addition, Society members have a duty to facilitate the enforcement of this Code of Professional Responsibility.

Rules

R7.1. A member has the duty to know and abide by all rules of ethical and professional conduct prescribed in this Code of Professional Responsibility.

Application for Rule 7.1

A7.1a. Society members are advised to review the Code of Professional Responsibility at least annually.

R7.2. A member shall not sponsor as a candidate for Society membership any person known by the member to engage in business or professional practices that violate the rules of this Code of Professional Responsibility.

R7.3. A member shall not directly or indirectly condone any act by another member prohibited by this Code of Professional Responsibility.

Application for Rule 7.3

A7.3a. If requested, a Society member should serve on such committees, boards, or hearing panels as are prescribed by the Society for administration or enforcement of the Code of Professional Responsibility. A Society member is obligated to disqualify him/herself from such service if he/she cannot not serve in a fair and impartial manner.

R7.4. A member shall immediately notify the Society if he/she is found in violation of any code of ethics to which he or she is subject and shall forward details to the Society.

R7.5. A member shall immediately notify the Society of any revocation or suspension of his/her license by a state or federal licensing or regulatory agency and forward details to the Society.

Application for Rule 7.5

A7.5a. If, after due process, a Society member is judged to have violated the code of ethics of another organization, he/she should notify the Society and provide such detail as may be necessary.

R7.6. A member possessing unprivileged information concerning an alleged violation of this Code of Professional Responsibility shall report such information to the appropriate enforcement authority empowered by the Society to investigate or act upon the alleged violation.

Applications for Rule 7.6

A7.6a. If a member believes that another member of the Society may have violated the Code of Professional Responsibility, the Society recommends, where feasible, that direct communication between the two members be the first step in addressing the problem.

A7.6b. The Society's Code of Professional Responsibility places responsibility upon all members to report violations of this Code. (See also Rule 7.6.)

R7.7. A member shall report promptly to the Society any information concerning the unauthorized use of an approved Society designation, degree, or credential.

Application for Rule 7.7

A7.7a. The Society logo may be imprinted on business cards and stationery used exclusively by the person who is a Society member. (See also Rule 4.6.)

MDRT Code of Ethics

Members of the Million Dollar Round Table should be ever mindful that complete compliance with and observance of the Code of Ethics of the Million Dollar Round Table shall serve to promote the highest quality standards of membership. These standards will be beneficial to the public and the insurance and financial services profession.

Therefore, members shall:

1. Always place the best interests of their clients above their own direct or indirect interests.

2. Maintain the highest standards of professional competence and give the best possible advice to clients by seeking to maintain and improve professional knowledge, skills and competence.

3. Hold in the strictest confidence and consider as privileged, all business and personal information pertaining to their clients' affairs.

4. Make full and adequate disclosure of all facts necessary to enable their clients to make informed decisions.

5. Maintain personal conduct which will reflect favorably on the insurance and financial services profession and the Million Dollar Round Table.

6. Determine that any replacement of an insurance or financial product must be beneficial for the client.

7. Abide by and conform to all provisions of the laws and regulations in the jurisdictions in which they do business

Certified Financial Planner Code of Ethics and Professional Responsibility[1]

CONTENTS

Preamble and Applicability
Composition and Scope
Compliance
Terminology in this Code

Part I—PRINCIPLES
Introduction
Principle 1—Integrity
Principle 2—Objectivity
Principle 3—Competence
Principle 4—Fairness
Principle 5—Confidentiality
Principle 6—Professionalism
Principle 7—Diligence

Part II—RULES
Introduction

Rules That Relate to the Principle of Integrity
Rule 101
Rule 102
Rule 103

Rules That Relate to the Principle of Objectivity
Rule 201
Rule 202

---

1. Reprinted with permission from Code of Ethics and Professional Responsibility. Copyright © 2001 by Certified Financial Planner Board of Standards, Inc. All rights reserved. During the first half of 2002, the CFP Board solicited comments on proposed changes to its Code of Ethics and Professional Responsibility. The current status of the proposed changes is available online at the CFP Board's website (www.CFP-Board.org).

Rules That Relate to the Principle of Competence
Rule 301
Rule 302

Rules That Relate to the Principle of Fairness
Rule 401
Rule 402
Rule 403
Rule 404
Rule 405
Rule 406
Rule 407
Rule 408
Rule 409
Rule 410
Rule 411
Rule 412
Rule 413
Rule 414
Rule 415
Rule 416

Rules That Relate to the Principle of Confidentiality
Rule 501
Rule 502
Rule 503

Rules That Relate to the Principle of Professionalism
Rule 601
Rule 602
Rule 603
Rule 604
Rule 605
Rule 606
Rule 607
Rule 608
Rule 609
Rule 610
Rule 611
Rule 612

Rules That Relate to the Principle of Diligence
Rule 701
Rule 702
Rule 703
Rule 704
Rule 705

PREAMBLE AND APPLICABILITY

The *Code of Ethics and Professional Responsibility (Code of Ethics)* has been adopted by the Certified Financial Planner Board of Standards, Inc. (CFP Board) to provide principles and rules to all persons whom it has recognized and certified to use the CFP®, CERTIFIED FINANCIAL PLANNER™ and CFP certification marks (collectively "the marks"). The CFP Board determines who is certified and thus authorized to use the marks. Implicit in the acceptance of this authorization is an obligation not only to comply with the mandates and requirements of all applicable laws and regulations but also to take responsibility to act in an ethical and professionally responsible manner in all professional services and activities.

For purposes of this *Code of Ethics,* a person recognized and certified by the CFP Board to use the marks is called a CFP Board designee. This *Code of Ethics* applies to CFP Board designees actively involved in the practice of personal financial planning, in other areas of financial services, in industry, in related professions, in government, in education, or in any other professional activity in which the marks are used in the performance of their professional responsibilities. This *Code of Ethics* also applies to candidates for the CFP® certification who are registered as such with the CFP Board. For purposes of this *Code of Ethics*, the term CFP Board designee shall be deemed to include current certificants, candidates, and individuals who have been certified in the past and retain the right to reinstate their CFP certification without passing the current CFP® Certification Examination.

COMPOSITION AND SCOPE

The Code of Ethics consists of two parts: **Part I—Principles and Part II—Rules.** The Principles are statements expressing in general terms the ethical and professional ideals that CFP Board designees are expected to display in their professional activities. As such, the Principles are aspirational in character but are intended to provide a source of guidance for CFP Board designees. The comments following each Principle further explain the meaning of the Principle. The Rules in Part II provide practical guidelines derived from the tenets embodied in the Principles. As such, the Rules describe the standards of ethical and professionally responsible conduct expected of CFP Board designees in particular situations. This

Code of Ethics does not undertake to define standards of professional conduct of CFP Board designees for purposes of civil liability.

Due to the nature of a CFP Board designee's particular field of endeavor, certain Rules may not be applicable to that CFP Board designee's activities. For example, a CFP Board designee who is engaged solely in the sale of securities as a registered representative is not subject to the written disclosure requirements of Rule 402 (applicable to CFP Board designees engaged in personal financial planning) although he or she may have disclosure responsibilities under Rule 401. A CFP Board designee is obligated to determine what responsibilities he or she has in each professional relationship including, for example, duties that arise in particular circumstances from a position of trust or confidence that a CFP Board designee may have. The CFP Board designee is obligated to meet those responsibilities.

The Code of Ethics is structured so that the presentation of the Rules parallels the presentation of the Principles. For example, the Rules which relate to Principle 1—Integrity, are numbered in the 100 to 199 series while those Rules relating to Principle 2—Objectivity, are numbered in the 200 to 299 series.

COMPLIANCE

CFP Board requires adherence to this *Code of Ethics* by all CFP Board designees. Compliance with the *Code of Ethics*, individually and by the profession as a whole, depends on each CFP Board designee's knowledge of and voluntary compliance with the Principles and applicable Rules, on the influence of fellow professionals and public opinion, and on disciplinary proceedings, when necessary, involving CFP Board designees who fail to comply with the applicable provisions of the *Code of Ethics*.

TERMINOLOGY IN THIS CODE

Client denotes a person, persons, or entity who engages a practitioner and for whom professional services are rendered. For purposes of this definition, a practitioner is engaged when an individual, based upon the relevant facts and circumstances, reasonably relies upon information or service provided by that practitioner. Where the services of the practitioner are provided to an entity (corporation, trust, partnership, estate, etc.), the client is the entity, acting through its legally authorized representative.

CFP Board designee denotes current certificants, candidates for certification, and individuals that have any entitlement, direct or indirect, to the CFP certification mark.

Commission denotes the compensation received by an agent or broker when the same is calculated as a percentage on the amount of his or her sales or purchase transactions.

Conflict(s) of interest(s) denotes circumstances, relationships or other facts about the CFP Board designee's own financial, business, property and/or personal interests which will or reasonably may impair the CFP Board designee's rendering of disinterested advice, recommendations or services.

Fee-only denotes a method of compensation in which compensation is received solely from a client with neither the personal financial planning practitioner nor any related party receiving compensation which is contingent upon the purchase or sale of any financial product. A related party for this purpose shall mean an individual or entity from whom any direct or indirect economic benefit is derived by the personal financial planning practitioner as a result of implementing a recommendation made by the personal financial planning practitioner.

Personal financial planning or financial planning denotes the process of determining whether and how an individual can meet life goals through the proper management of financial resources.

Personal financial planning process or financial planning process denotes the process which typically includes, but is not limited to, these six elements: establishing and defining the client-planner relationship, gathering client data including goals, analyzing and evaluating the client's financial status, developing and presenting financial planning recommendations and/or alternatives, implementing the financial planning recommendations and monitoring the financial planning recommendations.

Personal financial planning subject areas or financial planning subject areas denotes the basic subject fields covered in the financial planning process which typically include, but are not limited to, financial statement preparation and analysis (including cash flow analysis/planning and budgeting), investment planning (including portfolio design, i.e., asset allocation, and portfolio management), income tax planning, education planning, risk management, retirement planning, and estate planning.

Personal financial planning professional or financial planning professional denotes a person who is capable and qualified to offer objective, integrated, and comprehensive financial advice to or for the benefit of individuals to help them achieve their financial objectives. A financial planning professional must have the ability to provide financial planning services to clients, using the financial planning process covering the basic financial planning subjects.

Personal financial planning practitioner or financial planning practitioner denotes a person who is capable and qualified to offer objective, integrated, and comprehensive financial advice to or for the benefit of clients to help them achieve their financial objectives and who engages in financial planning using the financial planning process in working with clients.

PART I—PRINCIPLES

Introduction

These *Code of Ethics'* Principles express the profession's recognition of its responsibilities to the public, to clients, to colleagues, and to employers. They apply to all CFP Board designees and provide guidance to them in the performance of their professional services.

Principle 1—Integrity

A CFP Board designee shall offer and provide professional services with integrity.

As discussed in Composition and Scope, CFP Board designees may be placed by clients in positions of trust and confidence. The ultimate source of such public trust is the CFP Board designee's personal integrity. In deciding what is right and just, a CFP Board designee should rely on his or her integrity as the appropriate touchstone. Integrity demands honesty and candor which must not be subordinated to personal gain and advantage. Within the characteristic of integrity, allowance can be made for innocent error and legitimate difference of opinion; but integrity cannot co-exist with deceit or subordination of one's principles. Integrity requires a CFP Board designee to observe not only the letter but also the spirit of this *Code of Ethics.*

Principle 2—Objectivity

A CFP Board designee shall be objective in providing professional services to clients.

Objectivity requires intellectual honesty and impartiality. It is an essential quality for any professional. Regardless of the particular service rendered or the capacity in which a CFP Board designee functions, a CFP Board designee should protect the integrity of his or her work, maintain objectivity, and avoid subordination of his or her judgment that would be in violation of this *Code of Ethics.*

Principle 3—Competence

A CFP Board designee shall provide services to clients competently and maintain the necessary knowledge and skill to continue to do so in those areas in which the CFP Board designee is engaged.

One is competent only when he or she has attained and maintained an adequate level of knowledge and skill, and applies that knowledge effectively in providing services to clients. Competence also includes the wisdom to recognize the limitations of that knowledge and when consultation or client referral is appropriate. A CFP Board designee, by virtue of having earned the CFP certification, is deemed to be qualified to practice financial planning. However, in addition to assimilating the common body of knowledge required and acquiring the necessary experience for certification, a CFP Board designee shall make a continuing commitment to learning and professional improvement.

Principle 4—Fairness

A CFP Board designee shall perform professional services in a manner that is fair and reasonable to clients, principals, partners, and employers and shall disclose conflict(s) of interest(s) in providing such services.

Fairness requires impartiality, intellectual honesty, and disclosure of conflict(s) of interest(s). It involves a subordination of one's own feelings, prejudices, and desires so as to achieve a proper balance of conflicting interests. Fairness is treating others in the same fashion that you would want to be treated and is an essential trait of any professional.

Principle 5—Confidentiality

A CFP Board designee shall not disclose any confidential client information without the specific consent of the client unless in response to proper legal process, to defend against charges of wrongdoing by the CFP Board designee or in connection with a civil dispute between the CFP Board designee and client.

A client, by seeking the services of a CFP Board designee, may be interested in creating a relationship of personal trust and confidence with the CFP Board designee. This type of relationship can only be built upon the understanding that information supplied to the CFP Board designee will be confidential. In order to provide the contemplated services effectively and to protect the client's privacy, the CFP Board designee shall safeguard the confidentiality of such information.

Principle 6—Professionalism

A CFP Board designee's conduct in all matters shall reflect credit upon the profession.

Because of the importance of the professional services rendered by CFP Board designees, there are attendant responsibilities to behave with dignity and courtesy to all those who use those services, fellow professionals, and those in related professions. A CFP Board designee also has an obligation to cooperate with fellow CFP Board designees to enhance and maintain the profession's public image and to work jointly with other CFP Board designees to improve the quality of services. It is only through the combined efforts of all CFP Board designees, in cooperation with other professionals, that this vision can be realized.

Principle 7—Diligence

A CFP Board designee shall act diligently in providing professional services.

Diligence is the provision of services in a reasonably prompt and thorough manner. Diligence also includes proper planning for, and supervision of, the rendering of professional services.

PART II—RULES

Introduction

As stated in **Part I—Principles,** the Principles apply to all CFP Board designees. However, due to the nature of a CFP Board designee's particular field of endeavor, certain Rules may not be applicable to that CFP Board designee's activities. The universe of activities performed by a CFP Board designee is indeed diverse and a particular CFP Board designee may be performing all, some or none of the typical services provided by financial planning professionals. As a result, in considering the following Rules, a CFP Board designee must first recognize what specific services he or she is rendering and then determine whether or not a specific Rule is applicable to those services. To assist the CFP Board designee in making these determinations, this *Code of Ethics* includes a series of definitions of terminology used throughout the *Code of Ethics*. Based upon these definitions, a CFP Board designee should be able to determine which services he or she provides and, therefore, which Rules are applicable to those services.

Rules That Relate to the Principle of Integrity

Rule 101

A CFP Board designee shall not solicit clients through false or misleading communications or advertisements:

- **Misleading Advertising**: A CFP Board designee shall not make a false or misleading communication about the size, scope, or areas of competence of the CFP Board designee's practice or of any organization with which the CFP Board designee is associated.

- **Promotional Activities**: In promotional activities, a CFP Board designee shall not make materially false or misleading communications to the public or create unjustified expectations regarding matters relating to financial planning or the professional activities and competence of the CFP Board designee. The term "promotional activities" includes, but is not limited to, speeches, interviews, books and/or printed publications, seminars, radio and television shows, and video cassettes.

- **Representation of Authority**: A CFP Board designee shall not give the impression that a CFP Board designee is representing the views of the CFP Board or any other group unless the CFP Board designee has been authorized to do so. Personal opinions shall be clearly identified as such.

Rule 102

In the course of professional activities, a CFP Board designee shall not engage in conduct involving dishonesty, fraud, deceit or misrepresentation, or knowingly make a false or misleading statement to a client, employer, employee, professional colleague, governmental or other regulatory body or official, or any other person or entity.

Rule 103

A CFP Board designee has the following responsibilities regarding funds and/or other property of clients:

- In exercising custody of, or discretionary authority over, client funds or other property, a CFP Board designee shall act only in accordance with the authority set forth in the governing legal instrument (e.g., special power of attorney, trust, letters testamentary, etc.).
- A CFP Board designee shall identify and keep complete records of all funds or other property of a client in the custody of, or under the discretionary authority, of the CFP Board designee.
- Upon receiving funds or other property of a client, a CFP Board designee shall promptly or as otherwise permitted by law or provided by agreement with the client, deliver to the client or third party any funds or other property which the client or third party is entitled to receive and, upon request by the client, render a full accounting regarding such funds or other property.
- A CFP Board designee shall not commingle client funds or other property with a CFP Board designee's personal funds and/or other property or the funds and/or other property of a CFP Board designee's firm. Commingling one or more clients' funds or other property together is permitted, subject

to compliance with applicable legal requirements and provided accurate records are maintained for each client's funds or other property.

- A CFP Board designee who takes custody of all or any part of a client's assets for investment purposes, shall do so with the care required of a fiduciary.

Rules That Relate to the Principle of Objectivity

Rule 201

A CFP Board designee shall exercise reasonable and prudent professional judgment in providing professional services.

Rule 202

A financial planning practitioner shall act in the interest of the client.

Rules That Relate to the Principle of Competence

Rule 301

A CFP Board designee shall keep informed of developments in the field of financial planning and participate in continuing education throughout the CFP Board designee's professional career in order to improve professional competence in all areas in which the CFP Board designee is engaged. As a distinct part of this requirement, a CFP Board designee shall satisfy all minimum continuing education requirements established for CFP Board designees by the CFP Board.

Rule 302

A CFP Board designee shall offer advice only in those areas in which the CFP Board designee has competence. In areas where the CFP Board designee is not professionally competent, the CFP Board designee shall seek the counsel of qualified individuals and/or refer clients to such parties.

Rules That Relate to the Principle of Fairness

Rule 401

In rendering professional services, a CFP Board designee shall disclose to the client:

(a) Material information relevant to the professional relationship, including but not limited to, conflict(s) of interest(s), changes in the CFP Board designee's business affiliation, address, telephone number, credentials, qualifications, licenses, compensation structure, and any agency relationships, and the scope of the CFP Board designee's authority in that capacity.

(b) The information required by all laws applicable to the relationship in a manner complying with such laws.

Rule 402

A financial planning practitioner shall make timely written disclosure of all material information relative to the professional relationship. In all circumstances such disclosure shall include conflict(s) of interest(s) and sources of compensation. Written disclosures that include the following information are considered to be in compliance with this Rule:

(a) A statement of the basic philosophy of the CFP Board designee (or firm) in working with clients. The disclosure shall include the philosophy, theory and/or principles of financial planning which will be utilized by the CFP Board designee.

(b) Resumes of principals and employees of a firm who are expected to provide financial planning services to the client and a description of those services. Such disclosures shall include educational background, professional/employment history, professional designations and licenses held, and areas of competence and specialization.

(c) A statement of compensation, which in reasonable detail discloses the source(s) and any contingencies or other aspects material to the fee and/or commission arrangement. Any estimates made shall be clearly identified as such and shall be based on reasonable assumptions. Referral fees, if any, shall be fully disclosed.

(d)   A statement indicating whether the CFP Board designee's compensation arrangements involve fee-only, commission-only, or fee and commission. A CFP Board designee shall not hold out as a fee-only financial planning practitioner if the CFP Board designee receives commissions or other forms of economic benefit from related parties.

(e)   A statement describing material agency or employment relationships a CFP Board designee (or firm) has with third parties and the fees or commissions resulting from such relationships.

(f)   A statement identifying conflict(s) of interest(s).

Rule 403

A CFP Board designee providing financial planning shall disclose in writing, prior to establishing a client relationship, relationships which reasonably may compromise the CFP Board designee's objectivity or independence.

Rule 404

Should conflict(s) of interest(s) develop after a professional relationship has been commenced, but before the services contemplated by that relationship have been completed, a CFP Board designee shall promptly disclose the conflict(s) of interest(s) to the client or other necessary persons.

Rule 405

In addition to the disclosure by financial planning practitioners regarding sources of compensation required under Rule 402, such disclosure shall be made annually thereafter for ongoing clients. The annual disclosure requirement may be satisfied by offering to provide clients with the current copy of SEC form ADV, Part II or the disclosure called for by Rule 402.

Rule 406

A CFP Board designee's compensation shall be fair and reasonable.

Rule 407

Prior to establishing a client relationship, and consistent with the confidentiality requirements of Rule 501, a CFP Board designee may provide references which may include recommendations from present and/or former clients.

Rule 408

When acting as an agent for a principal, a CFP Board designee shall assure that the scope of his or her authority is clearly defined and properly documented.

Rule 409

Whether a CFP Board designee is employed by a financial planning firm, or an investment institution, serves as an agent for such an organization, or is self-employed, all CFP Board designees shall adhere to the same standards of disclosure and service.

Rule 410

A CFP Board designee who is an employee shall perform professional services with dedication to the lawful objectives of the employer and in accordance with this *Code of Ethics*.

Rule 411

A CFP Board designee shall:

    (a)   Advise the CFP Board designee's employer of outside affiliations which reasonably may compromise service to an employer, and

    (b)   Provide timely notice to the employer and clients, unless precluded by contractual obligation, in the event of change of employment or CFP Board certification status.

Rule 412

A CFP Board designee doing business as a partner or principal of a financial services firm owes to the CFP Board designee's partners or co-owners a responsibility to act in good faith. This includes, but is not limited to, disclosure of relevant and material financial information while in business together.

Rule 413

A CFP Board designee shall join a financial planning firm as a partner or principal only on the basis of mutual disclosure of relevant and material information regarding credentials, competence, experience, licensing and/or legal status, and financial stability of the parties involved.

Rule 414

A CFP Board designee who is a partner or co-owner of a financial services firm who elects to withdraw from the firm shall do so in compliance with any applicable agreement, and shall deal with his or her business interest in a fair and equitable manner.

Rule 415

A CFP Board designee shall inform his or her employer, partners or co-owners of compensation or other benefit arrangements in connection with his or her services to clients which are in addition to compensation from the employer, partners or co-owners for such services.

Rule 416

If a CFP Board designee enters into a business transaction with a client, the transaction shall be on terms which are fair and reasonable to the client and the CFP Board designee shall disclose the risks of the transaction, conflict(s) of interest(s) of the CFP Board designee, and other relevant information, if any, necessary to make the transaction fair to the client.

Rules That Relate to the Principle of Confidentiality

Rule 501

A CFP Board designee shall not reveal—or use for his or her own benefit—without the client's consent, any personally identifiable information relating to the client relationship or the affairs of the client, except and to the extent disclosure or use is reasonably necessary:

(a) To establish an advisory or brokerage account, to effect a transaction for the client, or as otherwise impliedly authorized in order to carry out the client engagement.

(b) To comply with legal requirements or legal process.

(c) To defend the CFP Board designee against charges of wrongdoing.

(d) In connection with a civil dispute between the CFP Board designee and the client.

For purposes of this rule, the proscribed use of client information is improper whether or not it actually causes harm to the client.

Rule 502

A CFP Board designee shall maintain the same standards of confidentiality to employers as to clients.

Rule 503

A CFP Board designee doing business as a partner or principal of a financial services firm owes the CFP Board designee's partners or co-owners a responsibility to act in good faith. This includes, but is not limited to, adherence to reasonable expectations of confidentiality both while in business together and thereafter.

Rules That Relate to the Principle of Professionalism

Rule 601
A CFP Board designee shall use the marks in compliance with the rules and regulations of the CFP Board, as established and amended from time to time.

Rule 602
A CFP Board designee shall show respect for other financial planning professionals, and related occupational groups, by engaging in fair and honorable competitive practices. Collegiality among CFP Board designees shall not, however, impede enforcement of this *Code of Ethics*.

Rule 603
A CFP Board designee who has knowledge, which is not required to be kept confidential under this *Code of Ethics*, that another CFP Board designee has committed a violation of this *Code of Ethics* which raises substantial questions as to the designee's honesty, trustworthiness or fitness as a CFP Board designee in other respects, shall promptly inform the CFP Board. This rule does not require disclosure of information or reporting based on knowledge gained as a consultant or expert witness in anticipation of, or related to, litigation or other dispute resolution mechanisms. For purposes of this rule, knowledge means no substantial doubt.

Rule 604
A CFP Board designee who has knowledge, which is not required under this Code of Ethics to be kept confidential, and which raises a substantial question of unprofessional, fraudulent or illegal conduct by a CFP Board designee or other financial professional, shall promptly inform the appropriate regulatory and/or professional disciplinary body. This rule does not require disclosure or reporting of information gained as a consultant or expert witness in anticipation of, or related to, litigation or other dispute resolution mechanisms. For purposes of this Rule, knowledge means no substantial doubt.

Rule 605

A CFP Board designee who has reason to suspect illegal conduct within the CFP Board designee's organization shall make timely disclosure of the available evidence to the CFP Board designee's immediate supervisor and/or partners or co-owners. If the CFP Board designee is convinced that illegal conduct exists within the CFP Board designee's organization, and that appropriate measures are not taken to remedy the situation, the CFP Board designee shall, where appropriate, alert the appropriate regulatory authorities, including the CFP Board, in a timely manner.

Rule 606

In all professional activities, a CFP Board designee shall perform services in accordance with:

(a) Applicable laws, rules, and regulations of governmental agencies and other applicable authorities.

(b) Applicable rules, regulations, and other established policies of the CFP Board.

Rule 607

A CFP Board designee shall not engage in any conduct which reflects adversely on his or her integrity or fitness as a CFP Board designee, upon the marks, or upon the profession.

Rule 608

The Investment Advisers Act of 1940 requires registration of investment advisers with the U.S. Securities and Exchange Commission and similar state statutes may require registration with state securities agencies. CFP Board designees shall disclose to clients their firm's status as registered investment advisers. Under present standards of acceptable business conduct, it is proper to use registered investment adviser if the CFP Board designee is registered individually. If the CFP Board designee is registered through his or her firm, then the CFP Board designee is not a registered investment adviser but a person associated with an investment adviser. The firm is the registered investment adviser. Moreover, RIA or R.I.A. following a CFP Board designee's name in advertising, letterhead stationery, and business cards may be misleading and is not permitted either by this Code of Ethics or by SEC regulations.

Rule 609
A CFP Board designee shall not practice any other profession or offer to provide such services unless the CFP Board designee is qualified to practice in those fields and is licensed as required by state law.

Rule 610
A CFP Board designee shall return the client's original records in a timely manner after their return has been requested by a client.

Rule 611
A CFP Board designee shall not bring or threaten to bring a disciplinary proceeding under this Code of Ethics, or report or threaten to report information to the CFP Board pursuant to Rules 603 and/or 604, or make or threaten to make use of this Code of Ethics for no substantial purpose other than to harass, maliciously injure, embarrass and/or unfairly burden another CFP Board designee.

Rule 612
A CFP Board designee shall comply with all applicable renewal requirements established by the CFP Board including, but not limited to, payment of the biennial CFP Board designee fee as well as signing and returning the Terms and Conditions of Certification in connection with the certification renewal process.

Rules That Relate to the Principle of Diligence

Rule 701
A CFP Board designee shall provide services diligently.

Rule 702
A financial planning practitioner shall enter into an engagement only after securing sufficient information to satisfy the CFP Board designee that:

(a) The relationship is warranted by the individual's needs and objectives.

(b) The CFP Board designee has the ability to either provide requisite competent services or to involve other professionals who can provide such services.

Rule 703

A financial planning practitioner shall make and/or implement only recommendations which are suitable for the client.

Rule 704

Consistent with the nature and scope of the engagement, a CFP Board designee shall make a reasonable investigation regarding the financial products recommended to clients. Such an investigation may be made by the CFP Board designee or by others provided the CFP Board designee acts reasonably in relying upon such investigation.

Rule 705

A CFP Board designee shall properly supervise subordinates with regard to their delivery of financial planning services, and shall not accept or condone conduct in violation of this *Code of Ethics*.

What You Should Know about Buying Life Insurance[*]

Life insurance is the foundation of financial security for youand your family. It protects your financial resources against the uncertainties of life so you can plan for the future. Choosing a life insurance product is an important decision, but it can be complicated. As with any major purchase, it is important that you understand your needs and the options available to you.

The American Council of Life Insurers (ACLI) has prepared this guide to help you know what questions to ask when you're buying life insurance. ACLI is a trade association of 383 life insurance companies, backed by an industry with 250 years of experience protecting American families. Its members collectively provide about 70 percent of the life insurance in the United States.

Why do I need life insurance?—Life insurance provides cash to your family after you die. The money your dependents receive (the death benefit) can be an important financial resource—to help pay the mortgage, run the household, and ensure that your dependents aren't burdened with debt. Having a life insurance policy might mean your family won't have to sell assets to pay outstanding bills or taxes. What's more, there is no federal income tax on life insurance benefits. If protection is not your primary goal, you should consider other financial products.

Where do I begin?—Start by evaluating your family's needs. Gather all your personal financial information and estimate what your family will need after you're gone. Include ongoing expenses (day care, tuition, or retirement) and immediate expenses (medical bills, burial costs, and estate taxes). Your family also may need money to help them readjust...perhaps to pay for a move, or job hunting expenses. Remember, life insurance provides financial protection.

How Much Life Insurance Will I Need to Purchase?

While there is no substitute for evaluating needs, one rule of thumb is to buy life insurance equal to five to seven times your annual income.

---

[*] Reprinted with permission from the American Council of Life Insurers (ACLI)

What are the different types of insurance?—Life insurance generally falls into two categories: term insurance and permanent insurance.

What is term insurance?—Term insurance provides protection for a specific period of time, from one to 30 years. It pays a benefit only if you die during the term. Depending on the policy, the premium may remain constant during its term or increase each year. Some term insurance policies can be renewed when you reach the end of the term, but the premium rates will generally increase. Many policies require that you present evidence of insurability at renewal to qualify for the lowest rates.

What is permanent insurance?—Permanent insurance provides lifelong protection. As long as you pay the premiums, the policy will remain in force, and the death benefit will be paid. These policies are designed and priced for you to keep over a long period of time. If you don't intend to keep the policy for the long term, this may be the wrong type of insurance for you. Permanent policies are known by a variety of names: whole, ordinary, universal, adjustable, and variable life. Their cash value or cash surrender value, which is not found in term insurance policies, provides you with some options.

- You can cancel or "surrender" the policy—in total or in part—and receive the cash value as a lump sum. If you surrender your policy in the early years, there may be little or no cash value.
- If you need to stop paying premiums, you can use the cash value toward premiums to continue your current insurance protection for a specified time, or to provide a lesser amount of protection covering you for your lifetime.
- You usually can borrow from the insurance company, using the cash value in your life insurance as collateral. Unlike loans from most financial institutions, the loan is not dependent on credit checks or other restrictions. You ultimately must repay any loan with interest, otherwise your policy may lapse, or your beneficiaries will receive a reduced death benefit.

With all types of permanent policies, the cash value of a policy is different from the policy's face amount. The face amount is the money that will be paid at death. Cash value is the amount available if you surrender a policy before your death.

What are the types of permanent insurance?—Whole life or ordinary life is the most common type of permanent insurance. The premiums generally remain constant over the life of the policy and must be paid periodically in the amount indicated in the policy. The cash value grows based on a fixed interest rate set in the policy. Universal life or adjustable life allows you, after your initial payment, to pay premiums at any time, in virtually any amount, subject to certain minimums and maximums. You also can reduce or increase the death benefit more easily than under a traditional whole life policy. (To increase your death benefit, the insurance company usually requires you to furnish satisfactory evidence of your continued good health.) Variable life provides death benefits and cash values that vary with the performance of a portfolio of investments. You can allocate your premiums among a variety of investments offering different degrees of risk and reward—stocks, bonds, combinations of both, or accounts that guarantee interest and principal. You will receive a prospectus in conjunction with the sale of this product. The cash value of a variable life policy is not guaranteed and the policyholder bears that risk. However, by choosing among the available fund options, you can allocate assets to meet your objectives and risk tolerance. Good investment performance will lead to higher cash values and death benefits. If the specified investments perform poorly, cash values and death benefits will drop. Some variable policies contain a guarantee that death benefits cannot fall below a minimum level.

What Are the Advantages and Disadvantages of Term and Permanent Insurance?

Term Insurance

Advantages
- Initial premiums generally are lower than those for permanent insurance, allowing you to buy higher levels of coverage at a younger age.
- It covers needs that will disappear in time, such as mortgages or college expenses.

Disadvantages
- Premiums increase as you grow older.
- Coverage may terminate at the end of the term or become too expensive to continue because of age or health status.
- The policy doesn't offer cash value.

Permanent Insurance

Advantages
- As long as the premiums are paid, protection is guaranteed for life.
- Premium costs can be fixed or flexible to meet personal financial needs.
- The policy accumulates a cash value against which you can borrow. (Loans must be paid back with interest or your beneficiaries will receive a reduced death benefit.) You can borrow against the policy's cash value to pay premiums or use the cash value to provide paid-up insurance.

Choosing a Company and Agent

Advantages
- The policy's cash value can be surrendered—in total or in part—for cash or converted to an annuity, (an insurance product that provides an income for a person's lifetime or a specific period of time.)
- A provision or "rider" can be added to a policy to give you the option to purchase additional insurance without taking a medical exam or having to furnish evidence of insurability. Other riders waive the premium if you become disabled, or allow you to collect all or part of the death benefit if you become terminally or chronically ill.

Disadvantages
- Required premium levels may make it hard to buy enough protection.
- It may be more costly than term insurance if you don't keep it long enough.

After you have considered your financial needs and become familiar with the basic types of life insurance, it's time to choose a company and agent.

Where do I purchase life insurance?—You can purchase life insurance at an insurance agency, a brokerage firm, a bank, or directly from a life insurance company on the Internet. Most companies have

Web sites describing their products and services, and some can direct you to an agent in your area.

How do I choose a company?—Contact your state insurance department for a list of companies licensed to do business in your state, then:

- Ask friends and relatives for recommendations.
- Conduct an Internet search.
- Talk to an insurance agent or broker.
- Research companies at a public library.

Once you've narrowed your search, check the company's financial condition by looking at its "rating." Rating agencies, including A.M. Best Company, Fitch Ratings, Moody's Investor Services, Standard and Poor's Insurance Rating Service, and Weiss Ratings, assess the financial strength of companies. Rating information is available on the Internet or in publications usually found in the business section of your public library.

How do I choose an agent?—Collect the names of several agents through recommendations from friends, family, and other sources. Find out: Is the agent licensed in your state? States require agents to be licensed to sell life insurance. Agents who sell variable products must also be registered with the National Association of Securities Dealers and have additional state licenses.

What company or companies does the agent represent? Some agents are "independent" and sell insurance for several different companies. "Captive" agents have an exclusive arrangement with a particular company and sell only their products and services. Ask the agent which companies he or she represents and what types of policies these companies sell.

Does the agent have any professional designations? Professional designations that life insurance agents may earn include Chartered Life Underwriter (CLU) and Life Underwriter Training Council Fellow (LUTCF). Agents who also are financial planners may have other designations, such as Chartered Financial Consultant (ChFC), Certified Financial Planner (CFP), or Personal Financial Specialist (CPA-PFS).

Is the agent a member of a professional association? The National Association of Insurance and Financial Advisors (NAIFA) is a key association for agents. It provides local educational seminars to keep agents up to date. Similar training and services for financial planners are available through the Society of Financial Service Professionals, and the Financial Planning Association.

The agent will begin by discussing your life insurance needs. He or she will ask questions about family income and your net worth. With the information you already have assembled about your personal goals and financial situation, you'll be able to discuss your insurance needs and options.

What can I expect an agent to do for me?—The agent should be willing and able to explain various policies and other insurance-related matters. You should feel satisfied that the agent is listening to you and looking for ways to find you the right type and amount of insurance at an affordable price. If you are not comfortable with the agent, or you aren't convinced he or she is providing the service you want, consult with another agent.

Will the agent ask questions about my health?—Be prepared at the initial meeting to answer questions about your health. For example, you can expect questions about your age, medical condition, medical history, family history, and personal habits. When you apply for life insurance, you also may be asked to have a medical exam. At times, a licensed medical professional will make a personal visit.

Always answer questions about medical history and health carefully and truthfully; this information is crucial for the company to evaluate your risk and establish a premium for your coverage. For instance, you will pay a lower premium if you don't smoke. On the other hand, if you have a chronic illness, you may be charged a higher premium. Also, in the event of a claim, accurate and truthful answers enable your beneficiary to receive prompt and full payment.

How do I know if a life insurance policy is right for me?—The agent will recommend a life insurance policy that will meet your needs. Look at the recommended policy with care to be sure it fits your personal goals. Often, an agent will provide a "policy illustration" that shows how the policy will work. Carefully study your agent's recommendation and ask for a point-by-point explanation. Make sure the agent explains items you don't understand. Because your policy is a legal document, it is important that you know what it provides.

If your agent recommends a term policy, ask:

- How long can I keep this policy? If I want the option to renew the policy for a specific number of years or until a certain age, what are the terms of renewal?
- Will my premiums increase? If so, when? Annually? Or after five or 10 years? • Can I convert to a permanent policy? Will I need a medical exam when I convert?

If your agent recommends a permanent policy, ask:

- Are the premiums within my budget?
- Can I commit to these premiums over the long term?
- How much will I receive if I surrender the policy? Permanent insurance provides protection for your entire life. If you don't plan to keep the policy for many years, consider another type. Cashing in a permanent policy after only a few years can be a costly way to get short-term insurance protection.

What does my policy illustration show?—A policy illustration shows premiums, death benefits, cash values, and information about other factors that may affect your costs. Your policy may provide for dividends to be paid to you as either cash or "paid-up" insurance. Or it could provide for interest credits that could increase your cash value and death benefit or reduce your premium. Dividends and credits are not guaranteed.

Your costs or benefits could be higher or lower than those in the illustration, because they depend on the future financial results of the insurance company. With variable life, your values will depend on the results of the underlying portfolio of investments. However, when figures are guaranteed, the insurance company will honor them regardless of its financial success. Ask your agent which figures are guaranteed and which are not.

If the illustration is for a variable life policy, be sure that the interest rate assumed is reasonable for the underlying investment accounts to which you would allocate your premiums.

Is a policy illustration a legal document, like a contract?—No, an illustration is not a legal document. Legal obligations are spelled out in the policy itself.

What else should I look for in a policy illustration?

- Is the classification shown (i.e., smoker/ nonsmoker, male/female) appropriate for me?
- When are premiums due—annually, monthly, or otherwise?
- Which amounts are guaranteed and which are not?
- Does the policy have a guaranteed death benefit, or could the death benefit change depending on interest rates or other factors?
- Does the policy pay dividends or provide for interest credits? Are those figures incorporated into the illustration?
- Will my premiums always be the same? Could the premium increase significantly if future interest rates or investment returns are lower than the illustration assumes?
- If the illustration shows that I will not have to make premium payments after a certain period of time, is there any chance I would have to resume payments in the future?
- Is the premium level sufficient to guarantee protection for my entire life?

What happens if I fail to make the required premium payments?—If you miss a premium payment, you typically have a 30- or 31-day grace period in which to pay the premium without consequence. If you die during the grace period, your beneficiaries would receive the death benefit minus the overdue premium. After the grace period, the policy will lapse. If you own a permanent policy, your company—with your authorization—can draw from your policy's cash value to keep it in force. However, this will result in lower cash values and a shortened coverage period.

What if I become disabled and can't pay the premiums?—Provisions or "riders" that provide additional benefits can be added to a policy. One such rider is a "waiver of premium for disability." With this rider, if you become totally disabled for a specified period of time, you don't have to pay premiums for the duration of the disability.

Are other riders available?—Yes. An "accidental death benefit," for example, pays an additional benefit in case of death resulting from an accident. Some companies provide "accelerated benefits," also known as "living benefits." This rider allows you, under certain circumstances, to receive the proceeds of your life insurance policy before you die. Such circumstances include terminal or catastrophic illness, the need for long-term care, or confinement to a nursing home. Ask your agent for information about these and other policy riders.

Do I have any recourse if my policy lapses?—Some life insurance contracts let you reinstate a lapsed policy within a certain period of time. However, you must provide evidence of insurability and pay overdue premiums (plus interest) as well as any outstanding policy loans.

When will the policy be in effect?—The date that insurance goes into effect could be different from the date the company issues the policy. If you decide to purchase the policy, always check precisely when the insurance becomes effective.

Is a "buyer's guide" available?—Most states require companies to provide a buyer's guide to explain life insurance terms, benefits, and costs. Ask your agent for a copy.

Tips on Purchasing Life Insurance

- Take your time. On the other hand, don't put off an important decision that would provide protection for your family.
- Make sure you fully understand the policy and are comfortable with the company, agent, and product.
- When you purchase a policy, make your check payable to the insurance company—not to the agent. Get a receipt.
- After you have purchased a policy, you may have a short "free-look" period—usually 10 days after receipt—during which you can cancel. Read your policy carefully. If you decide not to keep it, the company will give you an appropriate refund.
- Review the application information in your policy. Notify your agent or company promptly if there are any errors or omissions.
- If an agent or company contacts you and wants you to cancel your policy and buy a new one, contact your original agent or company.
- Surrendering your policy to buy another could be very costly; however, there are times that a switch to a new policy is appropriate.
- If you have a complaint about your agent or company, contact the customer service division of the company. If you are still dissatisfied, contact your state insurance department. Most

departments have a consumer affairs division that can be reached by a toll-free number.

- If you have your premiums automatically deducted from your bank account, let your insurer know when you change banks.
- Review your policy periodically—or when your situation changes—to be sure your coverage is appropriate.

Tips on Using the Internet

The Internet is a good resource for learning how life insurers help Americans accumulate, manage, and protect their assets. Company Web sites offer information on products as well as financial planning tools.

- If you are using the Internet, be sure you are on the official company site. Look for logos and seals that companies use such as TRUSTe, CPA WebTrust, BBB (Better Business Bureau) Online, or Verisign.
- If you purchase a policy over the Internet, you should receive e-mail confirmation immediately, as well as mail confirmation if you request it. You should receive your policy in the mail within 60 days of your purchase.
- If your insurer communicates with you or bills you electronically, alert the company of e-mail changes.

In addition to the Internet, you can find information about life insurance and other financial and retirement security products offered by life insurers—pensions, annuities, long-term care and disability income insurance, IRAs, and 401(k), 403(b), and 457 plans—from agents, state insurance departments, and public libraries. 101 Constitution Avenue, N.W. Washington, D.C. 20001 www.acli.com

Answer Key to Review Questions

Chapter 1 – Quiz Answers

Question Number	Answer
1	(a)
2	(b)
3	(b)
4	(c)
5	(b)
6	(a)
7	(b)
8	(b)
9	(c)
10	(c)

Chapter 2 – Quiz Answers

Question Number	Answer
1	(a)
2	(b)
3	(d)
4	(d)
5	(b)
6	(a)
7	(c)
8	(b)
9	(d)
10	(d)

Chapter 3 – Quiz Answers

Question Number	Answer
1	(c)
2	(c)
3	(d)
4	(a)
5	(b)
6	(b)
7	(a)
8	(b)
9	(b)
10	(d)

Chapter 4 – Quiz Answers

Question Number	Answer
1	(d)
2	(b)
3	(a)
4	(b)
5	(a)
6	(b)
7	(d)
8	(d)
9	(c)
10	(c)

Chapter 5 – Quiz Answers

Question Number	Answer
1	(b)
2	(d)
3	(c)
4	(a)
5	(c)
6	(c)
7	(a)
8	(c)
9	(c)
10	(b)

Chapter 6 – Quiz Answers

Question Number	Answer
1	(a)
2	(d)
3	(d)
4	(d)
5	(b)
6	(a)
7	(a)
8	(b)
9	(b)
10	(d)

Chapter 7 – Quiz Answers

Question Number	Answer
1	(d)
2	(d)
3	(c)
4	(c)
5	(c)
6	(d)
7	(c)
8	(c)
9	(d)
10	(d)

Chapter 8 – Quiz Answers

Question Number	Answer
1	(c)
2	(d)
3	(c)
4	(b)
5	(c)
6	(b)
7	(c)
8	(b)
9	(b)
10	(d)

Becoming an LUTCF

How to Qualify for the LUTC Fellow Designation

First

You must have completed 300 Designation Credits (DCs). LUTC's current core courses and courses in The American College/LUTC CFP Program earn 60 DCs each.

Twenty percent (60) of the total credits required to earn the designation may be elective credits. Elective credits may be earned by 1) completing continuing education modules that offer DCs OR; 2) by having earned the CLU, ChFC, CLF, CPCU, CFP, or FIC designation.

Second

Complete and pass the examination for LUTC's *Piecing Together the Ethical Puzzle* OR *Charting an Ethical Course* OR *Charting an Ethical Course for the Multiline Agent*. To order the text and exam, please call LUTC Customer Service at 1-877-655-5882.

While you may receive CE credit in most states for completion of any of these ethics courses, no DCs are granted.

Third

You must be a paid member in good standing of a local association of NAIFA in the year of conferment. For a membership application, contact your local association or NAIFA at **1-877-TO-NAIFA** (866-2432) before sending in your LUTCF application.

Fourth

You must complete and submit an LUTCF application to The American College and provide evidence of your membership in a local association of NAIFA. A copy of your current membership card is sufficient.

To ensure recognition at national and local conferment ceremonies in the fall, your application must be received at The American College no later than **August 1**.

Non-duplication of Designation Credit Policy

While LUTC courses successfully completed at any time in the past count toward the LUTCF, candidates cannot receive duplicate DCs for the same course or its replacement.

Diplomas

LUTCF diplomas are mailed directly to the designee.

Make Progress Toward the CLU, ChFC and CPCU Designations

Individuals holding the LUTCF designation who have completed the *Business Continuity Course* (or the former *Business Insurance Course*) **plus** the *Advanced Business Planning Course* (or the former *Advanced Sales Course*) will receive credit for The American College's HS 331 course, *Planning For Business Owners and Professionals*. If you have any questions, contact the Office of Student Services at 1-888-AMERCOL.

Individuals holding the LUTCF designation may receive Related Studies credit in the CPCU program by providing the American Institute for Chartered Property Casualty Underwriters a copy of his or her transcript or LUTCF diploma. For more information, contact the registrar at the Institute at 1-610-644-2100.

LUTCF Online Directory

As an LUTCF, you are eligible to have your name included in the LUTCF Online Directory.

To be included in the directory, indicate your request on the LUTCF application or register online at http://directory.lutc.com.

Your listing is a benefit of having earned the designation and includes your name, company name, address, phone number, and a link to your e-mail and homepage addresses.

THE AMERICAN COLLEGE
THE LEADER IN FINANCIAL SERVICES EDUCATION

270 S. Bryn Mawr Avenue
Bryn Mawr, PA 19010
1-877-655-5882
1-610-526-1180
Fax 1-610-526-1486
www.lutc.org

The LUTCF Designation

Applicant: Mail application to Registrar, The American College, 270 S. Bryn Mawr Avenue, Bryn Mawr, PA 19010. Please allow 4 - 6 weeks for processing. For more information about the designation, call 1-877-655-5882 or 1-610- 526-1180. Please type or print legibly. The name on the diploma will be printed as requested on this application. **This application should be submitted only upon successful completion of the 300 designation credits and an LUTC ethics course.**

Last Name: _____ First Name: _____ Middle Initial: _____

Mailing Address: _____ Apt./Suite Number: _____

City: _____

State: _____ Zip Code: _____

Office Phone: _____ Office Fax: _____

Social Security Number: _____ Date of Birth: (m/d/y) _____

E-mail Address: _____

Homepage Address: _____

Type legal name for engrossing on diploma: (First, Middle, Last) _____

IMPORTANT: *NAIFA dues must be paid in the year of conferment in order to qualify for LUTCF. (Attach proof of membership)*
I belong to the _____association of NAIFA.
I am a member of MDRT: ❑ Yes ❑ No
Primary Insurance Company: _____
Home Office City and State: _____

A. *I have successfully completed the following LUTC courses in the years indicated:*

Year

CURRENT COURSE OFFERINGS *(60 DCS EACH)*
(LUTC 201) Exploring Personal Markets _____
(LUTC 202) Meeting Client Needs _____
(LUTC 211) Disability Income _____
(LUTC 251/301) Business Continuity _____
(LUTC 252/302) Employee Benefits _____
(LUTC 255) Long-Term Care _____
(LUTC 261/311) Retirement Planning _____
(LUTC 271/321) Foundations of Estate Planning _____
(LUTC 281/331) Planning for Seniors _____
(LUTC 341) Building a Million Dollar Business _____

THE AMERICAN COLLEGE/LUTC CFP® PROGRAM
HS 318 Insurance and Financial Planning _____
HS 326 Planning for Retirement Needs _____

Year

FORMER COURSE OFFERINGS
Personal Insurance Course (120 DCs) _____
Business Insurance Course (120 DCs) _____
Advanced Sales Course (120 DCs) _____
Equities Marketing Course (60 DCs) _____
Financial Planning Skills (60 DCs) _____
Fundamentals of Financial Services (60 DCs) _____
Personal Estate and Retirement Plan (60 DCs) _____
Multiline Skills (60 DCs) _____
Professional Growth (60 DCs) _____
Advanced Estate Planning (60 DCs) _____
Advanced Business Planning (60 DCs) _____
Building a Million Dollar Business (60 DCs) _____

DESIGNATION CREDIT WAIVER

I have the following designation(s) and am eligible for a waiver of 60 DCs.
❑ CLU ❑ ChFC
❑ CLF ❑ CPCU
❑ CFP Certification
❑ FIC

B. I have completed and passed the examination for: ❑ *Piecing Together the Ethical Puzzle* **OR** ❑ *Charting an Ethical Course* **OR**
❑ *Charting an Ethical Course for the Multiline Agent;* written proof is enclosed. Please provide the following information regarding your completion of the ethics course requirement.
❑ If by seminar, name of moderator: _____ Date: _____ Location: _____
❑ If by self study, name of proctor: _____ Date: _____ Location: _____
❑ If through company, name of company: _____ Date: _____ Location: _____

C. Please add my name to the LUTCF Online Directory after my application has been approved. ❑ Yes ❑ No

To the best of my knowledge and belief, the statements made on this application are true and correct. In consideration of the award of the designation to me, I acknowledge and agree that NAIFA and The American College shall jointly have the authority to (1) establish and from time to time change the conditions under which the designation is to be awarded and used, and (2) suspend, revoke, or modify in writing my privilege to use the designation for good cause, of which they shall be the sole and final judge. I further agree that in addition to NAIFA's membership records, a decisive factor in the determination of my eligibility for the designation shall be the official records of The American College. I also promise that I will not use the designation except as authorized pursuant to this agreement.

Signature_____ Date_____

Certified Financial Planner Board of Standards, Inc. owns the marks CFP®, CERTIFIED FINANCIAL PLANNER™, and CFP (with flame logo)®, which it awards to individuals who successfully complete initial and ongoing certification requirements.

National Association of Insurance and Financial Advisors

Membership: Your Greatest Professional Investment

MEMBERSHIP AND TRANSFER APPLICATION

You've just made the best decision of your career. By joining your local NAIFA affiliate, you are not only making an investment in your professional career, but membership will increase your bottom line. NAIFA members enjoy a wealth of benefits including:

- A complimentary subscription to **Advisor Today** (formerly Life Association News)—your number one tool for new sales ideas

- Participation in **high quality, low cost professional meetings** and educational seminars to increase your skills and satisfy continuing education requirements.

- **Discounts up to 40%** on business resources — covering industry trends, client management software packages, and more!

- **Networking opportunities with your peers** to discover creative sales ideas that work best for them.

- **Professional recognition** through national public relations and media activities; also NAIFA members uphold a strict Code of Ethics proving their reputation as true insurance professionals.

- **Legislative representation** at the federal and state levels to protect your professional and future career interests.

- **Industry-wide recognition** through NAIFA's national awards program.

NAIFA is your professional association—ensuring you—of a future that will make your career both profitable and rewarding. For more information on benefits, please call your local association or call NAIFA's Member Services Department at 1-877-86-NAIFA (62432).

Your local NAIFA affiliate is a member of the State and National Association of Insurance and Financial Advisors. All applicants must join the local NAIFA affiliate where he/she lives or works. To apply for membership, read the Membership Acceptance Certificate on the back of this page, complete the attached application, sign the form, and submit with payment for the amount indicated on the back of the local copy. Checks should be made payable to your local NAIFA affiliate. We look forward to serving you as a NAIFA member!

And remember–NAIFA membership–is an investment in your future!

NAIFA MEMBERSHIP AND TRANSFER APPLICATION (Please Print Legibly)

FOR BANK/NAIFA USE ONLY	To Be Completed by Local Association*

SOCIAL SECURITY NO.   2. LOCAL ASSOCIATION NAME   3. ASSOCIATION NO.

To Be Completed by Local Association*

_____ New Member @ $ ____

_____ Reinstate @ $ ____

_____ Transfer Only (no dues required)

MEMBER TYPE   ____ Active   ____ Regular Associate   ____ Student Associate   5. APPLICANT'S FULL NAME Mr.___ Ms.___ Mrs.___ (First, Middle Initial, Last)

_____ Transfer/Renewal (dues enclosed)

_____ Former Association (include State location)

DESIGNATION(S) -- Limit Two   7. TITLE   8. MAIL SHOULD BE SENT TO: ____ Business ____ Home

PRIMARY COMPANY   10. FIRM/AGENCY NAME

BUSINESS ADDRESS (include country if outside USA)   Street   City, State, Zip   12. BUSINESS PHONE   13. BUSINESS FAX

_____ Credit Card Charge by NAIFA*

_____ Bank Draft by NAIFA*

*Attach completed Payment Option Card

Code ____

HOME ADDRESS (please complete for our legislative database)   Street   City, State, Zip   15. TOLL-FREE NUMBER

7. E-MAIL ADDRESS   18. MONTH/YEAR OF INITIAL LICENSE

To the best of our knowledge, the applicant named is entitled to and worthy of acceptance by this local association.

9. PRODUCER /AGENT TYPE ____ Ordinary ____ Multiline ____ Health ____ Home Service ____ Bank Agent   ____ Other (please specify) ____

Active Sponsor Signature (1)

21. APPLICANT SIGNATURE   22. DATE   APPLICATION APPROVAL

Active Sponsor Signature (2)

MEMBER ACCEPTANCE CERTIFICATE

In consideration of my acceptance as a member of this local association, I certify that:

a. I consent to be governed by the Bylaws and to conform to the Association's Code of Ethics and to the duly adopted policy positions of the Association.

b. I have never been found guilty of any violation of any insurance law or regulation, or any other State or Federal law (except minor traffic violations), and have never been disciplined by, or expelled from, or refused membership in any NAIFA affiliate or other association or organization. (Attach full written explanation of any exceptions to the foregoing.)

c. I agree that neither the Association nor its individual members, officers, directors, agents or employees shall be liable to me, individually or jointly, if this application for membership is rejected or for the consequences of any disciplinary action which may be sought or taken against me under the Local Association's Bylaws or Amendments thereto or any disciplinary or penal action which may be sought or taken against me under the laws of this or any other state or jurisdiction, or for any statement which the Local Association or any of said individuals may issue relative to any such action; provided, however, that nothing herein contained shall exonerate the Local Association or any of said individuals from liability to me for its or their gross negligence or willful misconduct.

d. My enclosed total payment includes local dues and $7.00 for an annual subscription to Advisor Today (formerly Life Association News). See page included in application for state association publication subscription rates.

e. I am currently licensed as a life and/or health insurance professional by the State of (explain if otherwise licensed or if no license is required).

f. I understand and agree that my application for membership will be declined if it does not obtain a majority vote of the Board of Directors, or in the opinion of the Board of Directors, I am or will be unable or unwilling to conform to any of the foregoing requirements.

Non-Deductibility of Lobbying Expenses Disclosure Statement

While association dues payments may be deductible by members as an ordinary and necessary business expense, dues are not deductible as charitable contributions for federal income tax purposes. The portion of your dues that the NAIFA federation spends in lobbying activities is $27.00 and is not deductible from your federal income taxes.

The portion of your dues attributable to state association lobbying expenses is also non-deductible from your federal income taxes. See page included in this application for the amount corresponding to your state.

For First Year Licensees and Student Associate Members. Federal law requires NAIFA to notify members of that portion of their total dues which is not deductible. Because your dues may be waived at the national, state and/or local level, you will shortly receive notification in a letter via NAIFA's New Member Welcome Packet regarding the portion of total dues you paid, if any, that are not deductible for federal income tax purposes.

DUPLICATE
CE CERTIFICATION REQUEST

When you successfully complete your LUTC course, you are automatically issued certification for the approved number of continuing education credits for your resident state. In many states, your grade report will meet the requirement for certification. In other states, specific certification forms will be issued within six to eight weeks of the final examination. There is no additional charge for this certification in your resident state.

Many states maintain reciprocal agreements. Meeting the continuing education requirement in a participating resident state will satisfy the requirements for continuing education in participating nonresident states in which you are licensed. In very few instances will other states require separate certification.

As a licensed agent, you are responsible for knowing and meeting the continuing education requirements of all states in which you are licensed.

If you need additional certificates for states other than your state of residence, for certification for PACE or CFP, or because you have misplaced the certificate provided to you, you may order additional certificates by completing the form below. **The fee for each additional/replacement certificate is $15.** (Note: This does **NOT** cover applicable roster fees.)

CONTINUING EDUCATION CERTIFICATION REQUEST
(Please allow six to eight weeks for processing.)

Name _____ Soc. Sec. _____

Address _____

City _____ State _____ Zip _____

Daytime Phone _____

Course Title _____ Taken: ❑ Fall ❑ Spring Year _____

States for which certification is requested: _____

_____ ❑ PACE ❑ CFP

State License Number _____

Enclosed please find my check for $ _____ for the _____ certificates requested.

Please charge my request for _____ certificates to my ❑ VISA ❑ Master Card

Account Number _____ Expiration Date _____

Name on Card _____ Signature _____

(Please Print)

Mail your request to: **The American College**
Continuing Education Administration
270 S. Bryn Mawr Avenue
Bryn Mawr, PA 19010

Index

A

Advance premium arrangements, 8-8
Agency principles, 4-3
Agent authority. *See* Types of agent authority
Agent licensing, 3-9
Agent obligations, 4-7
    Account for premiums, to, 4-11
    Avoid conflicts of interest, to, 4-8
    Business transaction execution, of, 4-10
    Careful solicitation, of, 4-9
    Carrier and possible abuses, to, 4-12
    Follow principals' instructions, to, 4-9
    Full disclosure of information, of, 4-10
    Loyalty, of, 4-8
    Perform with skill and care, to, 4-10
    Product carrier, to, 4-7
Apparent authority, 4-5
Applying professional expertise to facts to develop strategies, 6-7
    Determining suitability, 6-7

B

Behaving professionally, 5-8
Benefit(s) of full disclosure, 7-15

Disclosure in the application, 7-20
Documenting full disclosure, 7-17
Postsale disclosure, 7-20
What to document, 7-18

C

Case study: a trip to Aruba, 7-13
Case study: investment advice—NASD rules, 3-32
Changing face of the financial services industry, 1-4
Changing marketplace, 1-7
    Changing demographics, 1-9
    Changing legal environment, 1-9
    Educated consumers, 1-7
    Integration of financial services, 1-11
    Technological advancements, 1-8
Characteristics of a professional, 5-4
    Behaving professionally, 5-8
    Requirements for a profession, 5-6
Client education, 7-4
    Client education is selling, 7-4
    Client learning styles, 7-5

Tools for educating clients, 7-5
Codes of ethics. *See* Professional codes of ethics
Compliance and ethics. *See* Revisiting compliance and ethics
Constituencies. *See* Ethical obligations to six constituencies
Current status of the regulation of rebates, 8-22

D

Decision procedure, 2-24
Disclosure
    Application, in the, 7-20
    Full, 7-11
    Postsale, 7-20

E

Emergence of financial planning services, 3-17
Employee Retirement Income Security Act (ERISA), 3-11
Ethical behavior, 6-3
Ethical missteps. *See* Two ethical missteps
Ethical obligations to six constituencies, 2-27
    Allied professionals, 2-28
    Client, 2-27
    Company, 2-27
    Oneself and others related to us, 2-28
    Profession 2-27
    Society and its laws, 2-28
Ethical principles, 2-20
Ethical requirements facing the financial services industry. *See* Major ethical requirements

facing the financial services industry
Ethical sales, 7-3
Ethical sensitivity exercise, 2-3
Ethically sound sales process. *See* Six necessary steps in an ethically sound sales process
Ethics as a set of beliefs of what is right or wrong, 2-16
Ethics defined, 2-11
Ethos, 2-12
Evaluating our ethical beliefs, 2-18
Examples of inappropriate replacement, 8-17
Express authority, 4-4

F

Fair dealings, 6-5
    Understand the client's current financial condition, 6-5
    Understand the client's investment objectives, 6-6
False advertising, 7-9
Forgery, 1-17
Four basic ethical principles, 2-20
Fraud, 1-17
Full disclosure, 7-11

G

Golden Rule, 2-13, 5-23

H

I

Illustrations, 8-3
    Illustration history and evolution, 8-3
    Illustration use, 8-5

Illustrations—what are they? 8-4
Implied authority, 4-4
Improper licensing, 1-15
Insider information, 3-30
Insolvency, 1-18
Integrity, 5-21
Investment risk, 6-11
    Overview of investment considerations, 6-11
    Seven investment decision factors, 6-11
    Types of investment risk, 6-14

J

Judging the client's situation, 6-23
    Continuing service, 6-23
    Fact finder format and compliance considerations, 6-25
    Practical aids for determining suitability and finding facts, 6-23
    Supplementary information, 6-26

K

L

Lack of competency, 1-16
Law and ethics, 3-3
    Business law and business ethics, 3-5
    Law and compliance, 3-6
Laws and regulations that govern the insurance industry, 3-8
    Federal role in insurance regulation, 3-10
    State role in insurance regulation, 3-8
    Laws and regulations that govern other financial services, 3-11
    Federal regulation of registered products, 3-12
    Mandated securities continuing education, 3-16
    NASD rules of conduct, 3-15
    National Association of Securities Dealers, 3-14
    Rules of conduct—an application to insurance agents, 3-15
    Similarities between life insurance and securities sales, 3-11
Legal obligations and the roles of consultants and financial planners, 3-17
Licensing agent, 3-9

M

Major ethical requirements facing the financial services industry, 1-18
    Honest marketing, 1-20
    Identifying and meeting customer needs, 1-19
    Proper identification of skills, 1-19
Making of today's financial services environment, 1-5
McCarran-Ferguson Act, 3-9
Misrepresentation, 7-6
Misuse of illustrations, 1-13
Model regulations on illustrations, 8-6

N

NAIC replacement guidelines, 8-15
NASD rules of conduct, 6-27
National Association of Insurance Commissioners (NAIC), 3-10
National Association of Securities Dealers (NASD), 3-14
Need for ethical training, 1-21

O

Obligations of agent. *See* Agent obligations
Other marketplace practice issues in today's selling environment, 8-23
　Dividend description, 8-24
　Guaranty fund advertising, 8-24
　NASD endorsement, 8-24
　Product identification, 8-23
　Unauthorized practice of law, 8-25

P

Penalties for unethical behavior, 2-15
Practical application, 5-22
　Agent of the client, 5-25
　Client education, 5-24
　Client-focused service, 5-25
Procedures for using illustrations in the sales process, 8-7
　Advanced premium arrangements or premium offset: "the vanishing premium," 8-8
　Documentation of illustration use, 8-10

Illustration Questionnaire (IQ), 8-7
Illustrations and policy comparisons, 8-8
Regulation of illustrations for specialized policies, 8-10
Replacement versus twisting, 8-15
Product misrepresentation, 1-14
Production identification, 8-23
Professional codes of ethics, 5-19
　Codes applicable to the financial services professional, 5-19
　Common themes among professional codes, 5-19
Professional competitive integrity, 5-28
　Summary of professional responsibilities, 5-29
Pros and cons of laws prohibiting rebating. *See* Rebating
Purpose of ethical rules, 2-17

Q

Questions to ascertain the ethics of an action. *See* Six questions to ascertain the ethics of an action

R

Ratification, 4-5
Reason for this course, 1-3
Rebating, 8-18
　Pros and cons of laws prohibiting rebating, 8-18
　Why rebating should be allowed, 8-20
　Why rebating should not be allowed, 8-19

Replacement, 8-14
    Examples of inappropriate
        replacement, 8-17
    NAIC replacement
        guidelines, 8-15
    Replacement versus
        twisting, 8-15
Registration as an investment
    advisor, 3-19
    Avoiding registration as an
        RIA for insurance
        agents, 3-26
    Compensation test, 3-22
    Future regulatory trends and
        developments, 3-25
    Regulation under the Act,
        3-23
    RIA—Weighing the
        responsibilities,
        advantages, and
        disadvantages, 3-27
    Security advice test, 3-21
    Security business test, 3-21
    Who is subject to the
        Investment Advisers
        Act? 3-19
Regulation of financial planning
    professionals, 6-27
Regulation of illustrations for
    specialized policies,
    8-10
    Annuity products, 8-10
    Blended policies, 8-10
    Second-to-die policies, 8-10
    Senior citizen policies, 8-10
    Universal life policies, 8-10
Requirements for a profession,
    5-6
Responsibilities of
    professionalism, 5-11
    Attributes of professional
        behavior, 5-18
    Increased client service,
        5-11

    Increased need to be aware
        of ethical issues, 5-12
    Increased risk of legal
        liability, 5-13
    Practical steps to avoid legal
        liability, 5-14
Revisiting compliance and
    ethics, 4-14
    Acting to avoid punishment,
        4-16
    Compliance and
        professionalism, 4-18
    Compliance and the letter of
        the law, 4-16
    Compliance as reactive
        rather than proactive,
        4-17
    Compliance needs ethics,
        4-15
    Undermining ethics with
        compliance
        dependency, 4-16
Risk management, 6-22
Risk tolerance, 6-16
    Categories of investments,
        6-17
    Defining risk tolerance,
        6-16
    Risk spectrum, 6-17
    Risk tolerance assessment
        techniques, 6-19
Role morality, 2-26

S

Sales presentation, 7-3
Securities regulation, 3-12
    Investment Advisers Act of
        1940, 3-13
    Securities Act of 1933, 3-12
        1940, 3-13
    Securities Exchange Act of
        1934, 3-12

Six necessary steps in an
ethically sound sales
process, 8-12
 Clarify coverage
  components, 8-13
 Comply with regulations
  and mandated
  standards, 8-13
 Explain policy structure,
  8-12
 Explain who bears what
  risk, 8-13
 Gain client attention, 8-12
 Illustrate downside risk,
  8-13
Six questions to ascertain the
ethics of an action, 2-21
 Does it preserve my
  integrity? 2-24
 Is the action fair or just?
  2-22
 Is the action good for
  others? 2-22
 Is the action good or
  harmful for me? 2-21
 Is the action legal? 2-24
 Is there a commitment?
  2-23
Sources of positive law, 3-8
State regulation in the securities
and insurance
marketplace, 3-28
Suitability, 1-19

T

Twisting, 1-14
Two ethical missteps, 7-6
 False advertising, 7-9
 Misrepresentation, 7-6
Types of agent authority, 4-4
 Apparent authority, 4-5
 Express authority, 4-4
 Implied authority, 4-4
 Ratification, 4-5

U

Unauthorized insurance carrier,
8-25
Unauthorized practice of law,
5-12
Unethical practices in the
financial services
industry, 1-12
 Forgery, 1-17
 Fraud, 1-17
 Improper licensing, 1-15
 Insolvency, 1-18
 Lack of competency, 1-16
 Misuse of illustrations, 1-13
 Product misrepresentation,
  1-14
 Unnecessary replacement
  and twisting, 1-14

V

W

What is ethics? 2-3
Why ethical marketing practices
are important, 6-3
Why ethics is important, 2-14
Windowing, 1-17

X

Y

Your responses to ethical
dilemma scenarios, 2-6
 Areas of agreement, 2-6
 Areas of disagreement, 2-8
 How to score the exercise,
  2-11

Z